HERB COOKERY

BEE NILSON

Herb Cookery

PELHAM BOOKS

First published in Great Britain by
PELHAM BOOKS LTD
52 Bedford Square
London, W.C.1
1974

ISBN 0 7207 0743 9

Printed in Great Britain by
Northumberland Press Limited, Gateshead
in ten on eleven and a half point Granjon and
bound by the Dorstel Press, Harlow.

Contents

Foreword

In the first six chapters of this book I have included the sort of general information I like to have by me for handy reference. It includes notes on the common and botanical names of herbs, their growing habits and preferences for soil and sun, with recommended culinary uses for each. John Eric, my husband, has illustrated this by drawings of herbs grown in our London garden.

In addition, there are notes on how to buy, store, preserve, and use fresh, dried, and frozen herbs. While for those who are interested in health aspects of the use of herbs, there are some notes in the introduction.

When cooking, I find it useful to be able to look up suggestions for which herbs to add to which foods, so I have included a reference chapter on this.

The recipes have been tested in my own kitchen, and all served as part of normal meals for family and guests—with comments invited. They include ideas for using herbs to make everyday food more interesting and some for those who like to be more adventurous.

BEE NILSON

Introduction

With the exception of garlic, all the fresh herbs used in this book are ones I have grown in my London garden. A few, needing special care, have been grown in pots in a glassed-in but un-heated verandah. The dried herbs and seeds used have been partly those from my own growing and drying and partly commercial ones from the super-market.

The ease with which one can buy so many different herbs is something new for modern cooks and has lead to a revival of interest in this branch of cookery. The use of herbs in British cookery had declined steadily from Victorian times, so that to find British recipes using herbs freely a cook had to consult books written at the beginning of this century or earlier. To get the herbs, she had either to grow them herself or live where there was a herbalist's shop.

Some of our herbs are native to Britain, others come from Europe, many were brought by the Romans, while still others come from Asia. Growing herbs was very important in the Middle Ages, mostly in monastery and castle gardens. The plants were not only used for culinary purposes but also for medicines, and some were planted just for the bees.

Herbs were about the only flavourings available to cooks until Elizabethan times when spices were brought from the East. At first these were scarce and expensive and most people still had to rely on herbs.

Many writers suggest that the main reason why herbs and spices were so freely used by our ancestors was that they had very inadequate means of storing food, and strong flavourings were needed to mask staleness. Today we use them to give interest to the bland and tasteless mass-produced food which is gradually taking over in our shops and kitchens. Some people compensate for the lack of flavour by a free use of the ketchup and vinegar bottle but many others have discovered that using herbs is a more interesting way of adding flavour, and enables the enterprising cook to produce better food.

While the majority of cooks use herbs solely for their flavours, others consider they have important health-giving properties. Our ancestors believed that some of them had magical properties. The plants which contain hallucinatory drugs are believed to have been part of ancient witchcraft, but such plants are not culinary herbs.

The medicinal properties in culinary herbs are mainly carminative, helping to relieve feelings of dissention and flatulence in the intestine which result either from over-eating, gobbling, or an unwise selection of foods. Thus the use of such herbs in the flavouring of rich and indigestible dishes is good culinary practice. Angelica, balm, basil, mint, rosemary, coriander, sweet cicely, dill, fennel, anise, caraway, and sage all have carminative properties.

On the other hand it can be argued that the effect on health of using herbs in cooking can only be slight. Herbs contain only tiny amounts of the medicinally important ingredients. For use in medicine, concentrated extracts are prepared isolating the essential oils which form only about 0·1 to 0·3 per cent of the herb. These oils contain the carminative and other medicinal properties of the original herbs.

Some herbs are mildly antiseptic. These include garlic, mint, and thyme. The chief substance in oil of thyme is thymol, a more powerful antiseptic than carbolic acid. Before the development of modern drugs it was used for treating intestinal worms.

The essential oils of garlic and thyme affect the bronchial tubes and lungs and are often used in medicines for treating coughs and other bronchial complaints.

Some essential oils have an effect on the central nervous system. Those of garlic can be dangerous in large amounts. Garlic preparations are generally considered too powerful and dangerous to give to children.

The essential oils of wormwood or Artemesia absinthe have beneficial effects in small doses but are dangerous in large doses, for example, over-consumption of the drink Absinthe. The one of parsley is a stimulant in small doses, a depressant in large doses. Rue oil is toxic in large doses being a powerful irritant which can cause violent gastric pains, vomiting, and nerve derangement. The 1965 Food Standards Committee report on Flavouring Agents recommended that rue oil be prohibited for use in foods as a flavouring agent.

Sorrel is another herb containing a potentially dangerous substance, oxalic acid, poisonous in large doses. The same acid is found in rhubarb leaves in large enough amounts to make them poisonous. Spinach contains somewhat less oxalic acid than sorrel. Because sorrel has such a sharp flavour it is usually only eaten in small amounts.

Most essential oils are irritants to the gastro-intestinal tract, the kidneys, and bladder and some people are sensitive to quite small doses. This makes it just as important that herbal medicines should be prescribed by medically qualified people as is necessary with modern drugs.

However, in cooking we are not concerned with the concentrated essential oils but the whole herb and it is most unusual for anyone to find that culinary herbs used in moderation have any but beneficial and pleasurable effects.

One cannot claim that a high nutritive value is one of the benefits to be got from eating herbs. Their nutritive value is negligible. It is true that herbs like parsley contain more iron and vitamin C than many other plants but so little parsley is consumed at a time that the contribution to the total diet is negligible. In addition, herbs are usually chopped finely before being added to food and this process effectively destroys most of the vitamin C.

So forget about medicinal and nutritional values and enjoy herbs for their flavours, and for their beauty as garden plants.

Weights and measures

MEASURES

1 cup (c.)	= ½ an Imperial pint or 10 fluid ounces
	= 284 millilitres (when using millilitre measures count the cup a scant 300 millilitres)
1 tablespoon (tbs.)	= 15 millilitres or the size of a medicinal tablespoon
1 teaspoon (tsp.)	= 5 millilitres or the size of a medicinal teaspoon

IMPERIAL WEIGHTS AND MEASURES

16 ounces (oz.)	= 1 pound (lb.)
20 fluid ounces (fl. oz.)	= 1 pint (pt.)
2 pints	= 1 quart (qt.)
8 pints	= 1 gallon

AMERICAN MEASURES

1 American cup	= 8 fluid ounces or approx. 230 millilitres (British: 284 ml.)
1 American tablespoon	= ½ fluid ounce or approx. 14 millilitres (British: 15 ml.)
1 American teaspoon	= ⅛ fluid ounce or approx. 5 millilitres (British: 5 ml.)
1 American pint	= 16 fluid ounces (British: 20 fl. oz.)

If standard American cups and spoons are used with this book, the spoons can be taken as the same size as those used in the recipes, but count 1 cup as equivalent to 1¼ American cups.

METRIC WEIGHTS AND MEASURES

In all recipes British weights and many of the measures have been converted to the metric system. This has not been done with table-spoons and teaspoons because these are the same size as spoons used in many countries which use the metric system.

The conversions have been adjusted to give practical metric weights and measures which are still sufficiently accurate to give good results.

The following figures have been used.

1 ounce (oz.)	= 25–30 grammes (g.) (real value 28·35 g.)
1 pound (lb.)	= ½ kilogramme (kg.) (real value 453·6 g.)
	= 500 grammes
2 pounds	= 1 kilogramme (real value 2·2 lb.)
	= 1000 grammes
1 pint (pt.)	= ½ litre (l.) (real value 568·2 millilitres)
	= 5 decilitres (dl.)
1 inch (in.)	= 2½ centimetres (cm.) (real value 2·54 cm.)
	= 25 millimetres (mm.)
1 fluid ounce (fl. oz.)	= 25–30 millilitres (ml.) (real value 28·4 ml.)
1 litre (l.)	= 1000 millilitres or 10 decilitres
1 metre (m.)	= 1000 millimetres or 100 centimetres

OTHER USEFUL APPROXIMATIONS

⅛ pint	= 75 millilitres or 5 tablespoons
¼ pint	= 1½ decilitres or 150 millilitres
½ pint	= ¼ litre or 250 millilitres or 2½ decilitres
¼ pound	= 125 grammes
½ pound	= 250 grammes or ¼ kilogramme

ABBREVIATIONS USED IN THE RECIPES

°	= degrees Fahrenheit	min.	= minute/s
°C.	= degrees Centigrade	hr.	= hour/s
E.	= electric	in.	= inch/es
G.	= gas	g.	= gramme/s
tbs.	= level tablespoon/s	kg.	= kilogramme/s
tsp.	= level teaspoon/s	mm.	= millimetre/s
c.	= level cup/s	cm.	= centimetre/s
pt.	= pint/s	m.	= metre
oz.	= ounce/s	ml.	= millilitre/s
lb.	= pound/s	l.	= litre/s

Alphabetical list of culinary herbs with notes on the use of each and some hints on growing them

Although this chapter describes forty different herbs it is possible to produce well-flavoured and varied food with a much smaller collection.

Individuals have favourite herbs as well as ones they dislike so that a small collection which will suit one cook will not necessarily satisfy another. If I had space to grow only a few herbs my choice would be:

Bay	Marjoram	Sage
Basil	Mint	Savory
Chervil	Parsley	Tarragon
Chives	Rosemary	Thyme
Fennel		

I would buy garlic, horseradish (dried or fresh), caraway seeds, and coriander seeds. The rest of my forty I like to have but regard as dispensable.

For those who have strong likes and dislikes for certain flavours it is useful to know which herbs have similar flavours. To classify herbs thus is to a large extent misleading because no two herbs are exactly alike. The flavour they seem to have in common will be accompanied by a variety of other flavours which together make an individual herb unique. For example, all mints have a 'minty' flavour but they have other flavours as well which make them distinct from one another. Two other herbs with a minty flavour, costmary and catmint, are different again.

Anise is a flavour disliked by many people and can be detected in the following herbs:

Anise	Cumin	Dill
Caraway	Fennel	Sweet cicely
Chervil		

Many herbs are sold as being suitable for growing in pots, window boxes, and tubs. Whether they will be successful depends on the growing conditions, primarily the amount of light available, especially indoors, or the amount of shelter if they are on a balcony or in a window box. Very many herbs have to struggle for existence if they are deprived of light or exposed to cold winds in draughty conditions. In these conditions you are unlikely to get a worthwhile crop.

In order to grow well, herbs really need over-head light, so a patio, balcony, glass-roofed porch or verandah, or a window box are all better than having the herbs indoors all the time on a windowsill. If this is the only place available, choose a south or west window and turn the plants round once a day to give them light on all sides and to keep them a reasonable shape.

Watering is very important too and in summer in a sunny position they may need water two or three times a day. If this is impossible, choose only the herbs which are listed as liking dry conditions; but even these will need watering every other day in hot weather.

Herbs liking dry conditions and suitable for pots

Lavender (dwarf)	Rosemary (dwarf)
Marigold	Sage
Nasturtium	Thyme

Herbs needing moisture and suitable for pots

Basil	Chives	Parsley
Chervil	Marjoram	

Herbs for large pots or tubs on patio or balcony

Angelica	Lavender	Tarragon
Bay	Mint	Verbena
Fennel	Rosemary	

When planting herbs in the garden it is as well to find out the height to which they may be expected to grow so that you don't plant tall ones in front of short ones. Find out, too, whether they like dry or moist soil, sun or shade, poor, ordinary, or rich soil. Many like to plant all herbs together in an ornamental herb garden. In this case conditions are liable to be right for some and far from ideal for others, unless the herb garden is large enough to supply varied growing conditions. It is better, in my opinion, to put the herbs among other plants, each according to its preferred conditions.

ANCHUSA ITALICA

This anchusa is worth growing in the herb garden if only for its attractive shape and small flowers of a beautiful deep blue. It has long, narrow, greyish-green leaves pointing upwards stiffly in a thick cluster from ground level. From this rise the flowering stems up to 3–5 ft. (90–150 cm.) in height. It begins to flower in June and, if the spent flower spikes are cut out, it will flower again later on.

It is a perennial but can die in a severe winter, especially if it is grown in cold, damp soil. It does best in well-drained soil in sun or partial shade. It can be grown from seed sown in May or you can buy a plant in the spring.

The flowers are the edible part, used as a garnish in cold drinks, salads, and other cold dishes. Use them either alone or mixed with other edible flowers. They are particularly effective floating on the top of a fresh fruit salad or decorating the whipped cream on a cold sweet.

ANGELICA
Archangelica is the cultivated species.
Sylvestris is wild angelica.

They are closely related plants, the wild one having thinner purplish stems while the cultivated has light green stems. Flowers of the wild species are white or flushed with pink, the cultivated are greenish white or green. The cultivated has the better flavour and is superior for culinary purposes.

Angelica is a handsome plant which will grow as tall as 8 ft. (2·4 m.) in the rich, damp soil it prefers, and in partial shade. It can also be grown in a tub.

It is a biennial, flowering in May of its second year, and seeding itself freely. If it is kept cut and not allowed to flower it will last more than the usual two years of a biennial and may be kept going for 3–4 years or longer.

All parts of the plant are aromatic and edible. It is grown commercially for the bright green hollow stems which are candied and used in cakes and confectionery. The leaves are used for flavouring many liqueurs, in the preparation of bitters, and with juniper berries to flavour gin, while the seeds impart a muscatel-like flavour to wine and are used in the preparation of vermouth. Angelica leaves are one of the flavourings used in liqueurs like chartreuse and kümmel, while the root, blended with wormwood and other herbs, is used in making absinthe.

Being a large plant, there isn't usually room for many of them in a small garden and one has to decide whether to let the angelica grow to its full handsome size and flower, or whether to keep cutting down the shoots for cooking. It takes a lot of the plant to produce enough for making candied angelica or marmalade, so, if you want the best of both worlds you need a minimum of two plants, one to cut and one to flower and seed itself for the following year.

RECOMMENDED USES:
Crystallising (candied) for cakes and garnishing sweet things.
Drinks: leaves in wine cups and cold fruit drinks to give a muscatel flavour.
Marmalade: stems and leaves to give a very distinctive and delicious flavour.
Fruit: leaves and young stalks added when stewing fruit or making fruit compôte.
Salads: add young chopped leaves.

ANISE
Pimpinella anisum, also known as sweet cumin

This is a difficult plant to cultivate in Britain unless it can be grown in a warm, sunny garden. Even then seeds will only ripen in an exceptional summer. As the seeds are the most important part of this herb it is not worth growing unless you have the right conditions.

It is an annual which dislikes being transplanted. Sow the seeds in late spring or early summer where the plant will grow. It grows to about 18 in. (45 cm.) high with dainty, finely divided leaves which can be used in cooking. It flowers in July with small white flowers in umbels.

The seeds intended for culinary use are usually sold finely ground like a spice. The anise flavour is very strong and one to which people are addicted or which they can't abide. It is a popular flavouring in

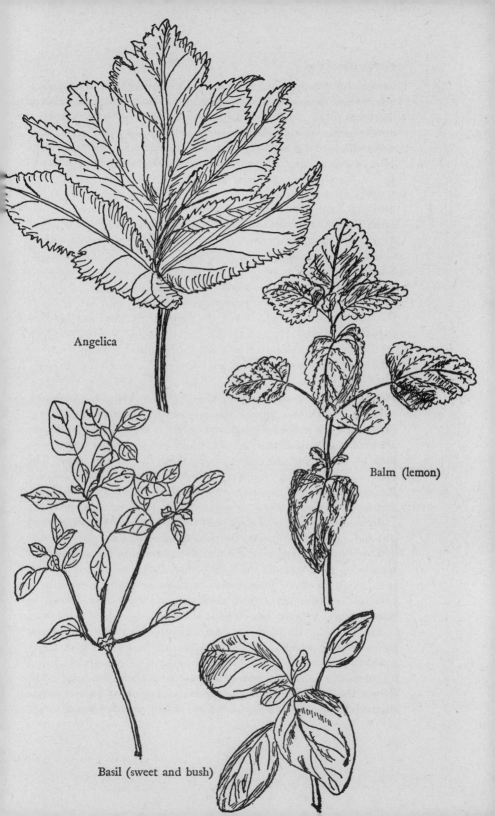

Angelica

Balm (lemon)

Basil (sweet and bush)

some parts of Europe, the nearest British equivalent to it being caraway. When flavouring foods with anise, avoid adding too much as
this tends to give the dish a peppery taste; ½–1 tsp. for 4 portions is
usually plenty. It keeps its flavour well when cooked.

An alternative to anise seed is to use the liqueur Anisette, specially
good in sweet dishes. Anisette contains the essential oils of the seeds.

RECOMMENDED USES:

Soups: ground seeds or fresh chopped leaves.
Fish: anisette or ground seeds in fish marinades.
Vegetables: green leaves chopped and sprinkled over vegetables in the
same way as parsley.
Salads: green leaves.
Breads: use ground seed as a spice.
Cakes, biscuits, and pastry: ground seeds used as a spice.
Desserts: ground seed or anisette for flavouring creams or other cold
sweets.

BALM or LEMON BALM
Melissa officinalis

Melissa is derived from the Greek word for a bee. When it is in flower,
from June to October, this herb is a favourite with the bees and was
planted for this purpose in monastery and castle gardens. The flowers
are small and insignificant, usually white, but sometimes tinged with
pink or yellow and borne in clusters along the upright stems. The
plant may be anything from 1–4 ft. (30–120 cm.) in height, depending on the situation; the leaves are a lightish green with serrated edges
and look not unlike some members of the nettle family. There is a
variegated variety of balm with gold-flecked leaves but this needs full
sun and a poorish soil if it is to retain the variegation.

The plant is a perennial, the tops dying down in the autumn and
coming up again in early spring. The easiest way of starting a clump
is to acquire a rooted piece; but it can also be grown from seed. It
grows very vigorously almost anywhere and even when grown in
partial shade the leaves have a good flavour.

The leaves are the only part used for food. They have an aromatic
lemon flavour which is fairly mild so this herb is used in larger
amounts than most others. For example, a small handful of leaves
(¼ pt. or 150 ml.) is not too much to flavour a salad for 4 people. The
flavour tends to be lost with prolonged cooking and it is better to add
the herb, chopped, towards the end of cooking or as a garnish.

Lemon balm retains its flavour reasonably well when dried or frozen.

RECOMMENDED USES:

Garnishing: fresh leaves have an attractive shape for garnishing cold sweet or savoury dishes. The leaves are delicious crystallised in the same way as mint leaves.

Soups: generous amounts added at the end of cooking.

Fish: add to a fish sauce instead of parsley.

Meat and poultry: for a lemon flavour add to casseroles at the end of cooking.

Salads: chopped or whole leaves mixed generously with other salad greens.

Desserts: use plenty of leaves to stew with fruit. It retains its flavour well for the short cooking time usually required for this. Leave in the fruit or remove.

Drinks: in white wine cups and iced fruit drinks. Fresh leaves for a herb tea.

BASIL
Ocimum basilicum is sweet basil
Ocimum minimum is bush basil

These are both annuals which are native to India and do not like the British climate. However, treated as half-hardy annuals (seed sown under glass with bottom heat in March) they can be planted out of doors in May in a sunny place sheltered from cold winds. If grown in pots under glass they are more vigorous plants with a better flavour. For a fresh supply of plants for the winter, sow seeds under glass in September.

Sweet basil has fairly large oval leaves, 1–3 in. (2–7 cm.) long, and will grow from 12–18 in. (30–45 cm.) high though it is better to keep it cut and producing new tender tops for the kitchen.

Bush basil has smaller leaves and grows 6–12 in. (15–30 cm.) high. Cutting the tops regularly for the kitchen helps to keep it in a well-shaped small bush.

The leaves of both species are very aromatic, sweet basil being considered the better of the two. It is one of the herbs used in mixtures for flavouring English pork sausages and, if used too generously in cooking, it makes everything taste like sausages. Used with discretion it is a wonderful herb which retains its flavour well in cooked dishes.

The leaves may be dried but lose a lot of flavour; freezing is a better method of preserving; best of all is to have a continuous supply of fresh leaves.

RECOMMENDED USES:

Condiments: make basil vinegar or use in mixed herb vinegar, in herb oils, in blends of dried herbs, in herb mustard, and spiced salt.

Soups: Basil is the traditional flavour for turtle soup; also good in tomato and thick meat soups.

Sauces: specially in tomato sauce and herb butter.

Eggs: in any egg dish but specially if tomatoes are included.

Cheese: good in hot cheese dishes or as one of the herbs used for flavouring soft cheese.

Fish: as one of the herbs for marinades and basting sauces; or for fish recipes containing tomatoes.

Meat and poultry: specially good in stews and casseroles containing wine and garlic. Use with other herbs for herb butters for grills.

Vegetables: specially good to flavour aubergines, tomatoes, peas, onions, beans, and beetroot.

Salads: in any salads, alone, or with other herbs; specially good in tomato salad.

Stuffings: with other herbs in fish and meat stuffings.

Pasta: add to meat or tomato sauces to serve with pasta or use to sprinkle on cooked pasta.

Drinks: goes best with tomato juice cocktails but can be added to fruit cups and iced fruit drinks.

BAY
Laurus nobilis, bay laurel, or sweet bay

In warm climates the bay tree can grow up to 60 ft. in height but it can be clipped and trimmed to keep it any height or shape you want. Trimming is best done between May and July. When grown in tubs, the bay is usually shaped as a standard and must be trained like this from very early on. Purchase a pot-grown plant of a shape you like and either keep it in a pot and eventually a tub, or plant it out in a spot protected from biting cold winds. It will withstand snow and frost but dislikes cold winds which kill many of its leaves and can kill the entire plant. In very cold districts it is wiser to grow the tree in a tub and move it to some shelter or under glass during the winter.

When planted out the tree should be watered freely for the first

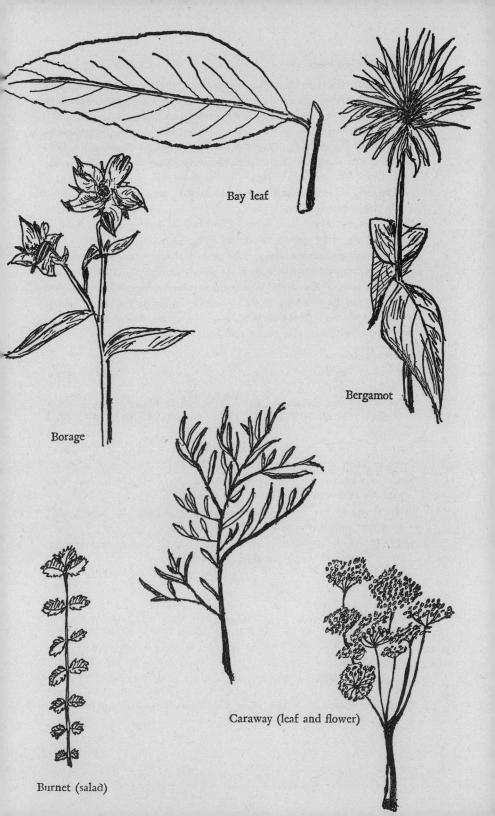

Bay leaf

Bergamot

Borage

Caraway (leaf and flower)

Burnet (salad)

month and thereafter for several months if the weather is dry. Once
it is established it will fend for itself out of doors but, when grown in
a tub, it needs the usual careful watering of all pot plants.

Bay leaves are 3–4 in. (8–10 cm.) long, dark green, and smooth,
often with a wavy edge. In May the tree has small greenish-yellow
flowers. The leaves are very aromatic and can be used for flavouring
both sweet and savoury dishes. Half a large leaf is usually sufficient
to flavour a stew or casserole for 4 people. Bay leaves are always added
at the beginning of cooking so that they have time to impart their
flavour to the other ingredients. They can be left in all the time or
removed when the dish is flavoured sufficiently.

Although fresh bay leaves can be picked all the year round, surplus
leaves, gathered when the tree is trimmed, can be dried for later use
and even pressed for dried flower arrangments. Dried leaves should
not be stored for too long as they soon lose a lot of flavour. To keep
a spray fresh for a short period, stand the stem in water or put the
leaves in a polythene bag in the refrigerator, or freeze them.

RECOMMENDED USES :

Garnishing: fresh leaves make attractive garnishes for cold sweet or
savoury dishes.

Condiments: best known as part of the classic bouquet garni; dried
leaves can be crushed or ground to add to other herbs for flavouring
mixtures.

Soups: as part of a bouquet garni for flavouring stock, or by itself in
many soups.

Sauces: cooked in the sauce and then removed; suitable for sweet or
savoury sauces; used in flavouring marinades.

Fish: in marinades; in the water used for poaching; in sousing and
pickling; in fish soups and stews; with kebabs.

Meat, game, and poultry: in stews and casseroles; in the water used
for boiling meat; in marinades; with kebabs.

Vegetables: in the water used for boiling vegetables, especially celery,
dried beans, and vegetable stews.

Desserts: leaves infused in the milk used for making custards, milk,
puddings, and cold sweets. Remove the leaf when the flavour is
strong enough.

BERGAMOT
Monarda, Bee balm, or Oswego tea

Many people who grow this plant for its lovely flowers and scent, or because the bees love it, never use it in cooking. It is a perennial, the tops dying down in winter. It belongs to the mint family, likes a moist situation, and will grow in shade or partial shade. It grows 2–3 ft. (60–90 cm.) high and has flowers of red, purple, pink, white, and sometimes other colours. The red bergamot (Monarda didyma), is usually regarded as the best for scent and its lemon-flavoured leaves.

Bergamot can be grown from seed but is most usually propagated by division of the roots in February or March, or by taking cuttings in July. A clump gradually increases in size but eventually the middle stops flowering and the clump then needs to be lifted, divided, the centre discarded, and the young pieces re-planted.

Both the leaves, which have a lemon scent, and the flowers in late summer, can be used for food. The leaves and flowers dry well and keep their fragrance and colour throughout the winter. Earwigs like the flowers so careful washing or soaking in water before use is advisable.

RECOMMENDED USES:
Garnishes: flowers in salads or to garnish sweet or savoury cold dishes.
Drinks: fresh leaves and flowers in white wine cups and iced drinks;
fresh or dried leaves to make a herb tea or to mix with Indian tea.
Salads: chopped leaves for flavouring.

BORAGE
Borago officinalis

This is an annual plant growing 1½–2½ ft. (45–75 cm.) high, easily grown from seed, and seeding itself freely. It prefers a sunny place with lime in the soil and does well on dry banks. It begins to flower in May or June, the flowers most often being either blue or white but they can be tinged with red or pink. They are bigger than anchusa flowers and a more attractive shape.

Flowers, leaves, and stems are all edible, having a decided cucumber flavour. The leaves are hairy and this makes all but the young leaves apt to be unpleasant to eat. Young leaves should be chopped before being added to salads. Seedlings, removed when the plants are thinned out, are tender and can be chopped for salads. The stems, too, are used in salads but should first have the outer skin peeled off; this is quite easy to do.

RECOMMENDED USES:

Garnishing: use the flowers to garnish any sweet or savoury dish.

Cheese: add finely chopped young leaves to soft cheese or yogurt to give a refreshing cucumber flavour.

Salads: flowers for garnishing; finely chopped young leaves and peeled stems for flavouring.

Drinks: Borage leaves are the traditional flavouring for Pimms No. 1, but leaves and flowers can be used in wine cups and cold fruit drinks of all kinds.

BOUQUET GARNI (also called a Faggot)

This is the traditional bouquet of herbs used in French cookery. It consists of a bay leaf, a sprig of parsley or some parsley stalks, and a sprig of thyme. These are either tied together with white cotton or tied in a muslin bag. Remove the bouquet before serving the food.

Dried herbs can be used and dried bouquets garnis are sold ready-made up in muslin bags. If these are stale they will be practically useless as flavouring agents and it can be better to make your own, especially if you grow the herbs and dry your own or store them in the freezer.

Other herbs are often included in flavouring bouquets, varying the herbs according to the food being cooked.

BURNET
Poterium sanguisorba; Primprinelle of French cooking; also called Garden or Salad burnet

Burnet is a hardy perennial which grows wild on chalky downs. It prefers a dry soil, not too rich, and will grow in partial shade. It is grown from seed or by division of roots in spring or autumn. It will seed itself although for use as a herb it needs to be kept cut and not allowed to flower. The leaves are very finely divided and grow in pairs along stems which come in a cup-like formation from the base of the plant. The flower stem rises about 1½–2 ft. (45–60 cm.) from the centre and has a greenish flower with purple-red stamens.

The leaves are the part eaten and regular cutting will provide plenty of young leaves. They have a cucumber-like flavour when young but, when old, are bitter. If kept cut it can be used throughout the winter.

RECOMMENDED USES:

Garnishing: a most attractive leaf for garnishing cold dishes or for floating in soups.

Sauces: in any sauce where a cucumber flavour would be appropriate; with other herbs in herb butters.

Salads: by itself or with other herbs in mixed salads.

Drinks: a refreshing flavour to add to cold milk and other cold drinks.

CAPER
Capparis spinosa

This plants grows wild in hot climates such as in North Africa and the Mediterranean area but does not grow successfully in temperate climates.

The caper grows into a small bush bearing beautiful flowers. The pickled capers sold for cooking are the buds, preserved in vinegar. Once a bottle of capers is opened the contents will keep for a long time provided enough of the liquid is left to keep the capers well covered.

Pickled nasturtium buds or seeds make very good alternatives to the caper (see page 91).

The caper spurge which grows in gardens in Britain is a Euphorbia and is poisonous, so don't be tempted to try pickling its buds.

RECOMMENDED USES:

Sauces: used in Tartare, Remoulade, Ravigote, vinaigrette, and Sauce Gribiche; also in caper sauce for serving with lamb or mutton.

Eggs: in stuffed eggs or egg salad.

Cheese: for flavouring soft cheese, e.g. Liptauer.

Fish: traditional in black butter sauce served with skate; with cold fish dishes; also good in sauces served with herrings, whiting, salmon, turbot, and conger eel.

Meat, game, and poultry: traditional in a sauce with boiled lamb or mutton; also good with chicken in a sauce or chicken salad; with liver and with pork.

Salads: in meat, chicken, egg, or fish salads or in the salad dressing served with these.

CARAWAY
Carum carvi

This is a biennial plant which grows to a height of about 2 ft. (60 cm.). It has finely cut fern-like leaves and small white flowers in umbels. It is grown from seed sown in March or April, will flower the following April or May, and then forms its fruits or seeds. When the seeds begin to ripen at the end of July or in August, the stems are cut down to the ground and the branches hung up in bundles to dry. Finally, the seeds are rubbed from the stalks and bottled. Provided they are fully ripe and dry caraway seeds will keep satisfactorily for a very long time.

It is not fussy about soil and position but does best in light soil in a sunny spot.

The green leaves can be used for flavouring as a green herb having a less pronounced flavour than the seeds. Caraway seeds have a distinctive anise-like flavour which some people dislike. Where caraway grows wild and is plentiful, the roots are used as a vegetable.

RECOMMENDED USES:

Soups: leaves or seeds as a herb flavouring; seeds used in herb dumplings to serve with soup.

Sauces: seeds added to mushroom sauce; leaves and young shoots to flavour a marinade.

Cheese: seeds used to flavour soft cheese.

Meat, game, and poultry: traditional in Goulash and many Central European recipes; sprinkled on duck and goose before roasting; sprinkled in the scored skin of pork before roasting.

Vegetables: a pinch of seeds used to flavour vegetables such as asparagus, beetroot, cauliflower, cabbage, potatoes, and marrow or courgettes.

Salads: leaves and young stems in green salads; seeds in cucumber salad.

Cakes: seed cake and sweet caraway biscuits; in bread.

CATMINT
Nepeta cataria, Catnep, or Catnip

This is a well-known garden perennial but is not often used for food.

It likes a good, rich soil containing lime and needs plenty of sun and protection from damp and cold winds.

The leaves are covered with a soft down which makes them look grey. The flowers can be blue, pink, or white. It can be grown from seed or by division of plants in the spring.

The whole plant has a minty flavour. The leaves, young shoots, and flowers are edible and can be dried. They are slightly bitter.

RECOMMENDED USES:

Sauces: leaves and young shoots for a minty flavour.
Meat, game, and poultry: leaves and shoots with other herbs.
Salads: leaves and young shoots.

CHERVIL
Anthriscus cerefolium

This is a hardy annual with flowering stems growing 12–18 in. (30–40 cm.) high, bearing small white flowers in umbels. The leaves are dainty, finely divided, and like lace in their delicacy. There is both a curled and a plain variety.

Chervil prefers a moist, fairly rich soil and partial shade, especially in hot weather. It is grown from seed sown from the end of February to October to give a succession of leaves. Once established it will seed itself freely, the seeds ripening in July. The leaves are cut when 3–4 in. long and, to keep the plants producing fresh leaves, cut some right down to the roots leaving a few to seed themselves.

Chervil wilts fairly soon after cutting and is not a good plant for marketing so it is difficult to find it in shops. If the leaves are washed as soon as they are gathered and the surplus water shaken off, they will keep in good condition for 1–2 days in a polythene bag or box in the refrigerator.

In mild districts chervil will remain green all winter but elsewhere it must be sown under glass for a winter supply. The leaves can be dried but lose flavour and it is better either to ensure a winter supply of fresh leaves or to freeze surplus leaves during the season.

The leaves are used for garnishing and flavouring in the same way as parsley but chervil has a very distinctive flavour with a hint of anise. It is better to chop chervil just before it is to be used and to add it to a dish just before serving rather than subject it to long cooking.

RECOMMENDED USES:

Garnishing: use chopped or as tiny pieces of leaf without stem, known as 'pluches'. These are floated on consommé and other soups or used to garnish cold dishes.

Condiments: use to make herb vinegar or oil.

Sauces: in Ravigote sauce; add to Béchamel instead of parsley; in vinaigrette sauce; in marinades.

Soups: add chopped just before serving; chervil royale for a garnish for consommé.

Eggs: one of the best herbs; as fines herbes (chervil, parsley, chives, and tarragon); good alone in cheese omelets; in baked egg dishes and stuffed eggs.

Cheese: to flavour soft cheese; with other herbs in hot cheese dishes.

Fish: as part of fines herbes used for flavouring any fish but specially mackerel, crab, lobster, mussels, and scallops.

Meat, game, and poultry: use with other herbs to sprinkle on stews and casseroles before serving; in accompanying gravies and sauces.

Breads, pastry, and batters: use with other herbs.

Salads: use alone or with other herbs; specially good with cucumber or chicken salads; add to salad dressings.

CHIVES
Allium schoenoprasum

These are the mildest-flavoured members of the onion family and indispensable for delicate foods which would be spoiled by using onion or garlic.

Chives are like tiny onions growing in clumps. Half a dozen of the small bulbs will soon increase to a sizeable clump. The leaves look like round grass and are the most important part for culinary use; but the bulbs, if large enough, can be used as a substitute for onions. The pinkish purple flowers are decorative and edible with a stronger onion flavour than the leaves, more like spring onions.

Chives can be grown from seed but a better way is to buy a small clump of the bulbs, and before long you will have as much as you can possibly use. The stock is increased by dividing the clumps yearly or even twice a year. Chives will grow in any good soil, in sun or partial shade, but need watering in dry weather to keep the leaves fresh and green. They can be grown in pots or window boxes.

They are perennials, the tops dying down in the winter, though they can be kept going under glass or can be cloched for leaves in January. Regular cutting is important to ensure a good supply of fresh green. When you have more than one clump cut each in rotation, cutting right down to the ground. A few clumps can be allowed

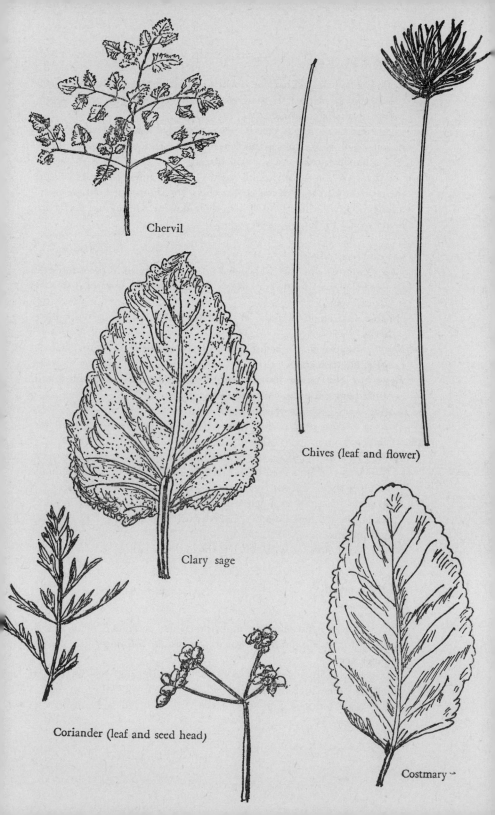

Chervil

Chives (leaf and flower)

Clary sage

Coriander (leaf and seed head)

Costmary

to flower and then either cut down or lifted, divided (6 bulbs in each piece), and re-planted. If watered freely, they will give fresh young foliage in the late summer.

Surplus chive leaves can be frozen at any time and retain their flavour very well. Freeze the leaves whole and, when using them, slice a bunch crosswise while still frozen.

Chives are almost invariably used chopped and it is better to add them at the end of cooking or use them for short-time cooking operations; otherwise they tend to lose their flavour. Onion and garlic are better to use for long cooking operations.

RECOMMENDED USES:

Garnishing: use the leaves chopped or scissor-snipped in the same way as parsley; use the flowers whole to garnish cold savoury dishes or float in soup.

Sauces: used alone to make chives sauces and butters or with other herbs.

Soups: chopped as a garnish particularly with potato soup, Vichyssoise, and fish soups.

Eggs: the best onion flavour for these; in omelets, scrambled and stuffed eggs; use alone or with other herbs.

Cheese: very good for flavouring soft cheeses.

Fish: as part of fines herbes with any fish recipe; in the fat used for shallow frying.

Meat, game, and poultry: in the fat used for shallow frying of steaks, chops, and escalopes; in herb mixtures to sprinkle in pan drippings and gravies; to flavour rissoles and other cooked meat recipes.

Vegetables: chopped as a garnish for any, specially good in mashed potato, boiled new potatoes, baked stuffed potatoes, celery, carrots, and turnips.

Salads: good alone or with other herbs in any salads.

CLARY SAGE
Salvia sclarea

This is a very handsome biennial (sometimes perennial) plant worth growing for its appearance, even if you decide you don't like it as a culinary herb.

It grows easily from seed sown in the spring, or you can buy a plant, and thereafter it will seed itself freely. It likes the sun and a well-drained soil if it is to survive the winter. It will grow from 3–5 ft. (90–150 cm.) tall, as a stately spire rising from a clump of large grey-green leaves not unlike foxglove leaves. The flowers, which last over a long period starting in June, are white with bluish or purple tones. They have a very pungent perfume. The leaves have a distinctive flavour which some people say is reminiscent of grapefruit. It is one of the more unusual herbs and needs to be used with discretion.

It can be used for flavouring in the same way as ordinary sage, as well as in claret or wine cups and chilled fruit drinks.

CORIANDER
Coriandum sativum or Chinese or Japanese parsley

Coriander is a very handsome annual growing 1½–2 ft. (45–60 cm.) high and flowering in July or August with white, pink, or pale mauve flowers in umbels. As soon as the round pea-like seeds begin to ripen the whole plant is cut down and hung up to dry. If the seeds are left they will very quickly fall.

Coriander likes sun and a dry soil. The seed can be sown in heat in March and planted out in May or it can be grown in pots or window boxes.

Both the seeds and leaves are used in cooking but they have entirely different flavours. The leaves have a mild flavour not unlike parsley while the seeds are strongly aromatic and spicy. The green seed has a most unpleasant smell and taste which disappears when it is fully ripe; the flavour improves as the seed ages and it is frequently toasted to bring out the full flavour. Prepared seeds are sold in shops stocking dried herbs.

The young green leaves are gathered as required and used like parsley. They can be dried or frozen.

The seeds are used whole as a flavouring in long cooking processes, or crushed.

RECOMMENDED USES:
Garnishing: the fern-like leaves used whole or chopped.
Cheese: crushed seeds in hot cheese dishes; chopped leaves in soft cheese.
Sauces: the leaves with other mixed herbs; crushed seeds in marinades or added to herb seasonings.
Soups: whole or crushed seeds; chopped leaves as a garnish.
Fish: seeds whole or crushed in any fish dish, especially curried fish.
Meat, game, and poultry: Crushed seeds or chopped leaves in minced

beef dishes; in beef pies and puddings; in beef stews and casseroles; crushed seeds rubbed into lamb for roasting or grilling; or with pork roasts or chops; in pilaus and other meat and rice dishes.

Salads: young leaves with other herbs.

Breads, biscuits, cakes: crushed seeds used as a spice.

Desserts: crushed seeds used to flavour jellies, creams, and other cold sweets.

COSTMARY
Chrysanthemum balsaemita or Alecost

Costmary is not native to Britain but has been grown here since the 16th century, mainly used for flavouring ale.

It is a perennial herb with large oval leaves, 6 in. (15 cm.) or more long and growing fairly close to the ground. The flower stalks rise 2–4 ft. (60–120 cm.) with clusters of yellowish and white flowers, though in temperate climates it often fails to flower and practically never seeds. It is best to buy a plant rather than seeds. It needs a light rich soil and plenty of sun. It grows vigorously, spreads, and can be divided in the spring or autumn.

The young leaves are used for flavouring, finely chopped. They have a minty flavour, rather bitter so that only tiny amounts can be used at a time, generally with other herbs. The leaves retain their flavour well when dried or frozen.

RECOMMENDED USES:

Soups: a little chopped and added at the end of cooking.

Eggs: a tiny bit with other herbs in omelets.

Meat, game, and poultry: a little in stews and casseroles for an unusual flavour, specially good with chicken, duck, game, goose, and veal.

Salads: add chopped young leaves, not too many.

Drinks: a pinch of chopped leaves to cold drinks for a bitter flavour.

CUMIN
Cuminum cyminum

Cumin is an annual growing about 6 in. (15 cm.) high with thread-like leaves and small white or pink flowers in June or July. The seeds ripen in August and resemble caraway seeds in flavour and appearance, though they are lighter in colour than caraway. The seeds have

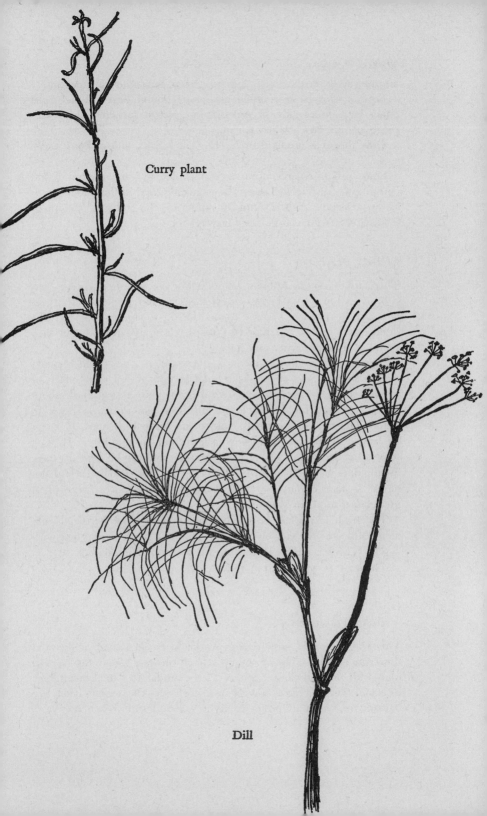

Curry plant

Dill

an unpleasant flavour when they are green, but lose it on ripening.

Seeds need to be sown under glass, with bottom heat and the plants either kept under glass or put out in a warm sheltered place with plenty of sun. Sow in early spring.

Only the seeds are used in cooking, in pickles, and in Far-Eastern cookery.

Some people regard cumin as replaceable by caraway, but I find cumin quite distinctive. However, it can be used in the same way as caraway; but if you are trying to reproduce the authentic flavour of Eastern dishes use cumin, not caraway.

CURRY PLANT

There are two quite different plants whose leaves taste of curry.

Chalcas koenigii (*Murraya koenigii*) is an Indian plant, the leaves of which are used in Madras curries and in Ceylonese cooking. The dried leaves can be purchased in shops selling Asian foods but they soon lose their pungent curry flavour.

Helichrysum angustifolium or *H. seculum*, is a plant which grows well in Britain. Start by buying a plant and put it in a sunny place, or in semi-shade, in poorish soil. It will grow into a large bush about 2½ ft. (75 cm.) high, with leaves of silver, not unlike lavender in shape. The flowers are small, golden, on long thin stems. It keeps its leaves all the year but they lack flavour in the winter. It is a most attractive plant to have in the garden and can be kept in shape by clipping in March or after flowering in July; but be careful not to cut it back beyond the new growths. When touched, the plant gives out a mild curry scent.

The fresh leaves can be used alone or with other herbs and are better added at the end of cooking. They are particularly good with egg and chicken dishes, in stuffing for poultry, or in salads.

The leaves can be dried or frozen.

DILL
Anethum graveolens

This plant is easily grown from seed and is an annual or biennial flowering either the first or second year. It grows 1½–2 ft. (45–60 cm.) high with finely divided feathery leaves similar to fennel but lighter in colour. It has yellow flowers in umbels and the fruit or seeds are flat and brownish. It prefers a light soil and sun. When the seeds begin to ripen the plant is cut down to the ground and hung up to dry. If you want leaves rather than seeds, keep the plant cut down and don't let it flower.

Both the leaves and seeds are used in cooking and have an anise flavour but are quite different from other herbs with a similar flavour. It is most like fennel but the flavour is less strong than fennel.

The leaves are best preserved by freezing, as much flavour is lost when they are dried. Commercial dried leaves, often called 'Dill weed', have more flavour than home dried dill.

RECOMMENDED USES:

Garnishing: small pieces of fresh leaf make an attractive garnish, more delicate than parsley; the flowers are edible and tiny sprays make attractive decorations for cold foods.

Condiments: seeds and leaves used to make dill vinegar which is very good; seeds used to flavour pickles, specially cucumber pickles.

Soups: add chopped dill at the end of cooking, specially to hot or cold cucumber soup and chicken soup.

Sauces: dill sauce for fish, lamb or mutton, chicken and pork; with other herbs in vinaigrette sauce and herb mayonnaise or salad dressings.

Eggs: chopped leaves in any egg dish alone or with other herbs.

Cheese: chopped fresh leaves to flavour soft cheese, alone or with other herbs.

Fish: leaves are suitable for any fish recipe but specially with salmon, mackerel, shrimps, and prawns; sprinkle over fish before grilling; use leaves or seeds to flavour marinades and basting sauces.

Meat, game, and poultry: seeds can be cooked with the meat, chopped leaves added at the end; good with chicken casseroles and with pork; dill sauce for boiled lamb or mutton.

Vegetables: leaves or seeds can be used as a flavouring with most vegetables, specially potatoes, peas, cauliflower, cabbage, green beans, and beetroot.

Salads: green leaves with any salad, specially good with cucumber.

Bread, biscuits, pastry: use whole or ground dill seeds either alone or mixed with spices.

FENNEL

There are two culinary fennels; *Foeniculum vulgare* is the one used as a herb for flavouring while the bulbous stem of Florence fennel or *Foeniculum dulce,* is used as a vegetable. Most Florence fennel is imported and is difficult to grow well in Britain but the herb fennel is an easy plant which grows wild in many parts of the country.

It is a hardy perennial which grows up to 4–5 ft. (120–150 cm.) in height, has feathery green leaves and umbels of yellow flowers from June to October. There is also one with bronze foliage. It can be grown from seed sown in April but pot-grown plants are also available from nurserymen. It needs to be grown in a sunny place if it is to develop its full flavour which is very aromatic with anise among its other flavours.

Every part of the plant is edible, the fresh leaves, stems, and ripe seeds being the most used. The leaves retain their flavour well for short-time cooking, otherwise add towards the end of cooking or use seeds.

If you want to have flowers and seeds it is a good plan to have several plants, some for flowers and some for cutting leaves and shoots. If these are cut to keep the plant about a foot high it will go on producing leaves all the season.

Leaves and stems can be dried, the latter being used for burning under grilled fish to give a distinctive flavour. Leaves and stems keep their flavour very well when frozen. For purposes of flavouring seeds are generally more satisfactory than dried leaves.

Although there are differences in flavour dill and fennel look very much alike. Fennel is a taller plant, the leaves usually a little darker, the flower heads less dense with fewer seeds which are grey compared with the brownish dill seeds.

RECOMMENDED USES:

Garnishing: fresh leaves are delicate garnishes; the flowers are edible and tiny sprays make a good decoration for cold dishes.

Condiments: seeds or leaves used for making herb vinegar or herb oil.

Soups: very good in fish soups using tender stems as well as leaves; crushed seeds also suitable.

Sauces: specially to serve with fish, shellfish, lamb or mutton, pork and veal; in vinaigrette sauce with other herbs; in marinades for fish.

Eggs: in sauces to serve with eggs; in omelets and scrambled eggs; for stuffed eggs.

Fish: one of the most useful herbs for all kinds of fish; dried stems for a flambé, chopped leaves to sprinkle over before grilling; in mayon-

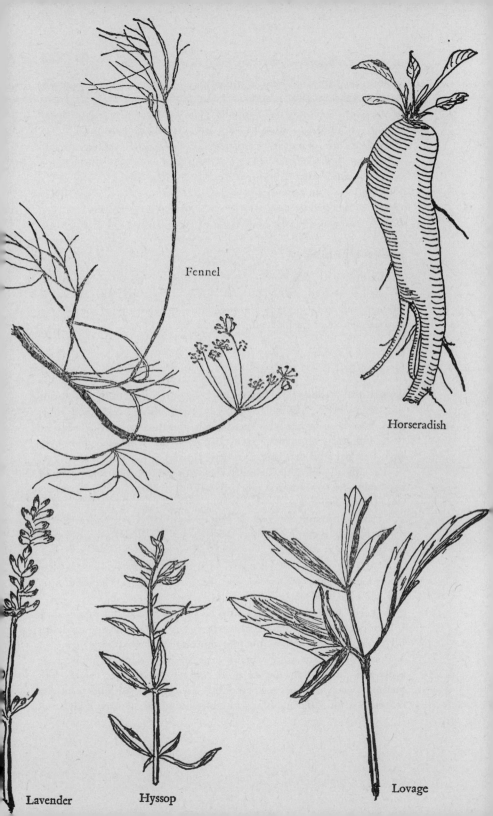

Fennel

Horseradish

Lavender

Hyssop

Lovage

naise for fish salads; for stuffings; in the water used for poaching fish, especially salmon and mackerel.

Meat, game, and poultry: specially good with the more fatty meats lamb or mutton, and pork; with liver and kidney; for veal.

Vegetables: use in sauces or sprinkle on cooked vegetables, specially beetroot, green beans, cabbage, parsnips, potatoes, and turnips.

Salads: in any, but very good with potato or fish salad.

Stuffings: for fish, lamb, veal, or pork.

Desserts: chopped green leaves or seeds in apple pie or tart.

Breads: use whole seeds; good with cheese biscuits.

FINES HERBES

A mixture of equal quantities of finely chopped fresh herbs consisting of parsley, chervil, tarragon, and chives. It is used a great deal in French cookery, especially for omelets and other egg dishes, but is also used in sauces, salads, and with poultry and fish.

GARLIC
Allium sativum

This is the strongest in flavour of all the onion family, so strong that many people dislike it intensely. Certainly since ancient times there have been people who hated garlic and those who were addicted to it. Horace is reputed to have claimed that it was more poisonous than hemlock and that eating it made him ill.

As with all the other strongly flavoured herbs, garlic needs to be used with discretion unless you are cooking for people who you know can stand a lot of it.

It can be difficult to grow in Britain as it likes a hot, dry climate and can rot in a damp summer. It needs a rich soil and a warm sunny place.

Fresh, dry bulbs will keep for six months so there is no problem about keeping imported garlic and there are many garlic products on sale such as dried garlic, garlic salt, and garlic vinegar.

A garlic bulb consists of many cloves encased in an outer skin. Individual cloves are planted in early spring and should be ready for lifting in July when they must be thoroughly dried for storage.

For cooking, the juice can be expressed by using a small garlic press and this and the use of garlic salt or dried garlic are the best methods when only a small amount is required. Fish and meat can be given a mild flavour of garlic by rubbing the surface with a cut clove prior to cooking; otherwise use a clove or piece of a clove crushed with the flat side of a knife; or whole cloves can be added during cooking. Unless you know that people like eating garlic as such it is better not to leave pieces of the clove in the food. This can cause real distress to those who are garlic-sensitive. For flavouring shallow fried food a clove can be cooked in the fat and then removed before cooking the food, or, for a stronger flavour, remove it after frying.

RECOMMENDED USES:

Condiments: garlic vinegar, oil, or spiced salt; powdered garlic.

Soups: can be used in any, especially meat soups, and garlic is traditional in fish soups of the Mediterranean countries and of Eastern cookery.

Sauces: used in many, sometimes in very large quantities, only for garlic addicts; small quantities are good in garlic butter for grills or sandwiches, mixed herb butters, in marinades for meat and fish, and in basting sauces.

Cheese: garlic juice or salt for flavouring soft cheese, best mixed with other herbs; a very little in hot cheese dishes.

Fish: traditional as a flavouring in the fish cookery of Eastern and Mediterranean countries, especially combined with other herbs and with tomatoes; also in the butter for dressing snails which have little flavour of their own.

Meat, game, and poultry: used with any of these as a flavouring by itself but better with other herbs as well; specially good with lamb, a few slivers of garlic inserted by the bone before roasting a leg; for grills of all kinds or in a butter to serve with them; in stews and casseroles; in accompanying sauces and gravies.

Vegetables: traditional in cooking tomatoes, sweet peppers, and aubergines; can be used with other vegetables but is too strong for most.

Salads: for a mild flavour use a little garlic oil or garlic vinegar in the dressing, or add a little garlic juice or some garlic salt.

Breads: sliced garlic and butter inserted in slits in a French loaf and baked; less crude in flavour is to use a garlic butter or mixed herb butter.

HORSERADISH
Armoracia rusticana

Horseradish is a perennial plant with a thick taproot and large leaves not unlike dock leaves, about 18 in. (45 cm.) long. In order to produce good-sized roots for the kitchen it needs rich soil and plenty of sun. It grows wild in many places. Once established it is hard to get rid of and can become troublesome in a small garden.

It is propagated by root cuttings planted in the late autumn or winter. Mature roots can be lifted in the autumn and stored in damp sand; or grated and dried; or grated and preserved in vinegar.

To use fresh horseradish, scrub the roots and then grate finely; or a more pleasant way, process pieces in the electric blender or in an electric shredder. Whichever way you do it, the very volatile and pungent juices get into the eyes and up the nose.

Fresh horseradish is sometimes served just plain grated but more often it is made into a hot or cold sauce. Bottled horseradish is available but a better product is made by buying dried horseradish and using this to make your own sauce by adding cream and other ingredients. A very good sauce is made by combining horseradish with apple.

RECOMMENDED USES:

Condiments: horseradish vinegar; grated and added to pickles, specially beetroot.

Sauces: make sauce with stock and add grated horseradish just before serving hot: cold, add to cream.

Eggs: horseradish sauce with hard-boiled eggs served hot or cold.

Fish: makes a good sauce for fatty fish like mackerel and herrings; or with smoked fish; add to mayonnaise for cold fish.

Meat, game, and poultry: traditional with roast beef, either plain grated or in a sauce; also with steaks or salt beef; with tongue or salt pork.

Salads: a little grated in any salad but specially with chicken, ham, egg, tomato, and beetroot.

HYSSOP
Hyssopus officinalis

This is one of the herbs not often used in the kitchen but worth growing for its beauty as a garden plant. It is a small evergreen bush growing 1–1 ½ ft. (30–45 cm.) tall with small dark-green leaves and flowers of blue, red, or white, from June to October.

It can be grown from seeds sown in April or from plants divided in the spring or autumn; or from cuttings in the spring. It needs a well-drained sunny place and an occasional trim to keep it in good shape.

The leaves, stems, and flowers are highly aromatic with a bitter flavour. Some describe it as minty, but it is a complex flavour. Because of the bitterness, it needs to be used with discretion.

Both flowers and leaves dry well and retain their flavour.

The flowers can be used for garnishing salads and other cold dishes. Small amounts of leaf can be used in soups, salads, and meat dishes.

LAVENDER
Lavandula (species and varieties)

This is another of the plants known to everyone, but not all know it as a culinary herb. Both the flowers and leaves are edible. They have a strong, hot flavour and must be used with discretion, for example, one flower head or four leaves, are plenty for 1 pt. (½ l.) of soup or stew (beef, chicken, lamb, or pork). A few leaves can be added with other herbs in a salad, and leaves and flowers make a herb tea.

Lavender is a hardy perennial shrub thriving in poor soil in full sun. There are lavenders of dwarf habit and those like the Old English lavender which grows 3 ft. (90 cm.) tall. After about five years a lavender bush loses its looks, becomes leggy, and needs replacing. Cuttings can be taken in spring or autumn and the new plants put out in their permanent positions the following autumn for the spring cuttings, and in spring for the autumn cuttings. The bushes can be kept a good shape by giving them a light clipping when the flowers have been gathered. If more drastic pruning is needed, do this in April.

Both leaves and flowers dry well.

LOVAGE
Levisticum officinale

Lovage is a hardy perennial growing 3–4 ft. high, more if it is a rich soil. It needs moisture to grow well, and either sun or semi-shade. It has large, deeply divided leaves and yellow flowers in umbels from July to August. It can be grown from seed or propagated by division of the root in autumn or spring. If the ground is kept well cultivated a plant will last for several years and, if allowed to seed will renew itself. To ensure plenty of young leaves, cut out at least the early flowers.

Leaves, stems, seeds, and roots are all edible. The predominating flavour is of celery, with a spicy background and a hint of lemon.

The leaves can be dried or frozen, and retain their flavour well.

It can be used in any recipe where you would normally add celery for flavouring, specially in stews, casseroles, and soups. The young leaves are good in salads and can be cooked with other vegetables. The shoots can be used for flavouring but are inclined to be a bit stringy for eating.

MARIGOLD
Calendula officinalis

This is the old-fashioned marigold, not to be confused with African and French marigolds more often seen in gardens today.

Calendula officinalis can be purchased as young plants in the spring or grown from seed sown in the autumn or spring. Once established, they will seed themselves freely and it is a good plan to leave a few of the early flowers on the plants to ensure well-ripened seed in August or September. When the plants have finished flowering in the autumn, scatter the seeds where you want the next crop to grow. Seeds sown in the spring make better plants if they are started under glass in March and planted out as young seedlings.

Marigolds do best in fairly poor soil, in sun or partial shade, and they make good pot plants.

The edible parts are the petals and young leaves though the latter need to be used sparingly because of their strong, bitter flavour and toughness. For salads, chop the leaves finely. The petals, too, are fairly tough and are better chopped if they are being used raw, for example, to add colour to a salad, alone or with other flowers. Petals can be added whole or chopped to cakes and buns for colour but do little for the flavour.

In fact, the best use for the marigold is as a garnish, using the beautiful orange petals to decorate sweet and savoury dishes. The orange colour can be extracted for use as a food colouring. The best way to do this is to simmer the petals in water or milk (about ¼ pt. or 150 ml. of petals to ½ pt. [250 ml.] of liquid). When the petals have begun to soften, put petals and liquid in the electric blender and process until smooth. Strain in case there are any large bits left. This liquid can be used for colouring sweet or savoury dishes.

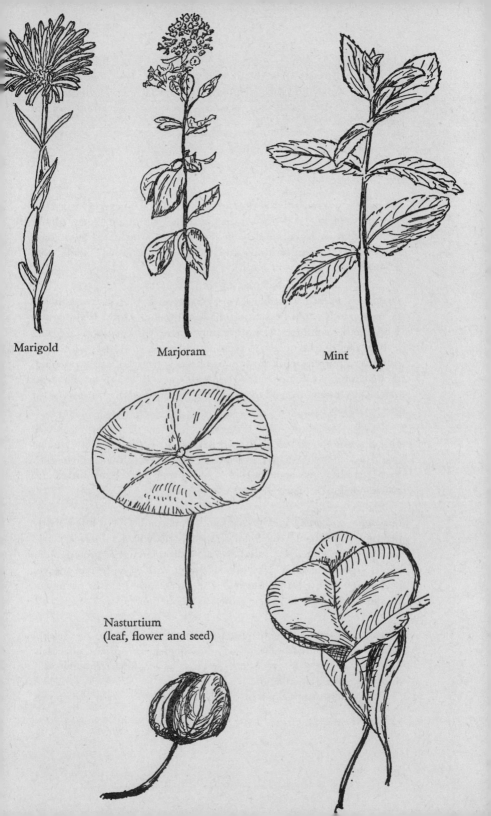

Marigold

Marjoram

Mint

Nasturtium
(leaf, flower and seed)

The petals retain their colour well when dried, best done by drying the whole flower and then stripping off the petals (see Drying). These can be used for garnishing savoury dishes, especially soups; or for sweet dishes.

MARJORAM
Origanum (species)

There are several different species of this herb. They prefer a light soil and sun but will grow quite well in semi-shade. They can be grown from seed sown under glass in April or propagated by division of the roots, and most kinds are available as pot-grown plants from a nursery specialising in herbs.

Origanum vulgare is wild marjoram, native to Britain where it can be seen growing in profusion on chalk or limestone hills. It also grows wild in other countries, including Italy where it is known as Orégano.

It is a hardy perennial growing 1–2 ft. (30–60 cm.) high with green leaves and purplish-pink flowers in bunches, from July to September; though for a good supply of fresh leaves it is better to keep at least one plant frequently cut to prevent it from flowering. It is one of the herbs loved by bees.

Origanum onites is pot or French marjoram. It prefers a hot climate but is a reasonably hardy perennial and can be grown under glass in winter. It grows about a foot (30 cm.) high with hairy leaves and whitish or pinky mauve flowers.

Origanum majorana is sweet or knotted marjoram. It is a less hardy perennial, a native of the Mediterranean, and will not survive a cold winter. It can either be treated as a half-hardy annual or grown under glass. It grows about 1½ ft. (45 cm.) high with greyish, hairy leaves and purple or whitish flowers. This marjoram has the strongest flavour of all, specially when grown in a hot climate.

Origanum aureum is golden marjoram of which there are several forms, all perennials. The leaves are golden in spring and early summer but revert to green as they grow larger. The following year they will come golden again.

The strength of flavour of any marjoram varies with the species and the climate but all are suitable for cooking; less is used of the strong ones.

Marjorams dry well but can lose flavour fairly quickly; freezing preserves the flavour better.

The leaves of all species are used in cooking and both the leaves and flowers are edible. If you have a strongly flavoured one use it sparingly or it can predominate over all other flavours.

RECOMMENDED USES:

Garnishing: small sprigs of leaves are attractive and the flowers can be used to decorate salads and other cold dishes.

Condiments: to make mixed herb vinegars and spiced salt; also in dried herb mixtures.

Soups: good in mixed vegetable soups, tomato, and goulash soups.

Sauces: in sauces for meat and poultry; in savoury butters for grills and vegetables; in basting sauces; tomato sauce and other sauces with pasta.

Eggs: add to omelets and other egg dishes.

Cheese: very good in any hot cheese dish.

Fish: dried marjoram sprinkled over fish for grilling; in marinades and basting sauces; in sauces to serve with fish; in recipes containing tomatoes.

Meat, game, and poultry: with any of these, added to stews and casseroles, sprinkled over meat before grilling or roasting (dried is best for this), in stuffings, and accompanying sauces or gravies.

Vegetables: fresh leaves added to vegetables during cooking or to sprinkle over cooked vegetables or use in the form of a herb butter for dressing cooked vegetables; especially good with green beans, Brussels sprouts, cauliflower, cabbage, carrots, mushrooms, spinach, tomatoes.

Salads: leaves for flavouring and flowers for garnishing: specially good flavour with tomato, cole slaw, and carrots.

Stuffings: for vegetables and poultry.

Pasta: sprinkle over cooked pasta or add to meat or tomato sauces to serve with it.

Breads: chopped fresh, or dried leaves.

Drinks: as a herb tea.

MINT
Mentha

There are very many species of this herb but not all of them are useful kitchen herbs. Some grow wild in Britain, usually near a stream or other moist place.

They are all hardy perennials, the foliage dying down in winter. Most of them prefer moisture, and a moderately rich soil, and partial shade. In order to get a good crop of leaves the beds need to be top dressed in winter after the tops have been cut down. It is advisable to renew the beds every three or four years, preferably planting in another part of the garden. This is particularly important if the mint suffers from rust. Mint is a very invasive plant but straying bits can easily be pulled out at the time of gathering; or you can prevent this wandering by confining the roots to an area bounded by slates driven in vertically. It can also be grown in large pots or tubs.

Mint is propagated by lifting and dividing roots in February or March; and you can buy rooted pieces in pots.

It can be preserved in a number of ways by drying (tends to lose flavour), by freezing (very good), or in vinegar for mint sauce.

Mint can be used in many ways other than the traditional British mint sauce with lamb, or mint cooked with new potatoes or peas. Other countries where its flavour is appreciated are Portugal, Spain, Italy, the Middle East, and India.

Mentha spicata, or spearmint, is the mint most often grown for traditional British cooking. The plant has slender dark green leaves and a purple flower.

Mentha rotundifolia is considered to be a better flavour than *spicata*, the variety Bowles mint being particularly good. It has long, woolly grey-green leaves.

Mentha rotundifolia variegata or Apple mint, because of its strong scent of apples, has decorative white and green leaves.

Other mints with a similar flavour to *M. spicata* are *M. cordifolia*, an early variety with wrinkled, heart-shaped leaves, *M. sylvestris* or horse mint with grey downy foliage, and *M. raripila* with smooth leaves.

Mints with special flavours are: Pineapple mint (green and gold foliage), Eau de Cologne mint (bronze-tinged leaves), Ginger mint (gold variegated leaves); all suitable for flavouring drinks, fruit and sweet dishes, or making mint tea.

Mentha pulegium or Penny Royal is a carpeting mint for shady places and among paving stones.

RECOMMENDED USES:

Garnishing: whole or chopped leaves; crystallised leaves for sweet dishes or for sweetmeats.

Condiments: mint vinegar; minted salt; mint sauce; mint jellies.

Soups: to flavour and garnish green pea, potato, cucumber, and chicken soups.

Sauces: mint sauce for lamb and mutton; for sauces with poultry, fish, and shellfish; in salad dressings, specially with cucumber.

Eggs: Mint with parsley makes a good mixture for any egg dish.

Cheese: to flavour soft cheese and yogurt.

Meat, game, and poultry: mint sauce with roast lamb or mutton; with duck and orange; with grilled lamb.

Vegetables: Chopped and sprinkled on cooked vegetables, specially beans, aubergines, cabbage, lentils, mushrooms, potatoes, marrow, courgettes, and spinach.

Salads: chopped in any mixed salad, also with cucumber or potato salads.

Stuffings: for lamb, fish, or veal.

Breads and Pastry: chopped mint in quick breads; mint and currant pasties.

Sweet dishes: chopped leaves with fruit, apples, gooseberries, fruit salad, grapefruit; in lemon or orange sorbets; in lemon jelly.

Drinks: mint juleps; cold fruit drinks; mint tea; claret cups; mint lemonade; mint syrup; yogurt and mint drink.

NASTURTIUM
Tropaeolum majus

These annuals can be low-growing, about 9 in. (23 cm.) high, or climbers. They need poor soil and plenty of sun to flower well, producing bright yellow-orange-red flowers throughout the summer. Even in deep shade they will grow well but produce leaves, not flowers. The one drawback is that they are very susceptible to attacks of black fly. Seeds are sown in the spring where the plants will grow. Small plants can be purchased for putting out in May.

Leaves, flowers, and seeds are all edible. The leaves are not unlike watercress in flavour, but more peppery. They are very good in salads or sandwiches, made like cucumber sandwiches.

The flowers make a beautiful garnish for salads, cold meat or fish dishes, and cold sweets. Wash them very carefully under running water to remove any insects; then shake gently to dry them.

The unripe seeds are preserved in vinegar as a substitute for capers. The flowers are used in a mixed herb vinegar.

PARSLEY
Petroselinum crispum

Some people find this hardy biennial difficult to grow. It can take several weeks for the seeds to germinate and it is often better to sow in pots than in the open. If the seeds can be given some bottom heat they will germinate in about two weeks. Young plants will transplant quite satisfactorily but mature plants are more difficult. Parsley grows well in pots or in a window box. It prefers a moist ordinary alkaline soil and semi-shade. In its first year it provides plenty of leaves but in the second year it flowers and then goes to seed. To have a continuous supply of fresh leaves parsley should be sown twice a year in April or May and again in July or August.

Some parsleys have deeply curled leaves, others are finely divided but not curled and this kind often has more flavour. When picking parsley always take the older leaves from the outside to allow young ones to grow from the centre.

Parsley tends to absorb other flavours and can only be used in large amounts where the basic flavour is bland, for example, parsley sauce made with milk or stock; or use in small amounts with other herbs, for example, in a bouquet garni. The stalks have more flavour than the leaf and are the better part to use for flavouring, leaving the leaf for garnishing.

Parsley can be dried but loses a lot of flavour in the process. Freezing is a better method of preserving. Freeze leaves and stems separately. The frozen leaves can be crumbled in the fingers or chopped while frozen. The stalks can be dried and powdered to give a green food colouring, or the juice can be squeezed from the leaves and used as a colouring.

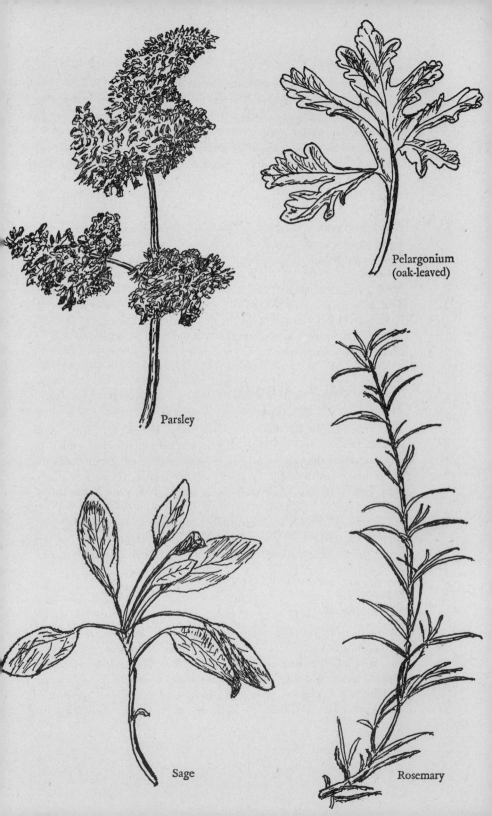

Pelargonium
(oak-leaved)

Parsley

Sage

Rosemary

RECOMMENDED USES:

Garnishing: fresh sprigs; sprigs fried in deep or shallow fat or oil; chopped or scissor-snipped.

Sauces: parsley sauce; as part of a bouquet garni for flavouring stock for sauces or the sauce itself; parsley or Maître d'hôtel butter; and with other chopped herbs.

Soups: parsley soup; as a garnish; mixed with other herbs for flavouring.

Eggs: good with any egg dish alone, or mixed with chives.

Fish: parsley sauce made with fish stock for serving with poached or boiled fish; parsley or Maître d'hôtel butter for grills; with other herbs.

Meat, game, and poultry: most commonly used as a garnish or as part of a bouquet garni for stews, casseroles, boiled meats; parsley or Maître d'hôtel butter for grills, or mixed herb butter.

Stuffings: specially for poultry and fish but used in others as well.

Bread: with other herbs.

PELARGONIUM CAPITATUM
'Oak-leaf' geranium

This pelargonium has finely divided leaves, like an oak leaf, small pinkish flowers, and a perfumed lemony scent. It is either grown in a pot which is the way to buy it, or may be planted out of doors for the summer and brought in again for the winter. It needs a sunny place and to be kept well watered in the summer, very little in the winter.

Leaves can be used for flavouring sweet dishes, either fresh leaves steeped in warm milk or other liquid used in the recipe, or the leaves dried and powdered to use as a spice in cakes or cold sweets.

ROSEMARY
Rosmarinus officinalis

Rosemary is an upright evergreen bush which, in favourable conditions, can grow to 6 ft. (1·8 m.) but is more often seen 3–4 ft. (90–120 cm.) high. It can be kept compact and free flowering by trimming annually after flowering or by the frequent cutting of sprigs for the kitchen. It is sometimes grown as a hedge and can be kept clipped.

It needs poor, well-drained, light soil and a warm, sheltered position. Provided these conditions are met it does quite well in semi-shade. It has narrow, tough leaves, dark green above and silver below, with pale blue flowers in April and May.

Rosemary can be grown in pots or tubs but for this, *R. o. pyramidalis*, which is a smaller variety is a better choice or *R. o. prostrata*, but the latter is a more delicate one which needs the protection of glass in the winter unless the garden is very warm all the year.

Rosemary can be grown from seed, cuttings, or layers. The cuttings are easy to strike, even rooting in water. They are best taken in late spring after flowering, and the cuttings should be from non-flowering shoots. They will also strike if taken in August or September.

It is one of the herbs which can be gathered fresh all the year round and is worth growing for that reason alone. The leaves can be dried but must then be crushed finely as they become unpleasantly tough and spiky to eat. Sprigs can be frozen and used as fresh rosemary.

This herb has a pungent flavour which some people find rather strong while others delight in it. For a very mild flavour just one or two leaves or a pinch of dried rosemary per portion is sufficient for a stew or soup. Fresh young leaves, very finely chopped, can be added to food at the end of cooking, or used in salads. A sprig of rosemary is often cooked under a roast leg of lamb or put inside a chicken; dried rosemary is rubbed into grills and dried or chopped fresh used in marinades.

The flowers are edible too, and make attractive garnishes.

RECOMMENDED USES:

Garnishing: flowers for fruit or wine cups and salads; sprigs for garnishing cold savoury dishes.

Condiments: rosemary vinegar and oil; spiced salt; mixed powdered herbs.

Soups: with other herbs in minestrone and meat soups.

Sauces: to serve with meat; rosemary butter for grills; in marinades and basting sauces for meat and fish.

Eggs: dried, in omelets and scrambled eggs, specially if tomatoes, ham, or bacon also included.

Fish: use dried or finely chopped fresh to flavour grills; or use in marinades or basting sauces.

Meat, game, and poultry: for beef grills or casseroles; in stuffings for chicken or duck; with partridges; one of the best herbs for lamb or mutton; good also with pork, veal, bacon, and ham.

Vegetables: use finely chopped fresh leaves or dried to flavour peas, sweet peppers, tomatoes, or vegetable stew.

Salads: finely chopped fresh leaves used sparingly alone or mixed with other herbs.

Pasta and batters: sprinkle cooked pasta with chopped fresh or dried, or use in a sauce; also in rice dishes; with other herbs in batters.

Breads: chopped fresh or dried with other herbs.

Cakes and desserts: chopped in a rich fruit cake or Christmas pudding. Flowers to garnish a fruit salad.

Drinks: in wine and fruit cups; rosemary tea.

SAGE
Salvia
(See also Clary Sage)

There are many different salvias grown in the flower garden for decoration and quite a number of species and varieties for culinary use.

The most common of these is *Salvia officinalis* or common sage. The broad-leaved or non-flowering form is one of the best. It is a perennial evergreen shrub, 1–2 ft. (30–60 cm.) high, with grey-green leaves. A plant lasts 3–4 years before becoming leggy and unsightly when it can be renewed by cuttings taken in spring or autumn, or by layering long side shoots to make new bushes. It will grow almost anywhere and thrives in partial shade but prefers a well-drained, good soil.

The narrow-leaved or flowering sage is most often grown as an annual or biennial but it can also be grown as a perennial and renewed by cuttings. Its leaves have a slightly stronger flavour than the broad-leaved sage. The flowers are a mixture of pink, blue, and lilac.

Salvia officinalis var. purpurea, or red sage, is a beautiful evergreen shrub with purple leaves and a royal blue flower. The flavour is milder than either of the grey-leaved sages. It can be kept clipped into a compact shape and frequently renews itself by self-rooted layers.

Golden variegated sage is another decorative variety with a mild sage flavour. It is less robust than the others, needing a sunny warm position and protection from frost and cold winds. It can be propagated from cuttings in the same way as the broad-leaved sage.

Sage leaves dry or freeze well and retain a good flavour. A crop of leaves for preserving can be gathered from the broad-leaved sage in May and another in August. Gather the other sages just before they flower in June or July.

Although the sages are evergreen, it is my experience that they have little flavour in very cold weather and it is often better then to use dried or frozen leaves.

RECOMMENDED USES:

Garnishing: Top sprays or large leaves of the grey-leaved sages make attractive decorations for savoury dishes, purple and variegated sages are even better, purple leaves, finely chopped, are attractive in salads. Sage flowers can also be used.

Condiments: spiced salt; herb mustard; dried herb mixtures; sage jelly.

Soups: in vegetable soups like minestrone, alone, or with tarragon and rosemary; in onion soup.

Sauces: sage and onion sauce; with other herbs in sauces or gravies for pork and poultry.

Eggs: in omelets, specially with ham and tomatoes; in herb pastry for egg quiches.

Cheese: in hot cheese dishes; to flavour soft cheese and cheese spreads.

Meat, game, and poultry: chopped fresh, or dried, in minced beef recipes; with chicken, goose, duck, or turkey; with grouse, pigeon, hare, or rabbit; lamb and mutton; liver; tripe; pork and ham; veal.

Vegetables: with haricot or butter beans; stuffed onions; stuffed tomatoes or sprinkled on grilled tomatoes; in vegetable stews.

Salads: in tomato salad; with other herbs in any salad.

Stuffings: sage and onion; sage and apple.

Bread and pastry: dried or chopped fresh, alone or with mixed herbs; good in cheese loaf or scones.

Drinks: sage tea.

SAVORY

Satureja hortensis or Summer savory
Satureja montana or Winter savory

Summer savory is a bushy hardy annual growing 6–18 in. (15–45 cm.) high. The leaves are narrow and pointed and the small flowers pale lilac. Seeds are sown in April, preferably in light soil with plenty of sun. It is ready to use from June onwards and, as the plants are cut, they produce fresh shoots. It can be grown under glass in pots or in a window box.

Winter savory is a hardy perennial growing about 12–15 in. (30–48 cm.) high with leaves like the Summer savory and pinkish mauve flowers. It can be grown from seed though the plants grow slowly and it takes a year to make a good-sized plant. It can be increased by division of the roots in spring or autumn, by taking cuttings in April or June, and by layering. Provided Winter savory is grown on poor, dry soil in a sunny position it will withstand even a severe winter.

Savory dries well, keeping its flavour as it does when frozen. The flavour is pungent; some compare it with marjoram, others with thyme, but it has a unique flavour, different from either of these.

RECOMMENDED USES:

Condiments: in mixed herb vinegar; spiced salt; in mixed dried herbs for seasoning.

Soups: in any, but specially meat soups, pea, bean, and lentil.

Sauces: with other herbs in marinades and basting sauces; in sauces to serve with vegetables, specially broad beans.

Eggs: in omelets, scrambled eggs, and stuffed eggs.

Fish: to sprinkle on grills or use in marinades or basting sauces.

Meat, game, and poultry: in minced beef recipes; beef stews and casseroles; with chicken, lamb, pork, and veal.

Vegetables: chopped fresh and sprinkled on cooked vegetables or in a sauce to serve with them, specially broad beans, carrots, peas, cauliflower, and beetroot.

Salads: with other fresh herbs, particularly with salads containing peas and beans, or with beetroot salad.

Breads and pastry: with other herbs, fresh or dried.

SORREL

Rumex acetosa is the wild sorrel of Britain
Rumex scutatus is French sorrel, also called garden sorrel

Wild sorrel is a hardy perennial which will grow to a height of 3ft. (90 cm.) with leaves shaped like an arrow-head. It is not unlike a dock in its habit of growth, even to the small pinkish brown flowers. It needs rich soil and a moist sunny place for good leaf production.

Garden sorrel is a perennial trailing plant with small leaves, also shaped like an arrow-head but less pointed than those of the wild

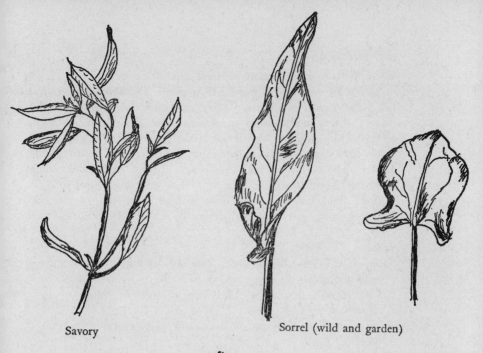

Savory

Sorrel (wild and garden)

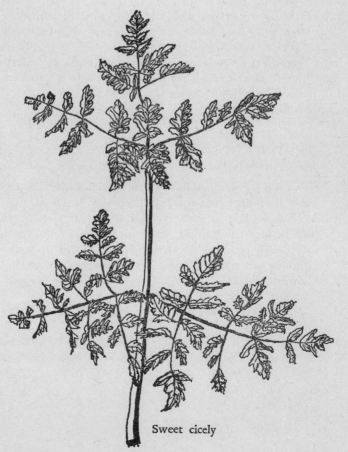

Sweet cicely

sorrel. It likes a dry, warm soil and sun.

Sorrels are used in cooking for their sharp, acid flavour, wild sorrel being the sharper of the two. They are soft watery leaves and cook down to a very small volume so two or three plants are needed to give a worthwhile amount. The usual method of cooking is to stew the leaves in butter, without added water, until the sorrel forms a pulp. If over-cooked it loses flavour. Because of its high oxalic acid content it should be cooked in either an aluminium or stainless steel pan.

Both sorrels can be grown from seed or by division of an established plant. Pot-grown plants are usually available from nurserymen.

RECOMMENDED USES:

Soups: it makes a delicious soup, preferably with milk or a mixture of milk and a delicate-flavoured white stock.

Sauces: sorrel purée added to Béchamel sauce or thick cream, to serve with pork or goose.

Eggs: a purée to stuff omelets; or stuff eggs; or raw, chopped in omelets.

Fish: a purée served with any fish, including salmon.

Meat, game, and poultry: a purée served with boiled chicken; with pork or veal cooked any way.

Vegetables: a few leaves cooked with beans or cauliflower; sorrel purée as a vegetable on its own (but only in small amounts).

Salads: a few young leaves in a mixed salad.

Stuffings: for fish.

SOUTHERNWOOD
Artemesia abrotanum, Old Man, or Lad's Love

This is a popular grey-leaved hardy perennial but although the leaves and shoots are edible it is not much used as a herb.

It grows into an attractive bush up to 5 ft. (1·5 m.) tall, though it can be kept down to 2 ft. (60 cm.) by clipping in March and again in July. It can be used to make a low hedge. It prefers a light to medium soil and will grow in sun or semi-shade. Even in full sun, however, it seldom produces its small yellow flowers, unless the summer is an exceptional one.

It is easily propagated by soft cuttings taken in the summer or hard-wood cuttings in the autumn.

The plant is very aromatic but many people dislike the smell and bitter taste. The leaves are used to make a herb tea (fresh or dried leaves). To experiment with it try a few chopped leaves in salads, alone or with other herbs and, if you like it, try it in other dishes including sweet ones which seem to go best with this herb.

SWEET CICELY
Myrrhis odorata, Anise Chervil, or Giant Sweet Chervil

This is a hardy perennial herb which grows wild in Scotland and northern England. It is slow growing but in a few years can reach 5 ft. (1·5 m.) When it is established, it produces white flowers in umbels in May, and the seeds are black. It seeds itself freely but can also be propagated by root division in early spring. It prefers a shady place with damp, rich soil and shelter from cold winds.

The light green leaves are lacy and fern-like. The whole plant is edible, including the seeds, has a slight anise flavour, and is sweetish. It is most appreciated when used in sweet dishes or salads. The root can be boiled and used cold in salads.

The leaves lose a lot of flavour when dried; less when frozen.

RECOMMENDED USES:
Garnishing: the leaf is most attractive for decorating sweet or savoury dishes.
Salads: chopped leaves alone, or with other herbs for flavouring salads; boiled cold root.
Fruit: add leaves to the syrup used for stewing fruit.
Cakes: use chopped leaves as a flavouring.

TARRAGON
Artemisia dracunculus (French tarragon)
Artemisia dracunculoides (Russian tarragon, sometimes called false tarragon)

The difference between these two tarragons is that the Russian grows taller with brighter green leaves but usually has less flavour than French tarragon and, under some conditions, can have very little flavour at all.

French tarragon is a perennial growing 2–3 ft. (60–90 cm.) high on slender, branching shoots with narrow olive-green leaves. It has tiny yellow-grey flowers in July or August but seldom produces seed in a temperate climate.

It is propagated by division of the roots in April or May. A clump lasts about four years but before this, start a new plantation to take over when the old one is discarded. Lift pieces of the old clump with a fork and plant the pieces a foot apart. Tarragon likes a warm, dry situation, preferably in full sun, though I find it still has a good flavour even when grown in half shade. The tops die down in the autumn when the plant should be mulched with compost which will help to protect the roots if the winter is severe.

The leaves are the aromatic part and can be gathered from early spring onwards. For preserving, gather in July. Tarragon loses flavour when dried but retains it very well when frozen. A few roots can be lifted and put under glass for a winter supply of leaves.

RECOMMENDED USES:

Garnishing: the leaves are very decorative for making designs on cold savoury dishes such as food in aspic or chaufoid sauce; or for decorating mayonnaise used for masking salad or hors d'oeuvre; also for garnishing soups.

Condiments: tarragon vinegar or oil; spiced salt; tarragon mustard; mixed herb vinegar.

Soups: in clear soup; chicken and fish soups.

Sauces: in sauces for fish, poultry, and other meat; in mayonnaise for cold fish; tarragon butter for grills; herb sauce; herb butters; Ravigote sauce; tarragon sauce, cold tomato sauce, melted butter sauce.

Eggs: in omelets, scrambled eggs, baked egg dishes.

Cheese: in hot cheese dishes.

Fish: in sauces to serve with any fish, specially salmon, mackerel, crab, lobster, mussels, scallops.

Meat, game, and poultry: in beef stews and casseroles; specially good with chicken; also with lamb or mutton, pork or ham, and veal.

Vegetables: in a sauce to serve with the vegetable or chopped and sprinkled on the cooked vegetable, specially with asparagus, beetroot, mushrooms, potatoes, peas, onions, and tomatoes.

Salads: in any salad but particularly with endive, orange, tomato; also with chicken and fish salads.

Stuffings: for chicken.

Drinks: in tomato juice.

THYME
Thymus vulgaris is common garden thyme
Thymus citriodorus is lemon-scented thyme

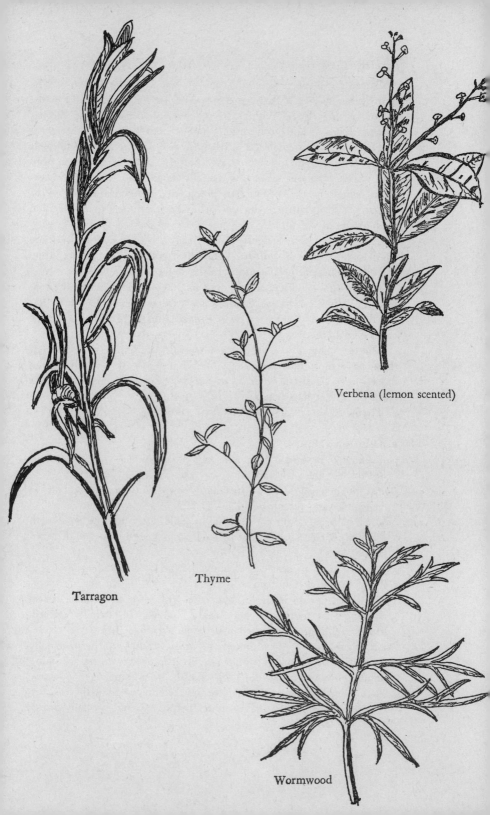

Tarragon

Thyme

Verbena (lemon scented)

Wormwood

These two evergreen perennials are the best for kitchen use. The many other species of thyme are grown either for their flowers or the colour of their leaves which can be silver-grey, golden, or varying shades of green, and with various habits of growth.

Thymus vulgaris makes a small bush 6–8 in. (15–20 cm.) high. It prefers warm, light soil containing compost, and needs shelter from cold winds. The leaves are tiny, usually dark green, and the flowers pink, from May to August. It is propagated either by sowing seeds, layering, taking cuttings during spring and summer, or by division of the roots in spring.

Lemon thyme has a lighter green leaf and makes a smaller more compact bush than *T. vulgaris*. There is a golden variety. The growing conditions and propagation are the same as for *T. vulgaris*.

Thyme can be dried and retains its flavour well either dried or frozen. Thyme can be picked from the garden during the winter but the flavour then is not very good and it is really better to use dried or frozen thyme.

The best parts to use are the young tips which have not flowered; these have most flavour and can be chopped stalk and all. When older pieces are used, or dried thyme, it is better to strip the leaves from the rather harsh stalks.

Thyme retains its flavour well during cooking.

RECOMMENDED USES:

Condiments: in mixed herb vinegar; herb powders for flavouring; spiced salt; herb mustard.

Soups: in a bouquet garni for many soups and stock; specially in vegetable, and tomato soup.

Sauces: in herb butter to serve with grills; in sauces to serve with fish; in marinades and basting sauces; in tomato sauce and mixed herb sauces.

Eggs: sparingly in omelets, scrambled eggs, and baked eggs.

Cheese: in hot cheese dishes.

Fish: lemon thyme is the best to use; with crab or lobster; in fish stuffings; in marinades and basting sauces; to sprinkle on fish before grilling; with baked fish; good with herrings.

Meat, game, and poultry: one of the most widely used herbs, chiefly as part of a bouquet garni but also with minced beef, for seasoning lamb chops or cutlets, for pork chops, and in stuffings; for game such as grouse, pigeon, and pheasant; lemon thyme with veal.

Vegetables: to sprinkle on vegetables before serving, specially beans, carrots, leeks, onions, and marrow; to sprinkle on halves of tomato before grilling.

Salads: use small amounts finely chopped with other herbs.

Stuffings: either common or lemon thyme in any.

Pasta and rice: in meat and other sauces served with pasta; with other herbs to flavour risotto, pilaff, and other rice dishes.

Breads and pastry: dried or chopped fresh, alone, or with other herbs.

VERBENA
Lippia citriodora or Lemon-scented verbena

This verbena is a tender, deciduous shrub which, in a warm climate, will grow to 10 ft. (3 m.). Against a south-facing wall in the warmer parts of Britain, it can be grown out of doors, but in most parts it is better grown as a pot plant under glass, being put out of doors in the warmer months.

As a pot plant it needs to be watered freely from March to September, but very little during the winter. In February it is pruned, the shoots being cut down to within an inch of their base. This treatment controls what can be a straggly and unsightly plant. Pinching out the tops of shoots during growth also helps to keep the tree in shape.

It is propagated by cuttings of young growth during the spring or summer.

The lemon-scented leaves are narrow, pointed, and crinkled. It has small mauve flowers.

The leaves retain their aroma very well when dried or frozen, less well when cooked. Either the fresh, frozen, or dried leaves can be used in almost any recipe where a lemon flavour is required though, because of its rather scented flavour, it is usually appreciated more in sweet dishes than in savoury ones.

RECOMMENDED USES:

Sauces: in sweet ones, or with fish or chicken.

Sweet Dishes: to flavour the milk for milk puddings and custards; in fruit salad; chopped and sprinkled on jellies and other cold desserts; to flavour cakes.

Drinks: in claret cups and cold fruit drinks; fresh or dried leaves used for a herb tea, alone or mixed with mint leaves.

WORMWOOD
Artemisia absinthium or Old Woman

Wormwood is a perennial, growing up to 3 ft. (90 cm.) high but can be kept clipped to about 2 ft. (60 cm.) It has greyish-green stems and silvery-green leaves, finely divided. The flowers are insignificant, yellowish-green.

It grows well in semi-shade but the soil needs to be poor and dry to produce a good silvery colour.

Wormwood is strongly aromatic and very bitter. Thus many people grow it for its beauty as a garden plant rather than for use as a herb.

Commercially it is used for making the liqueur absinthe, and for flavouring vermouth. Herb teas can be made from it and drunk in small quantities. In large and concentrated doses wormwood is a narcotic poison.

It can be used as a herb in minute amounts, not enough to allow the bitterness to be obvious.

CHAPTER TWO

Buying, harvesting and preserving herbs

When buying seeds and plants, the best plan is to get them from a nursery specialising in herbs; otherwise from a general nursery or garden centre. In my experience it is unusual for the non-specialist firm to keep more than a few of the most popular herbs.

Three specialist firms that should be able to supply more unusual seeds and plants are:

> E. and A. Evetts
> Ashfields Herb Nursery
> Hinstock
> Market Drayton
> Shropshire

> The Old Rectory Herb Garden
> Ightham
> Kent

> Laxton and Bunyard Nurseries Ltd.
> Sealand
> Chester CH1 6BA

The time for sowing most seeds under glass is about March, out of doors from April onwards, putting out plants in spring, or early summer for the tender ones. If you intend to grow the plants permanently in pots or tubs, pot-grown plants can be purchased at any time. Re-pot into larger ones when the herbs need it, that is, when the pot is full of roots.

If you are unable to grow fresh herbs, try to find a shop or market where you can at least buy some of them fresh. For example, it is often possible to buy fresh chives, mint, parsley, and bay leaves. Small greengrocers catering for foreign residents often have interesting fresh herbs as well as the more unusual dried ones.

To keep fresh herbs in good condition, wash and drain them well and store them in the refrigerator in a polythene bag or box; for longer storage, use the freezer (see p. 71).

Dried herbs are much easier to buy. It is best to purchase those in small, well-sealed drums or opaque bottles. If you buy small amounts fairly frequently you are likely to have better flavoured herbs than if you buy in large quantities which take many months to use up. When buying dried herbs it is important to be sure they are fresh, that is, have a good strong smell of the herb; stale ones have no odour or taste except that of hay or straw. Those sold as whole leaves or coarsely crushed leaves retain their flavour better than the finely crushed ones.

Dried herbs keep better if stored in opaque containers than if turned out into glass jars and exposed to the light. Keep them well-sealed, dry, cool, and away from strong light.

HARVESTING HERBS

They can be gathered for the kitchen at any time during the growing season; all the year round for evergreens. Young growing tips have the best flavour and are most tender. If you want to keep a constant supply of young leaves for culinary use, trim the tops of the plants regularly even if you do not want the herbs immediately. Surplus can be dried, frozen, or preserved in some other way. Never, of course, cut a plant right down until it has no leaves left, as this is the way to kill it. The exception to this are chives clumps which are cut to the ground in rotation. It is particularly important to keep plants like dill and fennel cut regularly to about 18 in. (45 cm.), otherwise they quickly produce flower heads at the expense of leaves. If you want flowers and seeds as well as leaves have one or more plants for cutting and others for flowering.

PRESERVING HERBS

Drying is still the most important method of preserving herbs commercially, but freezing is fast becoming a popular method for home preservation (see p. 71).

Making herb vinegars, oils, condiments, and pickles are other ways in which herb flavours are preserved (see p. 83). For crystallising, see p. 72 and marmalade, p. 73.

On the whole, commercially dried herbs have a good flavour. They are either dried by quick modern methods of dehydration or they are imported from countries with a hot climate where, not only do some herbs tend to have a stronger flavour to begin with, but conditions for natural quick drying are ideal.

Some dried herbs retain their flavour better than others, regardless of the method used, while some are very difficult to dry well under home conditions. The following list is meant as a guide though it is fair to say that with some of those I have listed as drying 'reasonably well' or 'poorly', the flavour of the commercial product is better than that of most home-dried ones.

Herbs which retain their flavour WELL

Anise seeds	Cumin seeds	Lovage
Bergamot	Dill seeds	Rosemary
Caraway seeds	Fennel seeds	Sage
Clary sage	Garlic	Savory
Coriander seeds	Horseradish	Thyme
and leaves	Hyssop	Verbena (lemon)
Costmary	Lavender	

Herbs which retain their flavour REASONABLY WELL
(that is, have a shorter storage life)

Balm	Catmint	Marjoram
Basil	Curry plant	Mint
Bay	Fennel leaves	Pelargonium

Herbs which retain their flavour POORLY
(that is, not worth drying)

Borage	Chives	Sweet cicely
Burnet	Dill leaves	Tarragon
Chervil	Parsley	

HOME DRYING METHODS

Herbs have their strongest flavour just before they flower and this is the time to gather them for drying; July or August for the majority. As the young growing tips have more flavour than the older leaves, about the top 4–6 in. (10–15 cm.) is a good compromise.

Gather the herbs in the morning after the dew has dried, and preferably when there has been no rain for two days. The herbs are then less watery and dry faster. Give them a preliminary washing only if they are dirty; and remove any damaged leaves.

Where to dry them is often a problem. Ideal conditions are a warm place to evaporate the moisture, and a good current of air to carry moisture away. The best temperature for quick drying (which retains most flavour and colour), is about 110–130°F. (45–55°C.). Ordinary oven drying is not recommended as temperatures are usually too high and much of the volatile flavour of the herb is lost as a result. If herbs are dried in a sunny place they tend to lose colour, but this is usually also the warmest place available and one has to forego colour for the sake of flavour. Provided it is dry and there is a good current of air, a shed, garage, unheated greenhouse, or a spare room are all suitable.

For drying, the herbs can either be tied in small bunches and strung over a line; or spread out flat on muslin or fine cotton placed over a rack (wire cake racks are suitable), turning the herbs daily to ensure even drying. Bunches of herbs should be small enough and tied sufficiently loosely for air to get at all parts.

The time required to dry them will vary depending on conditions and the type of herb, small herbs drying fastest. They can need only a few hours if the conditions are really ideal, but more likely it will be 1–3 days and, with large leaves, can be 2–3 weeks. Dry until the leaves feel quite brittle.

For maximum retention of flavour, do not crush the leaves until you want to use them. It is quite easy to crumble them as they are used, or, if a fine powder is wanted, to rub them through a sieve. When the herbs are dry, remove the leaves from the stalks and either store them in sealed polythene bags or in some container which has a tightly fitting lid. The bags or jars should be well filled and, in the case of bags, squeeze out air before sealing the bag tightly.

DRYING SEEDS (Coriander, fennel, dill, etc.)
Cut down the herbs when the seed heads are just beginning to lose their green colour. Hang them up to dry, preferably tied loosely in

paper bags to catch seeds as they fall, or with something below to catch the seeds. Alternatively, lay them flat on a piece of muslin and turn the herbs over daily. When the seeds are ripe and dry, rub them from the stalks, pick out pieces of stalk and leaf, or sieve, as appropriate. Store the seeds in the same way as dried leaves.

DRYING FLOWERS FOR GARNISHING

Most satisfactory are marigold, bergamot, chives, and lavender though there is no reason why any of the other edible flowers should not also be dried. Use the same methods as for drying leaves.

Dry marigolds as the whole flower, strip off the petals when they seem dry enough, and spread them out to finish drying. There is no need to rob the garden of marigold flowers in their prime but wait until the 'dead-heading' stage and then gather and dry.

Dry bergamot heads whole and then strip off the flowers, chives flowers are left whole, lavender can be left whole or stripped.

USING DRIED HERBS IN COOKING, see p. 80.

FREEZING HERBS

Herbs which dry satisfactorily (see p. 69), will also freeze well and those which are less satisfactory for drying are certainly worth freezing. Tarragon, chives, dill, chervil, and fennel are all excellent frozen and keep their flavour well until fresh leaves come again in the spring.

Herbs for freezing can be gathered at their time of maximum flavour, as described for drying, or frozen at any time when you have a surplus.

HOW TO FREEZE THEM

It is always better to freeze herbs whole rather than chopped. Some people advise a preliminary blanching in boiling water for a minute, then cooling in iced water before freezing but I omit this. I simply wash the herbs, drain them well, and freeze them while they are still fresh and unwilted.

I use three different methods of packing them for freezing:

1. Pack the herbs closely in polythene boxes and remove a few sprigs at a time as required, closing the box carefully each time.
2. Pack sprigs closely in polythene bags and close in the usual way. This method has the advantage that, when some of the herb is removed, the bag can be re-sealed closely with less air round the herbs than in a partially filled box.

The problem with this method is that if you freeze a lot of different herbs you need a good method of identification because all the bags look alike when the contents are frozen. Polythene boxes are easier to label conspicuously; but this is largely a matter of the labelling technique you use in your freezer.

3. For freezing just a few sprigs to be used up all together, put the herbs in a flat package of foil and seal the edges by rolling them over. This method means lots of little packages so some method of keeping each kind together is needed for example, putting the packages in a bag or box.

USING FROZEN HERBS IN COOKING, see p. 80.

CRYSTALLISING HERBS

Angelica is the most important herb used for crystallising. Large quantities of the plant are grown commercially for this purpose.

To be successful, young stems should be used as old ones are very stringy. To get plenty of young stems it is necessary to keep the plant well cut down and forego having angelica as an ornamental garden plant unless you have room for a number of plants.

Some people recommend crystallising lovage stems in the same way but I have never found this a very good idea, even the youngest of lovage stems being decidedly stringy.

Medium-sized green leaves like mint and balm can be crystallised and make attractive garnishes for sweet dishes or to serve instead of mints at the end of a meal.

HOW TO CRYSTALLISE ANGELICA

There are many different recipes for doing this, some following the commercial procedure, others simpler. The important thing, if you want the angelica to keep for any length of time, is to see that it absorbs plenty of sugar during the crystallising process. The recipe below is one I have found to be very satisfactory, especially for doing small quantities.

The cooking time will vary depending on the size and age of the shoots or stems used. It is simpler for the beginner to use fairly young, small stems.

1 *lb. angelica stalks* (½ *kg.*)

Wash, cut in lengths from 3–6 in. (8–15 cm.). Boil them in a little salted water until the stalks are just tender. Drain well, remove the outer skin, and put the stems in a shallow dish.

1 *lb. granulated sugar* (½ *kg.*)

Sprinkle evenly over the angelica, cover the dish and leave it for two days.

½ *pt. water* (250 *ml.*)

Put the angelica, sugar and water in a pan and stir until the syrup boils. Boil it very gently until nearly all the syrup is absorbed and the angelica is clear. It may be necessary to add a little more water during cooking if the syrup evaporates before the angelica is clear. Drain the angelica until it is cool enough to handle, then roll the pieces in granulated sugar to coat them well. Spread the pieces out on a wire cake rack and finish drying in a warm place or a very cool oven. Allow to become cold and store in covered containers.

CRYSTALLISED HERB LEAVES

Any small leaves can be prepared this way to use as a garnish for sweet dishes or to serve instead of sweets. Mint and lemon balm are the two best to use.

Beaten egg white   Granulated sugar

Wash the leaves and dry them carefully. Beat the egg white until frothy. Put the sugar in a saucer.

Use a pastry brush or a small paint brush to coat each leaf on both sides with egg white and then dip each side in sugar to coat. Arrange the leaves on a cake rack placed above a baking tray. Use a wire cake rack for this, not a plastic one. Cover the leaves with greaseproof paper and dry them in the oven at the lowest thermostat setting. Dry until they are crisp, then allow to become cold before storing them in an airtight box. These are not meant for long keeping but can be made a few days in advance.

SWEET ORANGE MARMALADE WITH ANGELICA

Quantities for just under 3 lb. of marmalade (1½ kg.). Try this small quantity first to see if you like it. Double this amount will yield 5 lb. of marmalade (2½ kg.).

1 *lb. fruit* (½ *kg.*) *made up of 2 sweet oranges and 1 lemon*
3 *oz. angelica stems* (75 *g.*) *or use some stems and some leaves*
1½ *pt. water* (1 *l.*)

Wash the fruit and angelica. Squeeze the juice from the oranges and lemons, discarding the pips. Slice or mince the skins finely. Put in a bowl with the juice and water. Slice the angelica in small pieces and tie it loosely in a muslin bag. Put this with the fruit. Cover and leave to soak for 24 hrs.

Bring to the boil and boil gently until the peel is quite soft, about 1½-2 hrs. Remove the bag of angelica, draining it into the orange mixture.

   2 *lb. sugar* (1 *kg.*)

Add to the pan and stir until the marmalade boils. Keep it boiling vigorously, stirring occasionally until a little sets when tested on a cold saucer. Leave to cool partially, stir to distribute the peel evenly, and pour the marmalade into clean pots. Cover when cold.

CHAPTER THREE

Which herbs for which foods

Alphabetical reference list of herbs recommended for different types of cooking and different foods.

This list is a summary of the information given in greater detail in Chapter One and the recipe section. It is for quick reference when you want ideas for adding herbs to your favourite dishes.

BASTING SAUCES
Herbs with a strong flavour which will survive high temperatures are best and dried ones are suitable. Basil, rosemary, thyme, garlic, bay, coriander seeds.

BEEF
Basil, bay, caraway (in goulash), coriander, garlic, horseradish, marjoram, parsley, rosemary, thyme.

BISCUITS
Plain and cheese: sage, chives, mint, marjoram, thyme, basil, dill or fennel seeds, cumin or caraway seeds.
Sweet: caraway seeds, verbena, sweet cicely, ground anise seeds.

BREADS
Dried or fresh herbs for making the bread; fresh herbs for spreading butters; use marjoram, basil, thyme, chervil, fennel and dill seeds, caraway seeds, crushed coriander seeds, ground anise seeds.

CAKES
Chopped fresh sweet cicely; ground anise seed or anisette; crushed coriander seeds; dill seeds; dried rosemary; caraway seeds.

CHEESE
Soft: caraway, chives, basil, mint, dill, sage, chervil, borage.
Hot Dishes: marjoram, tarragon, basil, thyme, sage, coriander, garlic.

DESSERTS (puddings and sweets)
Custards and milk puddings: bay, anise seed, lemon balm, verbena, pelargonium.
Fruit: mint, angelica leaves, verbena, fennel seeds, sweet cicely.
Jellies and creams: coriander seeds, mint, verbena, pelargonium, bay.

DRINKS
Herb Teas, pp. 255–6.
Fruit and Wine Cups: angelica leaves, balm, basil, borage, bergamot flowers, burnet, mint, verbena, rosemary, costmary (for bitters).

EGGS
Fines herbes (parsley, tarragon, chives, chervil), marjoram, lemon thyme, basil, mint, fennel, curry plant, rosemary, savory, sorrel, sage.

FISH
Parsley, dill, fennel, tarragon, chives, chervil, horseradish, garlic, marjoram, basil, capers, lemon thyme.

GAME
Strong-flavoured herbs are the best, thyme, sage, basil, rosemary, bay, marjoram.

HAM, see Pork.

LAMB AND MUTTON
Garlic, mint, rosemary, fennel, dill, thyme, basil, marjoram, savory, bay, tarragon, sage, coriander, capers.

MARINADES, see Basting sauces.

OFFAL
Sage, fennel, bay, rosemary, thyme, garlic, tarragon.

PASTA
Marjoram, thyme, basil, rosemary.

PASTRY
Marjoram, tarragon, thyme, chervil, dill, sage.

PORK AND HAM
Sage, marjoram, basil, rosemary, thyme, garlic, fennel, tarragon, caraway, dill, coriander, sorrel, capers.

POULTRY
Tarragon, parsley, lemon thyme, marjoram, rosemary, sage, basil, bay, capers, horseradish.

RICE
Sweet, see Desserts.
Savoury: Bay, chives, parsley, savory, thyme, marjoram, mint.

SALADS
Any fresh herbs; dried ones steeped in the oil used for making dressing.

SAUCES
Any fresh or dried herbs, the choice depending on the food the sauce will accompany. Add herbs during cooking, or just before serving (see p. 110).

SOUPS
Any fresh or dried herbs or mixtures, either cooked with the soup or as a garnish, depending on the herbs used (see p. 100).

STUFFINGS
Any herbs, fresh or dried, and appropriate to the meat, poultry, fish, or vegetables being stuffed.

VEAL
Chervil, parsley, tarragon, chives, rosemary, thyme, marjoram.

VEGETABLES
To cook with the vegetables (for flavouring): bay leaves, caraway seeds, parsley, savory, garlic, marjoram, thyme, basil, tarragon, sage.
To sprinkle on cooked vegetables (or add to a sauce): chervil, dill, parsley, chives, fennel, mint, basil, savory, marjoram, thyme.

CHAPTER FOUR

Preparing herbs for cooking

USING FRESH HERBS

When fresh herbs are added at the beginning of a cooking process, for example, making stock or soup, sauces, casseroles, or boiling meat and poaching fish, it is generally better to use whole sprigs rather than chopped herbs. These are then either lifted out or strained out before the food is served. When several different herbs are used together as in a bouquet garni, they are removed more easily if they have first been tied together with a piece of white cotton. If the tie is left long enough to hang over the edge of the cooking pot, retrieval is very easy.

It is advisable to wash fresh herbs before using them. The flavour of some is more volatile than others. Those which retain their flavour well during long cooking are the ones to add at the beginning, while those with a more elusive flavour are better added chopped, at the end of cooking.

Best herbs for long cooking are:

Angelica	Coriander	Parsley stalks
Anise	Fennel	Rosemary
Basil	Garlic	Sage
Bay	Lovage	Savory
Caraway	Marjoram	Thyme

Herbs it is better to add towards the end of cooking or use with short-time cooking:

Balm	Dill	Sorrel
Burnet	Horseradish	Sweet cicely
Chervil	Parsley	Verbena
Chives		

Somewhere between the two:

  Mint   Tarragon

If, when you have finished cooking a dish, the flavour is disappointing, it can always be reinforced by sprinkling the finished dish with some more of the same herbs, chopped.

CHOPPING FRESH HERBS

Dry them very thoroughly after washing. This is best done by rolling them up in a clean cloth or in absorbent paper towels. If this is not done, chopping will be difficult and the herb may become pulpy with the small pieces clumping together instead of staying separate. A similar thing can happen if a blunt knife is used for chopping; this bruises rather than chops.

Unless it is important for the appearance of the dish to have the herbs finely chopped, scissor-snipping is a better method as this bruises the herb less than chopping and retains more flavour. Hold the herbs in a bunch in one hand and snip finely with a pair of kitchen scissors. If convenient, do this directly over the food.

For chopping, the best tool is a really sharp cook's knife. Wood is the kindest chopping surface for preserving a sharp knife edge, otherwise use a modern plastic-coated board. Gather the herbs into a bunch and slice them roughly. Then hold the point of the knife on the board in one hand and use the other to work the knife blade up and down and to and fro across the herbs until they are finely chopped.

There are many devices sold for chopping herbs including little parsley mills, round wooden bowls with curved knives for chopping, cutting wheels, and a number of others. The electric blender is good for chopping herbs in a liquid such as a soup or sauce. Use just part of the liquid and avoid over-processing unless you want a green sauce or soup. For making stuffing, blend green herbs with the bread but be sure the herbs are dry or the bread will go soggy. The same method can be used for making herb-flavoured breadcrumbs for coating purposes.

The blender is also useful for chopping horseradish. Drop small pieces through the lid with the motor running; alternatively chop the horseradish with some of the liquid in the recipe.

QUANTITIES OF FRESH HERBS TO USE :
For a recipe for 4 people 1–3 tbs. chopped fresh herbs are usually

sufficient, the amount depending on the strength of flavour and personal taste.

EQUIVALENTS:

¼ *pt.* (150 *ml.*) *lightly packed leaves will give 3 tbs. chopped herbs, more if scissor-snipped*

This is useful to know if you are using the blender instead of chopping.

USING DRIED HERBS

Count ½ tsp. crushed dried herbs as being approximately equal to 1 tbs. chopped fresh herbs. This is only a rough guide, a lot will depend on the strength of flavour in the dried herb. How long it has been stored and under what conditions also makes a difference (see pp. 68–9).

If the dried herbs are to be added at the beginning of a long cooking process it is better to use whole leaves or seeds, tied together in muslin and removed before the food is served. If powdered or finely ground herbs are used, these should be added towards the end of cooking, otherwise a great deal of their flavour will be lost. If, before cooking, the herbs are soaked in some of the same liquid as is used in the recipe, and then crushed, this will help to bring out the flavour.

For salad dressings, basting sauces and marinades mix the dried herbs with some of the oil in the recipe and let this stand for a while to bring out the flavour. Or use herb oil, vinegar or wine (see pp. 83–90).

USING FROZEN HERBS

Use in the same quantities as for fresh herbs, and in the same way except that frozen herbs are unsuitable for garnishing because they lose their appearance when thawed.

Chop or slice the herbs while still frozen or simply crumble them in the fingers. If you are using them in a sauce, soup, or other recipe with liquid, it is a good idea to chop the frozen herbs in the blender, in a little of the liquid in the recipe.

Chopped frozen herbs can be added frozen to any hot dish and will thaw almost immediately.

For salads, sprinkle chopped frozen herbs into the salad and toss all in the dressing. The herbs will thaw in a minute or so.

HERBS FOR GARNISHING

For many people the only herb used for garnishing is parsley. For those who grow their own herbs there are many other possibilities.

Any fresh herbs can be used as a green garnish, scissor-snipped or chopped. Among the best for this are chives, mint, caraway, anise or coriander leaves, dill or fennel, marjoram, sage, savory, sweet cicely, tarragon, and nasturtium leaves.

Herb leaves with an interesting shape can be used as single leaves or small sprays. These are:

Balm leaves
Basil leaves or top sprigs
Bay leaves for sweet or savoury
Burnet sprigs
Caraway, fern-like leaves
Chervil sprays, tiny sprigs or
    pluches
Coriander, fern-like leaves
Curry plant for silver leaves
Dill and fennel for their
    feathery look
Mint leaves and top sprigs
Nasturtium leaves
Parsley sprigs
Pelargonium leaves
Rosemary sprigs
Sage, red, green or variegated
Sweet cicely, small sprigs
Tarragon single leaves
Wormwood for lacy grey leaves

Whether the garnish is edible depends on the particular herb. Obviously the tough or very strongly flavoured herbs will not usually be eaten; but the delicate ones can be, for example, floating on soup, decorating a salad, set in a jelly, and so on.

Edible herb flowers make most attractive garnishes and are much neglected. Some can be dried for winter use (see pp. 61–71). The best flowers to use are:

Anchusa italica, rich blue
Bergamot, red, pink, purple
Borage, blue, white, or pink
Caraway, dill, fennel, tiny pieces
    of the umbels
Chives, lavender colour
Curry plant, bright yellow
Hyssop, many colours
Lavender, heads or stripped
Marigold petals
Marjoram, pink to lavender
Nasturtium, yellow, orange,
    red
Rosemary, pale blue
Sage, deep blue or red sage
Thyme, lavender colour

Careful washing or soaking is necessary as flowers tend to harbour insects. Holding them under a running cold tap is a good way. Shake gently and drain well before using. They can be kept fresh in a polythene box in the refrigerator.

Mixed flowers, chopped if large ones, make a pretty garnish scattered over salads. Sprays of leaves and flowers can be set in clear jelly to garnish cold sweet or savoury dishes.

HERBS FOR COLOURING FOODS

For those who dislike using commercial food colourings in cooking, herb juices are a good alternative, always provided the flavour of the juice is appropriate to the dish being coloured. This does rather limit the use of many of them to savoury dishes, with a few exceptions such as mint for green colouring, or marigold petals for orange.

The best way of extracting the colour is to put the herb in an electric blender with a minimum amount of water and process until pulped, then strain through muslin. Alternatively, pound the herb in a mortar and squeeze it in muslin to extract the juice. For marigold petals see p. 46.

FRIED PARSLEY

This is a traditional edible herb garnish for hot dishes. Parsley may be fried in deep fat (not much at a time because it froths), or in butter. The essentials are to remove the stalks before frying, to dry the parsley very thoroughly, and not to have the fat too hot or cook for too long or the green colour will be lost.

CHAPTER FIVE

Condiments

Although herb condiments are perhaps most useful when fresh herbs are out of season, yet they have their uses as seasonings at all times of the year. Many are made commercially and can be found in the shops.

If you grow your own herbs, or even if you have to rely on dried ones, it is worthwhile making at least some of these just for variety. For those who have surplus fresh herbs, making your own condiments is an excellent way of preserving their flavours for the winter.

HERB OILS

These are for making mayonnaise, salad dressings, marinades, and basting sauces, but the oils can also be used in many other recipes. These include frying in shallow fat, especially as a preliminary stage in preparing casseroles.

Adding herbs to oil introduces some moisture so, when using it for frying, heat it slowly to drive off moisture and prevent undue splashing.

Any kind of salad or frying oil can be used. I think it is a waste to use a good olive oil for this purpose as its natural flavour is enough on its own.

Suitable herbs are:

Garlic	Coriander seeds
Basil	Fennel
Rosemary	Tarragon
Thyme	

Use a mixture of herbs or just one if you have a favourite, for example, garlic or basil.

QUANTITIES:

> ½ *pt.* (250 *ml.*) *oil*
> ¼ *pt.* (150 *ml.*) *fresh leaves or* 1–2 *cloves of garlic*
> *or* 1 *tbs. coriander seeds*

The exact quantity is not very important as you can always strain the oil when it is flavoured enough or add more of the herb and brew for longer if the flavour is weak.

To prepare herb oil, crush the herbs in a mortar with a little of the oil, then add this to the rest of the oil. Alternatively put the herbs and a little oil in the electric blender and process to chop the herbs.

Put the oil in a warm place and leave to infuse for 2–3 weeks or until well flavoured. Shake the bottle occasionally. Strain through muslin and bottle.

HERB MUSTARDS

These are particularly useful in cooking, for example, in making French or other dressings, in sauces using mustard as an ingredient, for making sandwiches and flavouring sandwich fillings. They are also useful as a table mustard to add interest to hot or cold meats.

They can be made with just one herb or with a mixture such as Herb Seasoning (p. 85). For mixing the mustard a herb vinegar or herb oil can be used instead of actually adding herbs to the mustard, thus producing a milder herb flavour.

BASIC RECIPE

Make this small quantity to try different herbs and double the recipe for a second making of any you particularly like.

> 3 *tbs. mustard powder*

Put in a small basin and mix to a stiff paste with cold water.

> ½ *tsp. salt*   ½ *tsp. sugar*
> 1½ *tsp. herb or wine vinegar*   Pinch of *pepper*
> ¼–½ *tsp. dried powdered herbs*   1½ *tsp. oil*

Unless the herbs are already in a fine powder it is as well to rub them through a sieve before adding them to the mustard. Mix all the ingredients into the mustard and store it in a covered pot or jar.

FRENCH MUSTARD WITH HERBS

   6 *tbs.* (90*ml.*) *dry mustard*
Put in a small basin and mix to a stiff paste with cold water.

   1 *tsp. sugar*   1 *tsp. salt*
   1 *tbs. olive oil*   2 *tsp. tarragon vinegar*
   1 *tsp. anchovy essence*   1 *tsp. mushroom ketchup*
   A good pinch of powdered
   marjoram

Add all ingredients to the mustard and mix thoroughly. If it seems a little stiff, add more vinegar. Store in a covered jar or mustard pot.

HERB SEASONING

Use this for flavouring any savoury dish. It is a good general flavouring but it has the disadvantage of all blends, that it can become monotonous if used often. It can be varied by the addition of spices, for example, nutmeg, mace, cloves, ginger, or allspice.

   Finely grated rind of 1 *lemon*
Spread this out on a saucer or piece of paper and put it in a warm place to dry. Do this if possible the day before you want to make up the mixture.

   1 *tbs. crushed dried marjoram*   ½ *tbs. dried thyme*
   ½ *tbs. crushed dried basil*   1 *tbs. dried savory*
   ¼ *tsp. powdered dried bay leaf*

If the crushed leaves are already fairly fine the mixture can simply be bottled as it is, but a better blend of flavours results if the ingredients are pounded together in a mortar or in an electric blender. The mixture can then be sieved to remove any remaining large pieces. Add the dried lemon rind, mix, and put in a covered jar.

   Use the mixture in approximately the proportions of ½ tsp. to a pint (½ l.) of sauce, soup, stew, and so on.

HERB VINEGARS

These are useful for making salad dressings, marinades and basting sauces, vinaigrette and other sauces containing vinegar, and for mixing mustard. Vinegars made with just one kind of herb are the most useful but a mixed herb vinegar is also worth making. Those who prefer to use lemon juice or wine in cooking will find it useful to make herb oils (p. 83), or herb wines (p. 88).

The best vinegars to use are either a white wine or cider vinegar. The flavour of malt vinegar is too strong for most herbs with the possible exception of mint, garlic, and horseradish.

There are several different ways of making herb vinegar. These include using precise quantities of herb to vinegar (½ pt. or 250 ml. of leaves to 1 pt. or ½ l. of vinegar). A simpler method is just to fill a bottle or jar loosely with sprigs of small-leaved herbs or leaves of larger herbs and add vinegar to cover. Pouring warm or hot vinegar over the herbs helps to extract the flavour when seeds are used instead of fresh herbs.

Herb vinegars can be made throughout the growing season whenever there are leaves to spare but the most flavour for fewest leaves results if they are picked just before the herb flowers. It is wise to pick the leaves after a couple of dry days when they contain less water and have a more concentrated flavour. If necessary, wash the leaves but dry them well before adding to the vinegar.

Any herbs with a fairly strong flavour are suitable. The recipes which follow are those I use for my own cooking and find useful.

BASIL VINEGAR

This is a traditional addition to turtle soup but is also good for flavouring many other foods.

Bruise the basil leaves in a mortar, or by crushing, and use enough to half-fill a bottle or jar, just loosely packed. Add cold vinegar to fill the jar or bottle, cover, and leave for about 14 days. Strain and bottle.

CORIANDER VINEGAR

This one has a slightly astringent flavour.

Bruise coriander seeds in a mortar or crush with a rolling pin.

Allow 2 or more tablespoons to each pint (½ l.) of warm vinegar. Cover and keep in a warm place for 14 days or until flavoured to your taste. Strain and bottle.

DILL VINEGAR

Loosely fill a jar or bottle with sprigs of dill and fill up with cold vinegar. Cover and leave for about 14 days. Strain and bottle.

FENNEL VINEGAR make in the same way as dill vinegar.

GARLIC VINEGAR

This makes one of a fairly strong flavour which needs to be used sparingly.

    1 oz. (25 g.) of garlic or about 8 good-sized cloves
    1 pt. (½ l.) vinegar

Skin and chop the garlic coarsely. Put it in a bottle with a pinch of salt and the vinegar. Cover and infuse for 14 days, shaking the bottle occasionally. Strain and bottle.

HORSERADISH VINEGAR

1½ oz. (40 g.) grated fresh horseradish	*1 tbs. finely chopped or grated onion*
A few grains of cayenne pepper	*A few celery seeds*
	1 pt. (½ l.) vinegar

Put all in a container, cover and steep for about 14 days. Strain and bottle.

MINT VINEGAR

Loosely fill a bottle or jar with sprigs of mint, or half-fill with leaves. Cover and leave for 2–3 weeks. Strain and bottle.

    This can be served with lamb in place of mint sauce or use as other herb vinegars.

NASTURTIUM FLOWER VINEGAR

This one has an unusual flavour and the flowers deepen the colour of the vinegar. Use full-blown flowers and wash them very carefully to remove any insects. Shake dry.

Flowers to fill a 1 pt. (½ l.)   *Vinegar to fill the jar*
   jar, loosely   *½ chopped shallot*
¼ clove of garlic

Cover the jar and leave to steep for about 2 months. Strain, add a pinch of cayenne pepper, and bottle.

TARRAGON VINEGAR

Method 1

Put enough sprigs of tarragon in a bottle to fill it loosely, cover the tarragon with vinegar, cork the bottle and leave for 2–3 weeks before straining; or leave the tarragon in the bottle and pour off the vinegar as required.

For a stronger vinegar, fill the bottle loosely with leaves instead of sprigs, strain before use.

Method 2

Sprigs of tarragon to loosely   *1 clove*
   fill 1 pt. (½ l.) jar   *Vinegar to fill the jar*
2 strips thinly pared lemon
   rind

Cover, and leave for 2–3 weeks. Strain and bottle.

MIXED HERB VINEGAR

Use thyme, marjoram, basil, savory, tarragon, chives, mint, selecting at least four different herbs.

Fill a 1 pt. (½ l.) jar with small sprigs or leaves of the chosen herbs. Do not pack down.

Add
   1 strip lemon rind
   A few slices of shallot or onion or some chopped chives

Add to the herbs and fill the jar with vinegar. Leave for 14 days or until the vinegar is well flavoured. Strain and bottle.

HERB WINES

These are not meant for drinking as wine but for use as flavourings. They are made in the same way as herb vinegars (see previous recipes), but using an inexpensive white or red wine or dry cider, instead of the vinegar.

They can be used in the same way as herb vinegars but, in addition, are suitable for general cooking in place of wine, for example, in sauces, casseroles, and other recipes. They are also very good for flavouring cold milk drinks, fruit juices, and fruit salads.

The three recipes which follow are different from those given for herb vinegars and are specially good in sweet dishes.

ANGELICA WINE

Angelica leaves give a flavour of muscatel to the wine.
  2 or more tbs. chopped angelica leaves
  ½ pt. (250 ml.) white wine or cider
Put in a bottle or jar and leave for 3–4 days. Strain and bottle.

LEMON VERBENA WINE

Good for jellies and other moulds, fruit salads, and fruit compotes; also for cold milk.
  2 tbs. chopped top sprigs of lemon verbena
  ½ pt. (250 ml.) dry cider or white wine
Put in a bottle or jar and leave for 3–4 days. Strain and bottle.

ROSEMARY WINE

  1 tbs. chopped fresh rosemary
  ½ pt. (250 ml.) dry cider or wine
Put in a bottle or jar and leave to infuse for 3–4 days. Strain and bottle.

MINT AND APPLE JELLY

To serve with hot or cold meats.
  3 lb. (1½ kg.) cooking apples
  Juice of 1 lemon
  3 or 4 sprigs of mint
To get a jelly with a good colour, use apples with a bright green skin. Wash the fruit and cut it in small pieces, removing any bad bits. Put in a pan and just cover with water. Add mint and lemon

juice. Boil gently for an hour or until the apples are well mashed down. Strain through a jelly bag.

Sugar   Green colouring or more mint

Measure the juice and add 1 lb. (½ kg.) sugar for each 1 pt. (½ l.) of juice. If desired, add a few drops of green colouring, but if a stronger mint flavour is preferred, hold a bunch of fresh mint leaves in the jelly for a little while when it is boiling. Stir to dissolve the sugar before bringing the jelly to the boil. Boil until a little sets when tested on a cold plate.

A little chopped mint can be added before potting the jelly. Cover while still very hot, or when quite cold.

MINT CHUTNEY

QUANTITIES FOR 2–3 lb. (1½–1¾ kg.).

2 *lb.* (1 *kg.*) *apples*	4 *oz.* (½ *c. or* 125 *g.*) *raisins*

Peel and core the apples and mince or chop them with the raisins.

1 *tsp. dry mustard*	4 *oz.* (½ *c. or* 125 *g.*) *brown sugar*
¼ *pt.* (150 *ml.*) *chopped mint*	2 *tsp. salt*
¾ *pt.* (400 *ml.*) *vinegar*	½ *tsp. pepper*

Put all the ingredients in a pan with the apples and raisins and cook slowly until the mixture is the consistency of thick jam. Put in small pots and cover when cold.

Keep for at least a month to mature before using.

MINT CHUTNEY (uncooked)

This does not keep a long time, 2–3 days in a cool place, several weeks in the refrigerator.

QUANTITIES FOR 1 lb. (½ kg.) jar

½ *pt.* (250 *ml.*) *mint leaves*	1 *lb.* (½ *kg.*) *sultanas or raisins*

Wash and drain the mint. Mince or chop mint and fruit together, finely.

1 *tsp. salt*	5–6 *tbs.* (75–90 *ml.*) *vinegar*
Pinch of cayenne pepper	

Add to the mint and raisins using enough vinegar to moisten to the consistency of thick jam. Pot and cover.

MINT JELLY (using gelatine)

This will keep several weeks in the refrigerator. Use in place of mint sauce.

QUANTITIES FOR ¾ pt.

¼ *pt.* (150 *ml.*) *hot water*   1 *tbs. gelatine*
Dissolve the gelatine in the water

2 *oz.* (¼ *c. or* 50 *g.*) *caster sugar*   1 *tbs. Lemon juice*
¼ *pt.* (150 *ml.*) *white wine vinegar*
Add to the water and gelatine and stir until the sugar dissolves.

¼ *pt.* (150 *ml.*) *chopped mint leaves*
Add and mix. Leave to cool until it begins to thicken, stir to distribute the mint evenly, and pour into small pots. Cover.

For decorating a platter of cold meats, set the jelly in several tiny moulds and unmould round the edge of the platter.

MINTED SALT

To use at table as a condiment or to use in flavouring foods, for example, grilled lamb cutlets or chops, green peas or pea soup, potatoes, cucumber soup or salad, and egg dishes.

2 *tbs. salt*   ½ *tbs. dried crushed mint*
Pound these together in a mortar, then sieve to remove any large bits of mint which remain. Store in a covered jar.

PICKLED NASTURTIUM SEEDS

Use these instead of capers—some say they are even better.

SPICED VINEGAR FOR THE PICKLE

3 *peppercorns*   1 *bay leaf*
1 *tbs. salt*   ½ *pt.* (250 *ml.*) *white vinegar*
Optional extras: grated horseradish, tarragon leaves and a few cloves

Bring the vinegar and flavourings to the boil, cover and infuse for 2 hrs. Strain and leave to become cold.

Put the vinegar in small bottles and add the nasturtium seeds as they are gathered, while they are still young and green. If necessary, wash them well first and then drain them very thoroughly before adding them to the vinegar. Fill the jars to within ½ in. (1 cm.) of the top of the vinegar. Leave at least a month before using the seeds.

SAGE JELLY (with gelatine)

This makes a delicious accompaniment to hot or cold roast pork and other meats. It can be made with either green or red sage, using the young growing tips.

Make in the same way as Mint jelly (p. 90).

SPICED SALT

To use at table as a condiment, or for cooking, for flavouring soups, casseroles, sauces, meat and fish for grilling, for sprinkling on roasts, and indeed, whenever salt is used and the flavour of herbs would improve the dish.

QUANTITIES FOR 5–6 oz. (150–175 g.) of spiced salt.

    2 *oz. (50 g.) free-running cooking salt*
    1 *oz. (25 g.) celery salt*
    ½ *oz. (15 g.) ground black pepper*

Mix these in a small bowl.

    ½ *oz. (15 g.) each of dried thyme, marjoram, and savory*
    1 *tbs. dried sage*

Pound these finely in a mortar or put them in the electric blender with all the other ingredients and blend to a powder. Add pounded herbs to the salt mixture.

    ½ *tsp. cayenne pepper*   ¼ *tsp. ground cloves*
    ¼ *tsp. ground mace*   ¼ *tsp. ground allspice*

Mix thoroughly with the other ingredients. Put in a bottle with a cork or lid. For table use, put the salt in a salt shaker.

CHAPTER SIX

Hors d'oeuvre and starters

ARTICHOKE HEARTS OR BOTTOMS

These make an excellent starter on their own or as part of a mixed hors d'oeuvre. Unless you have a lot of fresh artichokes to use up, it is more practical to buy canned hearts or bottoms. If fresh artichokes are used, boil in plenty of salted water until the leaves will pull out easily. Drain well and remove all leaves and the choke. Trim the remaining bottoms as necessary.

To use canned artichokes, drain well, rinse in cold water and drain again thoroughly. Mix them with French dressing and sprinkle generously with chopped, dill, or fennel and parsley.

ASPARAGUS FLAN WITH CHERVIL

See Vegetables, p. 191.

ASPARAGUS, FRESH OR CANNED

Boil fresh asparagus until just tender. Drain carefully and allow to become cold. Drain canned asparagus carefully. Arrange on a dish, pour over it some French dressing, or mask with mayonnaise. Arrange small sprigs of chervil on top of mayonnaise; sprinkle the French dressed ones with chopped parsley and tarragon.

BAKED EGG WITH HERBS

See p. 138.

BEANS, ITALIAN

See Vegetables, p. 193.

BEETROOT WITH HORSERADISH

This will keep for a week or more in a covered container.

2 *medium-sized cooked beetroot*   6 *peppercorns*
2 *tbs. grated fresh horseradish*   *Vinegar to cover*

Skin and dice the beetroot and put it in a jar or dish with the other ingredients. Cover with a lid and store in a cool place.

BEETROOT SALADS

See Salads, pp. 194-5.

BROAD BEANS

Serve these as part of a mixed hors d'oeuvre. Use either young fresh cooked beans which are allowed to become cold, or use canned beans. I find frozen broad beans have little flavour. Drain canned beans well and, if the skins seem rather thick, remove by pinching each one gently. Mix gently with French dressing and sprinkle sparingly with fresh chopped savory or lemon thyme; or generously with chopped parsley.

BUTTER BEANS

See White Bean Salad, p. 194.

CAULIFLOWER

Use flowerets of cold cooked cauliflower, cooked until only just tender. Arrange in a shallow dish, mask with mayonnaise and sprinkle with chopped mint, parsley, or chervil.

See also Cauliflower salads, p. 198.

CELERY, APPLE, AND BEETROOT SALAD WITH FENNEL

See Salads, p. 199.

CHICKEN AND HAM MOULD

This is suitable for serving on its own as a starter. See recipe, p. 181.

CHICKEN OR RABBIT TIMBALES

Suitable for serving on its own as a starter. See recipe, p. 182.

COURGETTE SALAD

To serve as part of a mixed hors d'oeuvre. See Salads, p. 201.

COURGETTES OR MARROW WITH TOMATOES

Very good as a starter on its own. Use the recipe on p. 201, making it with oil for serving the dish cold.

CUCUMBER AND DILL WITH YOGURT

Suitable for a starter on its own.
QUANTITIES FOR 4–6.
   ½–1 cucumber, peeled and thinly sliced
Arrange in a serving dish or individual dishes.
   ½ pt. (250 ml.) chilled plain yogurt   Salt and pepper
   2 tbs. finely chopped fresh dill
Mix and pour over cucumber.
Alternative. Dice the cucumber, mix with the other ingredients, and serve in cocktail glasses.

CUCUMBER AND GREEN PEPPER COCKTAIL

QUANTITIES FOR 4–6.
   1 lb. (½ kg.) cucumber   Salt and pepper
Peel the cucumber and cut it in small dice. Put in a shallow dish and sprinkle the cucumber with salt. Leave for 20–30 mins. Drain well, return to the dish and sprinkle with pepper.
   4 tbs. finely chopped green pepper
   ¼ clove of crushed garlic or to taste
   ½ pt. (250 ml.) thick yogurt or soured cream
Combine these and then add to the cucumber. Cover the dish and refrigerate until the cucumber is well chilled.
   Chopped fresh mint or other herbs
Serve the mixture in small glasses and sprinkle the tops generously with the herbs.

CUCUMBER À LA GREQUE

COOKING TIME 15 mins.   QUANTITIES FOR 4.

1 *lb. (1 large or ½ kg.) cucumber*
Peel and cut in quarters lengthwise. Cut out the seeds. Cut the
quarters in 1-in. (2½-cm.) pieces.

½ *pt. (250 ml.) water*	6 *tbs. (90 ml.) olive oil*
4 *tbs. (60 ml.) lemon juice*	*Salt and pepper*
1 *sprig of parsley*	*A few celery leaves*
1 *sprig of thyme*	1 *bav leaf*
1 *sprig of fennel*	12 *coriander seeds*

Put these in a fairly large pan and bring to the boil. Add the cucumber and boil gently for 10 mins. Use a perforated spoon to lift the
pieces of cucumber into a dish. Strain the liquid over them and
leave to become cold. Serve with some of the liquid as a dressing.

EGG MAYONNAISE WITH CAPERS

To serve on lettuce leaves as a starter, or plain, as part of a mixed
hors d'oeuvre.
  Shell cold, hard-boiled eggs and cut in halves lengthwise. Arrange
in a dish, cut side down, and mask with mayonnaise mixed with
chopped capers or pickled nasturtium seeds. Garnish with a few whole
capers and tiny sprigs of parsley.

FISH COCKTAIL

QUANTITIES FOR 3–4.

6 *oz. (175 g.) flaked, cooked white fish*   *Salt and pepper*
Put the fish in small glasses or dishes and sprinkle with salt and
pepper.

¼ *pt. (150 ml.) soured cream*   1 *tbs. lemon juice*
Whip together to mix well.

2 *tsp. chopped dill or fennel*   1 *tbs. chopped chives*
Mix into the cream and pour it on top of the fish. Refrigerate until
required, but do not prepare a long time in advance. Garnish with
  Tiny sprays of dill or fennel, tomato, cucumber, or lemon

FISH (BAKED) TO SERVE COLD

Suitable for a starter on its own. See Baked fish steaks to serve cold,
p. 145, and Baked fish to serve cold, p. 146.

FISH IN FENNEL SAUCE

See Fish, p. 151.

HARD-BOILED EGGS

See p. 140.

HERB QUICHE

To serve as a starter on its own. See p. 139.

HERRING (SALT) WITH DILL, PARSLEY AND SPICE

QUANTITIES FOR 4–8.

4 fillets of salt herring

Soak over-night or for 5–6 hrs. in plenty of cold water. Drain, rinse, and make sure there are no bones left in the fillets. Slice each fillet diagonally in ½-in. (1-cm.) slices and arrange these in a flat dish, each in the shape of the original fillet.

3 tbs. oil

1 tbs. concentrated tomato purée

¼ tsp. pepper

½ tsp. dried dill or 1–2 tsp. chopped fresh dill

½–1 tbs. sugar

1 tbs. mixed herb, or plain wine vinegar

1 tbs. water

¼ tsp. ground or crushed allspice

Mix all together and pour over the fish.

Chopped parsley

Sprinkle a little on top, not too much or it will mask the other herb flavourings.

LEEKS VINAIGRETTE WITH THYME

See Salads, p. 203.

LIVER PATÉ

To serve as a starter on its own. See p. 175.

MUSHROOM SALAD

To serve as part of a mixed hors d'oeuvre
  Small white mushrooms
  French dressing made with lemon juice
Wash and dry the mushrooms and slice them very thinly. Arrange
them in a flat dish and pour the dressing over them, using enough to
moisten them well. Leave to stand for half an hour or so for the
dressing to be absorbed by the mushrooms.
  Chopped chives and parsley
Sprinkle generously over the mushrooms and serve.
Alternative herbs: use marjoram, tarragon, or mint.

MUSSELS

To serve as a starter on their own or as part of a mixed hors d'oeuvre.
  Use fresh cooked, or canned mussels, well drained. Rinse canned
mussels and drain again. To cook fresh mussels, wash and scrub
well discarding any damaged or open shells. Put in a large pan
with a few spoonsful of water, cover and cook very gently until the
shells open, drain, cool and remove the mussels from the shells.
  Dress with a French dressing made with lemon juice and sprinkle
the mussels with chopped chervil, lemon thyme, or tarragon.

PEPPERS, SWEET

See Italian dish of green peppers, p. 206.

POTATO SALAD

See Salads, pp. 206–7.

RED CABBAGE

Serve pickled red cabbage mixed with grated fresh horseradish or
mix dried horseradish with it and leave to steep for several hours
before serving.

RICE SALAD

To serve as a starter on its own or as part of a mixed hors d'oeuvre.
See Salads, p. 216.

SAUERKRAUT SALAD

See Salads, p. 196.

SHRIMP AND ORANGE COCKTAIL

QUANTITIES FOR 4.

  2 *large oranges*   4 *oz.* (125 *g.*) *shelled shrimps*
  1 *tbs. chopped cucumber or gherkin*

Peel the oranges and remove all pith, pips, and membrane. Mix the pulp with the shrimps and cucumber or gherkin.

  4 *tbs.* (60 *ml.*) *mayonnaise*
  2 *tbs. chopped dill or* 1 *tbs. chopped basil*

Combine these and mix with the oranges and shrimps, using more mayonnaise if needed to moisten well.

  Shredded lettuce   *Sprigs of dill or leaves of basil*

Put some lettuce in the bottom of four glasses, put the mayonnaise mixture on top and garnish with the herb sprigs or leaves.

SOUSE OF COLD PORK

To serve as part of a mixed hors d'oeuvre (see p. 169).

TOMATO SALAD

See Tomatoes, p. 208.

TONGUE SALAD

To serve as part of a mixed hors d'oeuvre. Slice cooked or canned tongue very thinly and arrange, over-lapping, in a shallow dish. Combine French dressing with chopped marjoram, savory, chives, or parsley and use to moisten the tongue well.

CHAPTER SEVEN

Soups

Any herbs can be added to soup. At the beginning of cooking add those whose flavour will survive long, slow cooking (see p. 78), the others, towards the end of cooking or as a garnish. Canned and packet soups benefit greatly from the addition of herbs to give a more interesting flavour. Add chopped fresh or dried herbs as the soup is being heated.

HERBS SPECIALLY RECOMMENDED FOR HOME-MADE OR COMMERCIAL SOUPS:

Garnishing: Dried or fresh marigold petals, chervil pluches, any chopped fresh herb.

Stocks: Bouquet garni.

Chicken soup: Balm in generous amounts, chives, chervil, bay, mint, parsley, rosemary, tarragon.

Celery soup: Coriander leaves or seeds.

Consommé: Chervil pluches or Chervil Royale (p. 101).

Fish soup: Bay, chervil, dill, fennel, garlic, parsley, savory, thyme.

Lentil soup: Chervil, dill, lovage, savory, sorrel, thyme

Meat soups: Anise, balm, basil, bay, chervil, coriander, marjoram, rosemary.

Minestrone: Rosemary, sage, tarragon.

Mushroom soup: Fennel, parsley, tarragon.

Onion soup: Marjoram, rosemary, sage, tarragon, thyme.

Pea soup: Dill, mint, parsley, savory, tarragon, thyme.

Potato soup: Chervil, dill, lovage, nasturtium leaves, marjoram, parsley, thyme.

Tomato soup: Basil, marjoram, parsley, rosemary, tarragon, thyme.

Turtle soup: Basil.

Vegetable soup: Bay, balm, chervil, coriander, marjoram, parsley, thyme.

For an unusual flavouring in small amounts with other herbs: Hyssop, lavender, curry plant, sweet cicely.

CHERVIL AND EGG SOUP

COOKING TIME about 20 mins.   QUANTITIES FOR 4.

1 *oz. (25 g.) butter*   ½ *oz. (1 ½ tbs. or 15 g.) flour*

Melt the butter in a saucepan, add the flour, stirring and cooking until crumbly.

1½ *pt. (1 l.) stock. Use canned consommé or chicken stock*

Add to the pan, stir until it boils and boil gently for 15 mins.

1 *tbs. finely chopped fresh*   1 *small carrot, grated*
   chervil   *Salt and pepper*

Just before serving, add the chervil and carrot, with seasoning to taste. Serve the soup straight away as further cooking or keeping hot will cause the chervil to lose flavour.

4 *eggs*

Put a raw egg in each soup plate or bowl, add the very hot soup and stir to mix with the egg.

CHERVIL ROYALE

For garnishing consommé

COOKING TIME 1 hr.   TEMPERATURE E. 350° (180°C.) G.4
QUANTITIES FOR 4.

½ *pt. (250 ml.) loosely packed chervil leaves*
¼ *pt. (150 ml.) single cream*

Measure the leaves and then wash them. Shake off excess water and put them in a small pan with the cream. Bring to the boil, remove from the heat, cover and infuse for 20 mins., or until well flavoured with chervil.

2 *eggs*

Add to the infusion and whisk just enough to mix eggs and cream. Strain into a jug pressing the chervil to remove liquid. Pour into small, well-greased or oiled moulds, for example, timbale or castle pudding moulds. Stand the moulds in a baking dish with hot water coming half way up their sides. Cook until the custard is set, about 25–30 mins. Remove from the water and leave to become cold. Turn out of the moulds and cut in slices as thinly as possible without breaking the custard. From these slices stamp out small rounds with a biscuit cutter. Add these to hot consommé at serving time.

CHICKEN SOUP WITH CHIVES

Use concentrated cream of chicken soup and, when diluting it, use some single cream, evaporated milk, or yogurt, instead of all water. Heat just to boiling and add a generous quantity of fresh or frozen, finely chopped chives.

CHICKEN SOUP WITH MINT

COOKING TIME 20 mins.　　QUANTITIES FOR 3-4.

　1½ *pt.* (1 *l.*) *chicken stock*　1 *oz.* (2 *tbs. or* 25 *g.*) *rice*
Bring the stock to the boil, add the rice and boil gently for 15 mins.

　2 *tsp. potato flour*　1 *egg yolk*
　¼ *pt.* (150 *ml.*) *yogurt*
Mix the potato flour and egg yolk and gradually beat in the yogurt. Remove the soup from the heat and stir in the yogurt mixture. Return the pan to the heat and stir until the soup just comes to the boil. Remove from the heat and taste for seasoning.

　Salt and pepper　　*Chopped mint*
Season to taste and serve the soup sprinkled with plenty of chopped mint.

CONSOMMÉ WITH MUSHROOMS AND HERBS

COOKING TIME 5-10 mins.　　QUANTITIES FOR 4.

　2 *oz.* (50 *g.*) *mushrooms, sliced*　2 *tbs. lemon juice*
Put the mushrooms in a small dish and sprinkle the lemon juice over them. Leave for 5 mins. Frozen mushrooms can be used for this, sprinkling the lemon juice over them and leaving them to thaw.

　1½ *pt.* (750 *ml.*) *consommé or clear stock*
　Salt and pepper
Use canned consommé or beef broth or a well-flavoured home-made meat broth. Season to taste. Heat just to boiling and add the mushrooms.

　1 *tsp. chopped fennel, chives, or dill*
Sprinkle into the soup just before serving it.

CREAM OF MUSHROOM SOUP WITH TARRAGON

QUANTITIES FOR 2–3.
  A 15 *oz.* (452 *g.*) *can of cream of mushroom soup*
  5 *tbs.* (75 *ml.*) *dry cider or white wine*
  5 *tbs.* (75 *ml.*) *milk*   1 *tbs. chopped tarragon*
Put in a pan and heat to boiling, then serve.

FISH SOUP WITH DILL OR FENNEL

COOKING TIME ½ hr.   QUANTITIES FOR 4.
  1 *oz.* (25 *g.*) *butter or margarine*   2 *tbs. flour*
  1½ *pt.* (750 *ml.*) *fish stock*
Melt the fat in a saucepan, stir in the flour. Cook gently until it
looks mealy. Remove from the heat, add the stock, mix well and
continue heating and stirring until it boils. Boil gently for 5 mins.
  ¼ *pt.* (150 *ml.*) *milk*   ¼ *pt.* (150 *ml.*) *cream*
Add to the soup and heat.
  2 *tsp. lemon juice or to taste*   *Salt and pepper*
  2 *or more tbs. chopped dill or fennel*
Season to taste and add the chopped herbs just before serving.
Alternative herbs: Chervil, parsley, savory, thyme, garlic.

GREEN PEA SOUP WITH MINT

COOKING TIME 5–10 mins.   QUANTITIES FOR 4–6.
  8 *oz.* (250 *g.*) *fresh or frozen peas*
Cook the peas in a little lightly salted water until they are just
tender. Drain, keeping the cooking liquid. Either sieve the peas or
put them in the electric blender, using ¼ pt. (150 ml.) of the cooking
liquid to moisten the purée. Return to the pan.
  1 *pt.* (½ *l.*) *good chicken stock*
Any remaining pea stock can be used to make up the pint. Add the
stock to the purée.
  2–3 *sprigs of mint*
Chop finely or mix in the electric blender for a second, using some
stock to moisten it. Add the mint to the soup, bring to the boil and
simmer for a few minutes.
  1 *egg yolk*   1 *tsp. potato flour*
  ¼ *pt.* (150 *ml.*) *yogurt*   *Salt and pepper*
  Sugar

Mix egg yolk and potato flour and stir in the yogurt. Add a little of the hot soup, mix and pour into the remaining soup, stir until it just comes to the boil. Season to taste.

Diced crisp bacon
Use as an optional garnish.

ICED CUCUMBER SOUP

QUANTITIES FOR 4.

1 large or 2 small cucumbers   ½ *small onion*

Wash the cucumber and either grate it finely or put it in the electric blender. Peel and chop the onion very finely or blend it with the cucumber.

2 tbs. lemon juice
2 mint leaves, finely chopped or a little chopped sorrel
Add to the cucumber.

½ *pt. (250 ml.) melted aspic jelly or canned consommé*
Salt and pepper
Add to the cucumber, seasoning to taste. Put in serving dishes and chill in the refrigerator.

A few prawns or shrimps or some more chopped mint
Use these as a garnish when ready to serve the soup.

LAMB OR MUTTON SOUP

This is a good way of using up the bones and last bits of meat on a leg or shoulder; or you could make it with fresh scrag or neck of lamb or mutton.

COOKING TIME after the stock has been made, 20 mins.

QUANTITIES FOR 3–4.

Bones and meat   *1 onion*   *1 bay leaf*

If you are using cooked meat, remove meat from bones before making the stock; with fresh meat, leave the meat on the bones (1 lb. meat and bone or ½ kg. will be sufficient). Add onion and bay leaf and cook the bones or fresh meat in a pressure cooker for ½ hr. or boil with water to cover for 2 hrs. Strain, and remove freshly cooked meat from the bones. Cut either meat in small pieces.

1 small chopped onion   *2 tbs. oil*

Heat the oil in a saucepan and fry the onion until it begins to brown.

1 *oz.* (2 *tbs. or* 25 *g.*) *rice*	*Salt and pepper*
1½ *pt.* (750 *ml.*) *stock*	*The pieces of meat*

Plenty of chopped fresh mint, chervil, chives, or lovage

Add to the pan and simmer until the rice is cooked (10–15 mins.). Taste for seasoning.

Yogurt

As each portion of soup is served put a good tablespoon (more if liked) of yogurt in the middle.

LENTIL SOUP

COOKING TIME 2 hrs.	QUANTITIES FOR 4–5.
1 *oz.* (25 *g.*) *fat*	1 *carrot, diced*
1 *onion, sliced*	1 *turnip, diced*

Heat the fat in a saucepan, add the vegetables, cover, and cook gently for about 15 mins. shaking or stirring occasionally but not allowing the vegetables to brown.

2 *pt.* (1¼ *l.*) *stock*	1–2 *tsp. salt*
8 *oz.* (1 *c. or* 250 *g.*) *lentils*	*Fresh or dried thyme or savory*
Pinch of pepper	*to taste*
3 *or* 4 *bacon rinds or a ham*	
bone	

Add to the vegetables and boil gently until the lentils are tender. Either rub through a sieve or remove the bacon rinds or ham bone and pulp the soup in the electric blender. Return to the pan.

½ *pt.* (250 *ml.*) *milk*

Add to the soup and re-heat, tasting for seasoning.

Alternative herbs: Chervil, dill, lovage, or sorrel.

ONION SOUP

To serve hot or cold.

COOKING TIME about ¾ hr.	QUANTITIES FOR 6–8.
2 *tbs. oil*	2 *large onions*

Skin the onions and chop them finely. For a large amount like this it is worthwhile using the electric blender or mincer. Heat the oil in a saucepan and stew the onion in it for 10 mins., without browning.

3 *pt.* (1½ *l.*) *white stock*	*Celery salt*

Add to the onion, bring to the boil, cover and simmer for about ½ hr. or until the onion is tender. If a completely smooth soup is preferred, it may be sieved or blended at this stage.

   2 *tsp. potato flour*   6 *tbs.* (90 *ml.*) *fresh, or soured*
   1 *tsp. wine vinegar*   *cream*
                ½ *tsp. sugar*

Mix the potato flour to a smooth paste with the cream, add the other ingredients and stir this into the soup. Just bring to the boil.

   Salt and pepper
   2–4 *tbs. chopped marjoram, sage, or thyme, or a mixture*

Season the soup and stir in the herbs. Serve hot, or cool and then store in the refrigerator to serve cold.

PARSLEY SOUP

COOKING TIME about 15 mins.   QUANTITIES FOR 4–6.

   2 *oz.* (50 *g.*) *butter*   4 *tbs.* (60 *ml.*) *finely chopped onion*

Melt the butter in a large saucepan and stew the onion in it gently until it is softened but not brown.

   2 *tbs. flour*

Add to the pan and stir and cook for a minute.

   2 *pt.* (1¼ *l.*) *milk or milk and white stock mixed*
   Salt and pepper

Stir the liquid into the pan and stir until the soup boils. Boil gently for 5 mins. Season to taste.

   About ¼ *pt.* (150 *ml.*) *chopped parsley*

Add enough parsley to make the soup really green. Make sure it is hot, and serve.

POTATO SOUP

COOKING TIME ½ hr.   QUANTITIES FOR 4.

   4 *medium-sized* (1 *lb.* or ½ *kg.*) *potatoes*
   1 *oz.* (25 *g.*) *butter or margarine*

Peel and slice the potatoes fairly finely. Heat the fat in a saucepan. Add the potatoes, cover and stew gently for about 15 mins. without allowing the potatoes to brown. Stir or shake the pan frequently.

   1½ *pt.* (1 *l.*) *water*   3 *or* 4 *sprigs of mint, dill, or marjoram*

Add to the potatoes, bring to the boil and cook until the potatoes are tender. Sieve the potatoes or pulp them in the electric blender.

   ½ *pt.* (250 *ml.*) *milk or single cream*   *Salt and pepper*

Add the milk or cream and re-heat the soup, seasoning to taste.

   Herb leaves or chopped herbs to garnish.

POTATO AND ONION SOUP

If this is made with chicken stock, the combination of ingredients gives the soup a pleasant gamey flavour.

COOKING TIME ¾–1 hr.   QUANTITIES FOR 6 or more.

2 medium-sized onions, chopped
1 lb. (½ kg.) potatoes, peeled and sliced
1 oz. (25 g.) butter or margarine

Melt the fat in a saucepan and stew the vegetables in it for about 10 mins. Shake or stir occasionally but do not allow to brown.

1½ pt. (750 ml.) chicken stock

Add to the vegetables, bring to the boil, cover, and boil gently until the vegetables are tender, about 30–40 mins. Either sieve the soup or pulp it in the electric blender.

2 good tbs. marjoram leaves   ½ pt. (250 ml.) milk

Either chop the marjoram or blend it with the milk. Add to the soup. Heat just to boiling.

Salt and pepper   A knob of butter
A little Worcester sauce

Season to taste, add the butter and stir to melt it.
Alternative herbs: thyme or sage.

SAUERKRAUT SOUP

COOKING TIME about 20 mins.   QUANTITIES FOR 4.

8 oz. (250 g.) sauerkraut   8 oz. (250 g.) potatoes

Drain the sauerkraut, then chop it fairly small. Peel and dice the potatoes.

¼ tsp. or more of caraway seeds   Salt
1–1½ pt. (½–¾ l.) white stock

Boil the vegetables with the stock and seasonings until the potatoes are tender. Mash the vegetables.

½ oz. (1½ tbs. or 15 g.) flour   A little cold stock or water

Blend the flour to a smooth cream and use it to thicken the soup. Boil for a couple of minutes.

1 egg yolk or 1 whole egg   Lemon juice to taste
½ pt. (250 ml.) soured cream   Pepper
*   or yogurt*

Beat the egg and cream or yogurt together and stir it into the soup. Stir until it is almost boiling. Season to taste and serve, sprinkled with
Paprika pepper

SORREL SOUP

This is a soup with a delicate flavour. Some recipes advise using chicken stock but I think this one using just milk and cream is better. It is better not to finish the soup until just before serving it as there is a tendency for the milk to curdle if the soup is kept hot for long.

COOKING TIME about ½ hr.   QUANTITIES FOR 4.

   2 oz. (6 tbs. or 50 g.) semolina   1 pt. (½ l.) milk

Heat the milk in the top part of a double boiler, sprinkle in the semolina and cook for about 25 mins., stirring often and adding more milk if it becomes a stodgy mixture.

   3 oz. (3 pt. loosely packed or 1½ l.) sorrel leaves
   A small knob of butter

Melt the butter and add the sorrel, cooking it over a gentle heat, stirring frequently until it is a soft pulp. Add to the cooked semolina and milk and rub through a sieve or put in the electric blender just long enough to make smooth. Leave the soup at this stage until just before serving.

   Double cream and milk to thin   Salt

Re-heat the soup with cream and milk to thin it, and season to taste. Do not boil at this stage.

Alternative: The soup may be finished with an egg yolk mixed with the cream.

TOMATO SOUP WITH TARRAGON OR BASIL

COOKING TIME 40 mins.   QUANTITIES FOR 3–4.

   1 onion, sliced   1 small carrot, chopped
   1 oz. (25 g.) butter or margarine

Fry the vegetables in the fat in a saucepan until the onions begins to colour.

   1 pt. (½ l.) stock   14–16 oz. (450 g.) can of tomatoes
   1 rasher bacon, chopped   ½ tsp. sugar
   1 tsp. salt   Bouquet garni
   Pinch of pepper   ½ tsp. paprika pepper

Add to the pan, cover and simmer for 20–25 mins. Rub through a sieve and return to the pan.

   1 tbs. flour   3 tbs. milk or cream

Mix to a smooth paste, add some of the hot soup, stir and return to the pan, stirring until the soup boils. Simmer for 5 mins. Taste for seasoning.

1 *tbs. chopped tarragon or basil*

Stir into the soup just before serving.

VEGETABLE SOUP WITH CHERVIL

COOKING TIME about 1 hr.   QUANTITIES FOR 4.

8 *oz.* (250 *g.*) *potatoes, thinly*   1 *oz.* (25 *g.*) *butter or margarine*
sliced   1 *large leek, sliced*

4 *oz.* (125 *g.*) *carrots, chopped*

Melt the butter or margarine in a saucepan, add the vegetables, cover and stew for about 10 mins. or until the vegetables begin to soften. Do not allow them to brown.

1½ *pt.* (750 *ml.*) *water   Salt and pepper*

Add to the pan, bring to the boil, and boil gently for 40 mins. or until the vegetables are quite soft. Either rub through a sieve or pulp in the electric blender. Return to the pan and re-heat.

2 *good-sized sprigs of chervil*

Wash, dry, and remove the leaves, chop them finely, and add to the soup. Alternatively, chop them in the blender, using a small amount of the soup as liquid. Add to the hot soup.

2 *tbs. cream*

Taste the soup for seasoning and add the cream just before serving.

VEGETABLE SOUP WITH MARJORAM

COOKING TIME about ¾ hr.   QUANTITIES FOR 4–5.

1 *lb.* (½ *kg.*) *fresh or frozen raw vegetables*

Include some onion, some root vegetables, celery, some green vegetables such as cabbage or sprouts, and any others available. Prepare the vegetables as for boiling, slicing or cutting them in dice. There is no need to thaw frozen vegetables.

1 *oz.* (25 *g.*) *fat or* 2 *tbs. oil*

Heat in a large pan, add the vegetables, cover and cook over a very gentle heat for about 10 mins., stirring or shaking the pan occasionally.

2 *pt.* (1 *l.*) *stock*   1 *tbs. chopped fresh marjoram, or*
Pinch of pepper   *more to taste*
2–3 *tsp. salt*

Add to the pan, bring to the boil, cover, and boil gently until the vegetables are tender. Taste for seasoning.

Grated cheese

Sprinkle each portion with grated cheese as the soup is served, or hand the cheese separately.

Alternatives: Put the cooked soup in the electric blender to make a smooth consistency, thin with stock as necessary. Instead of the marjoram use balm, chervil, parsley, sorrel, or thyme.

CHAPTER EIGHT

Sauces

Including salad dressings, herb butters, basting sauces and marinades

Any herbs can be used in sauces, the choice depending on the food the sauce will accompany. Such sauces are most appreciated when served with plainly cooked meat, fish, and vegetables and they are one of the best ways of adding interest to everyday food.

HERB SAUCES SPECIALLY RECOMMENDED ARE:

With eggs: chives; parsley; sorrel.

With fish: apple and horseradish; fennel; caper; chives; cold tomato; cream cheese and mayonnaise; cucumber; dill; green Dutch; herb; horseradish; melted butter; parsley; salsa verde; sauce gribiche; shrimp; yogurt; bearnaise.

With meat: apple and horseradish; apple and sage; bearnaise; caper; chives; cold tomato; fennel; herb; horseradish; mint; piquant; sage and lemon; salsa verde; sauce gribiche; soured cream; vinaigrette; yogurt.

With poultry: apple and sage; sage and lemon; fennel; apple and horseradish; chives; cucumber; green tarragon; herb; melted butter; parsley; piquant; soured cream; yogurt.

Cold fish, meat, and poultry (for salad dressings see pp. 126–7): apple and horseradish; chives, using cream and yogurt; cold tomato; cream cheese and mayonnaise; herb; horseradish; mint; remoulade; sauce gribiche; soured cream; bearnaise.

Vegetables: chives; fennel; melted butter; parsley, vinaigrette; yogurt.

Meat and fish fondues: bearnaise; chives; cold tomato; cream cheese and mayonnaise; dill; herb butters; herb sauce; salsa verde; soured cream.

APPLE AND HORSERADISH SAUCE

This is a thick uncooked sauce rather like a chutney in consistency and meant to be served with hot or cold meat, poultry, or fish. It will keep for 2–3 weeks, covered, in the refrigerator.

QUANTITIES FOR 4.

½ tsp. mustard powder   1 tsp. water

Mix the mustard to a smooth cream with the water.

2 medium-sized apples or 1 apple and 1 medium carrot
3 tbs. lemon juice

Peel the apple and carrot and grate fairly finely, mixing at once with lemon juice. Mix in the mustard.

1 tsp. sugar   2 tbs. grated horseradish

Add and mix well.

APPLE SAUCE WITH SAGE

To serve with pork or duck.

COOKING TIME about 5 mins.   QUANTITIES FOR 4.

8 oz. (250 g.) apples, peeled and sliced thinly
2 fresh sage leaves finely chopped, or more to taste
Sugar to taste

Put in a pan with just enough water to prevent sticking. Simmer until the apples are reduced to a pulp. Use hot or cold.

BEARNAISE SAUCE

For serving with grilled meat or fish but it can be used whenever a cold herb sauce is appropriate.

COOKING TIME a few mins.   QUANTITIES FOR 4–6.

1 tsp. finely chopped shallot or onion
A sprig each of tarragon and chervil
Pinch of salt   5 tbs. (75 ml.) white wine vinegar

Cut the herbs up roughly, put all the ingredients in the top of a double boiler, and boil over direct heat until the liquid is reduced to about a dessertspoonful. Remove from the heat and cool a little.

2 egg yolks   3 oz. (75 g.) melted butter

Add the egg yolks to the herbs and vinegar and put the pan over boiling water. Whisk to mix in the egg yolks and then add the butter and continue whisking until the sauce thickens. Rub it through a small nylon sieve and keep it warm but don't heat it any more or it will separate. (But don't despair if this happens. Cool the sauce by stand-ing the pan in cold water and whisking hard to make it smooth again.)

> 1 *tsp. each of chopped chervil and tarragon*
> *Cayenne pepper*

Add to the sauce and serve just warm, or cold.

BÉCHAMEL SAUCE

Using a bay leaf and other flavourings makes this a very special white sauce. It can be used in the same way, plain, or with fresh chopped parsley or other fresh herbs added.

COOKING TIME 15–20 mins.   QUANTITIES FOR 6–8.

> 1 *pt.* (½ *l.*) *milk*   1-*in.* (2½-*cm.*) *piece of celery*
> 1 *shallot or small onion*   1 *bay leaf*
> 2–3 *slices of carrot*   10 *peppercorns*

Peel the onion or shallot and clean the other vegetables. Put all the ingredients in a pan and bring to the boil. Remove from the heat and leave to infuse for 5 mins. Then strain. Rinse and dry the pan.

> 1½ *oz.* (40 *g.*) *butter or margarine*
> 1½ *oz.* (4½ *tbs. or* 40 *g.*) *flour*

Melt the fat in the pan and mix in the flour. Cook gently until mealy looking. Remove from the heat and gradually add the strained milk, whisking until the sauce is quite smooth. Return to the heat and stir until it boils. Cook gently for 5 mins., or longer over boiling water.

> 4 *tbs.* (60 *ml.*) *single cream*   *Salt*

Season to taste, and add the cream just before serving.

CAPER SAUCE

Although this sauce is most often served with boiled mutton it is also very good with other boiled meats such as tongue or bacon, and with boiled or steamed fish, in fact, with any food where a sharp flavour would be an improvement. Pickled nasturtium seeds can be used to replace the capers (see p. 91).

COOKING TIME 10–15 mins.   QUANTITIES FOR 4–6.

> 2 *oz.* (50 *g.*) *butter or*   2 *oz.* (6 *tbs. or* 50 *g.*) *flour*
> *margarine*

Melt the fat in a saucepan and add the flour. Stir and cook for a few minutes until the mixture looks crumbly. Remove from the heat.

> 1 *pt.* (½ *l.*) *fish or meat stock*

Gradually add to the pan, mixing or whisking all the time until the sauce is smooth. Return to the heat and stir until it boils, boil gently for about 5 mins.

  2 tbs. chopped capers   Salt and pepper
  1½ tbs. vinegar from the capers, or use lemon juice

Add to the sauce and serve hot.

Alternative: Use lemon juice instead of vinegar and add 1 tbs. anchovy essence.

CHIVES SAUCE No. 1

To serve with eggs, fish, poultry, or meat.

COOKING TIME 5–10 mins.   QUANTITIES FOR 4.

  1½ oz. (½ c. or 40 g.) *fresh breadcrumbs*
  1 oz. (25 g.) *butter*

Melt the butter in a small pan and cook the breadcrumbs gently in it until they are golden brown. Remove from the heat and cool a little.

  ¼ pt. (150 ml.) *white stock*   2 tbs. *finely chopped chives*

Add to the pan, stir and heat until boiling. Simmer for a minute or so for the breadcrumbs to absorb the stock and thicken the sauce.

  Salt and pepper

Season to taste and serve, adding more stock if the sauce has become too thick.

CHIVES SAUCE No. 2

This is good served with fish, grilled or boiled meats, chicken, vegetables, or with a meat fondue.

QUANTITIES FOR 4.

  1 tbs. French mustard   2 egg yolks
  1 tbs. wine vinegar   ¼ tsp. salt
  Pinch of pepper

Mix together until well blended.

  2 oz. (50 g.) *butter*

Soften until almost melted and then whisk into the egg mixture until the sauce is the consistency of mayonnaise.

  2 tbs. chopped fresh chives

Mix into the sauce and serve warm or cold.

Alternative: use other fresh herbs in place of the chives.

CHIVES SAUCE No. 3

Serve this with hot or cold meats, poultry, fish, or meat fondues.
QUANTITIES FOR 4 or more.

½ pt. (250 ml.) soured cream or thick yogurt
¼ tsp. salt   1 tbs. lemon juice
¼ tsp. freshly ground white pepper
1 tbs. chopped fresh chives

Combine the ingredients thoroughly and refrigerate until required.

COLD TOMATO SAUCE

For serving with grilled meat or fish, cold meats, or meat fondues.
QUANTITIES FOR 4.

3 tbs. concentrated tomato purée   3 tbs. yogurt
1 tbs. lemon juice   2 tbs. oil
½ tsp. salt   ½ tsp. sugar
Pepper to taste

Mix together thoroughly.

3 tbs. chopped fresh herbs (tarragon, chives, parsley, marjoram)

Mix with the sauce, cover and store in the refrigerator until the sauce
is well chilled.

CREAM CHEESE AND MAYONNAISE SAUCE

This is rather like a Tartare sauce but milder in flavour and less
oily. It is very good as a sauce for cold fish or meat and for meat or
fish fondues.
QUANTITIES FOR 4.

4 oz. (125 g.) cream cheese

Mash or sieve to make smooth.

2 tsp. or more of finely chopped fresh herbs
Salt and pepper   2–3 tbs. mayonnaise

Beat these into the cream cheese using enough mayonnaise to make a
thick creamy sauce.

CUCUMBER SAUCE WITH DILL

This is very good with grilled lamb cutlets, veal escalopes or chops,
grilled fish, or chicken cooked in any way.

COOKING TIME about 20 mins.   QUANTITIES FOR 4.

   8 oz. (250 g.) *cucumber*
Peel, cut in strips and then across to give small dice.
   ½ oz. (15 g.) *butter*
Melt in a small saucepan, add the cucumber and stew slowly until
it is almost soft.
   1 *tbs. flour*
Add and mix in.
   ¼ pt. (150 ml.) *white stock*
Stir in and bring to the boil. Simmer for 5 mins.
   2 *heaped tbs. chopped fresh dill*   *Salt and pepper*
Add to the sauce. There should be enough dill to make it look green.
   5 *tbs.* (75 ml.) *soured cream or use fresh double cream with a
      squeeze of lemon juice*
Add and heat the sauce just to boiling. Serve hot.

DILL SAUCE No. 1

To serve with grilled or fried fish steaks or small whole fish; or use
as a fondue sauce.
QUANTITIES FOR 4–6.
   4 oz. (125 g.) *sieved cottage cheese*   *Salt and pepper*
   2 *tsp. grated or very finely chopped onion*
   1 *tbs. or more of chopped fresh dill*
   A little cream to give the desired consistency
Combine the ingredients and chill the sauce in the refrigerator.
Alternative method: Put the unsieved cheese, a slice or two of onion,
and the dill sprigs in the electric blender with about ¼ pt. (150 ml.)
of cream. Mix until smooth and the onions and dill finely chopped.

DILL SAUCE No. 2

COOKING TIME 20 mins.   QUANTITIES FOR 4.
   1 *small onion finely chopped*   ½ oz. (15 g.) *butter*
Heat the butter in a small pan and fry the onion until golden
brown.
   1 *tbs. chopped parsley*   1 *tbs. chopped dill*
   1 *tbs. flour*
Add to the pan and mix well.
   ¼ pt. (150 ml.) *stock*   1 *tbs. lemon juice*
   Pinch of sugar   *Salt and pepper*

Stir into the other ingredients in the pan, stirring until it boils, and boil gently for 10 mins.

   2 *tbs. freshly chopped dill*
   ¼ *pt.* (150 *ml.*) *soured cream or use fresh double cream and a little more lemon juice*

Add to the sauce and heat without boiling. Serve hot.

FENNEL MAYONNAISE

To serve with grilled and fried fish or with a fish salad.
QUANTITIES FOR 4 or more.

   ¼ *pt.* (150 *ml.*) *mayonnaise*
   1–2 *tbs. finely chopped fresh fennel*

Just before serving the sauce, chop the fennel and combine it with the mayonnaise. Freshly chopped fennel always has more flavour than when it has been prepared in advance.

FENNEL SAUCE

To serve with boiled lamb or mutton, herrings, mackerel, salmon or other fish, poultry, rabbit, or vegetables.
COOKING TIME about 10 mins.   QUANTITIES FOR 4–8.

   1½ *oz.* (40 *g.*) *butter or margarine*
   1½ *oz.* (4½ *tbs. or* 40 *g.*) *flour*

Melt the fat in a saucepan, add the flour and mix and cook until it looks crumbly. Remove from the heat.

   1 *pt.* (½ *l.*) *white, fish, or vegetable stock*

Use a stock suitable for the meat, fish or vegetable. Stir it into the roux, whisking to make it smooth. Return to the heat and stir until it boils. Boil gently for 5 mins.

   1 *egg yolk*   1 *tsp. sugar*
   1½ *tbs. vinegar or lemon juice* Salt *and pepper*
   4 *tbs. finely chopped fresh fennel*

Mix the egg, sugar, and vinegar or lemon juice and add to the sauce. Stir and heat, to thicken without boiling. Add the fennel, season to taste, and serve.

GREEN DUTCH SAUCE

For serving with fish.
QUANTITIES FOR 4–8.

1½ oz. (40 g.) *butter or margarine*
1½ oz. (4½ tbs. or 40 g.) *flour*
1 pt. (½ l.) *milk or half milk and half fish stock*

Heat the fat in a small pan, add the flour and mix and cook until it looks crumbly. Remove from the heat. Add the liquid, stir well, return to the heat and stir until it is smooth and boiling, boil gently for 5 mins.

2 or more tbs. *chopped parsley*   Salt and pepper
Lemon juice to taste

Add to the sauce, seasoning to taste. Serve at once or cover when cold and store in the refrigerator for re-heating. The sauce should be really green with parsley, and should taste of it.

GREEN TARRAGON SAUCE (for the blender)

Serve this with fried, roast, or steamed chicken pieces.

QUANTITIES FOR 4.

½ pt. (250 ml.) *milk*   3 tbs. *white wine*
2 tbs. *cornflour*   5 tbs. (75 ml.) *fresh tarragon leaves*
Pinch of fresh or dried thyme Salt and pepper

Blend all together until the tarragon is finely chopped. Pour into a pan and stir until it boils; boil gently for 5 mins. Season to taste.

HERB SAUCE

For serving with grilled meat, poultry, or fish, with fondues, boiled or cold meat, poultry or fish, or as a salad dressing.

QUANTITIES FOR 6 or more.

½ small onion   A good sprig of parsley
A few tarragon leaves   A sprig of thyme
A few marjoram leaves

Skin the onion and chop it very finely. Wash, dry, and chop the herbs.

6 tbs. *olive oil*   2 tbs. *wine vinegar*
3 tbs. *lemon juice*   1 tsp. *sugar*
½ tsp. *salt*   Pinch of pepper

Mix all together and add the onion and herbs. Leave to stand a while before using.

Alternative method: Put all the ingredients, whole onion and uncut herbs, in the electric blender and mix until the herbs and onion are finely chopped.

HORSERADISH SAUCE (cold)

QUANTITIES FOR 4.

Pinch of paprika pepper   *2 tsp. dry mustard*
4 tbs. (60 ml.) grated fresh   *1 tsp. wine vinegar*
   horseradish

Mix these together until they are well blended.

4 tbs. (60 ml.) double cream, thick yogurt, or soured cream

Add to the first mixture and beat until creamy. Cover and store in the refrigerator for ½ hr. or so before using.

HORSERADISH SAUCE (hot)

This is for serving with hot boiled meats, steamed or grilled fish, and dishes like meat loaves and fish puddings.

COOKING TIME 8–10 mins.   QUANTITIES FOR 4.

¾ oz. (20 g.) margarine or   *1 tsp. dry mustard*
   butter   *½ pt. (250 ml.) stock or milk*
¾ oz. (3 tbs. or 20 g.) flour

Melt the fat in a saucepan, stir in the flour and mustard and cook for a few minutes. Remove from the heat, add the liquid, mix and return to the heat, stirring until the sauce thickens and boils. Boil for 5 mins.

½ tsp. salt   *1½ oz. (½ c. or 40 g.) grated*
3 tbs. (45 ml.) vinegar   *horseradish or more to taste*
                     ¼ tsp. sugar

Add to the sauce and serve hot.

MELTED BUTTER AND HERB SAUCE

To serve with fish, poultry, meat, or cooked vegetables.

QUANTITIES FOR 4.

2 oz. (50 g.) butter, melted   *1 tbs. chopped fresh herbs or*
2 tsp. lemon juice   *½ tsp. dried*
Pinch of pepper

Melt the butter and add the fresh herbs and seasoning just before serving; add dried herbs ¼–½ hr. before serving and keep the sauce warm.

MINT SAUCE

There are a number of different ways of making this traditional sauce. Some like very little vinegar in it, some like a lot, while others prefer to use lemon juice.

Proportions of ingredients should be according to personal taste and you may want to vary the recipes given below.

MINT SAUCE No. 1

QUANTITIES FOR 4 or more.
½ pt. (250 ml.) mint leaves
1–2 oz. (2–4 tbs. or 25–50 g.) caster sugar
5 tbs. (75 ml.) malt or wine vinegar

Chop the mint finely and mix it with the sugar and vinegar, stirring until the sugar dissolves. Leave to infuse for about 2 hrs. before serving.

Using the electric blender
Put the ingredients in the goblet and process at slow speed until the mint is finely chopped. Leave to infuse.

For the freezer
Use the above proportions of mint and sugar but instead of vinegar, pour just enough boiling water over the leaves to moisten them. Allow to cool and then put in a small container for the freezer. When required add the vinegar to the frozen mint and leave the sauce to thaw at room temperature.

Using mint preserved in vinegar
Put chopped mint in small jars and cover with cold vinegar. Seal and store in a cool, dark place. To make the sauce, remove as much mint as needed, add sugar to taste, and a little boiling water, then vinegar to taste.

MINT SAUCE No. 2

QUANTITIES FOR 4.
4 tbs. (60 ml.) chopped fresh mint   *2 tbs. caster sugar*
2 tbs. warm water   *8 tbs. (120 ml.) lemon juice*

Mix together until the sugar dissolves. Leave to infuse for at least ½ hr. before serving.

PARSLEY SAUCE

COOKING TIME 5–10 mins.   QUANTITIES FOR 4.

   2 oz. (50 g.) *butter*   1–2 oz. (3–6 tbs. or 25–50 g.) *flour*

Melt the butter in a small pan and add the flour. Mix and cook until the flour looks crumbly. Remove from the heat.

   ½ pt. (250 ml.) *stock or milk*

For the stock use the liquid from the accompanying food, for example, poached fish, boiled meat or vegetables. Add to the pan, stir and whisk until the sauce is smooth. Return to the heat and stir until it boils. Boil gently for 5 mins.

   4 tbs. or more *chopped parsley*   *Salt and pepper*
   Lemon juice or vinegar

Season the sauce to taste, using enough parsley to make it really green. Serve hot.

PIQUANT SAUCE

To serve with boiled meats such as beef, salt pork, bacon or ham, tongue, and poultry.

COOKING TIME 15 mins.   QUANTITIES FOR 4.

   1 tbs. *finely chopped onion*
   ¼ pt. (150 ml.) *dry white wine and wine vinegar mixed*

Use half wine and half vinegar or a little more wine than vinegar according to how sharp you like the sauce. Put in a small pan with the onion and boil rapidly until reduced by about half.

   ½ pt. (250 ml.) *stock from the meat*

Add to the pan and simmer for 10 mins.

   1 tbs. *potato flour*

Mix to a smooth cream with a little cold water and stir into the hot sauce. As soon as it boils, remove from the heat.

   2 tbs. *chopped parsley*   1 tbs. *chopped tarragon*
   1 tbs. *chopped chives*   2 tsp. *capers*
   1 *small gherkin, chopped*   *Salt and pepper*

Taste for seasoning and add salt and pepper as needed, and the herbs just before serving the sauce.

REMOULADE SAUCE

To serve with cold meat, poultry, or fish.

QUANTITIES FOR 4 or more.

  ¼ pt. (150 ml.) mayonnaise   ½ tsp. anchovy essence
  1 tsp. chopped gherkins   1–2 tsp. made mustard
  1 tsp. chopped fines herbes   1 tsp. chopped capers
  (parsley, tarragon, chervil)

Mix all together making sure there is plenty of mustard flavour.

SAGE AND LEMON SAUCE

To serve with duck, goose, pork, boiled ham or bacon.

COOKING TIME 35 mins.   QUANTITIES FOR 4.

  ½ oz. (15 g.) butter or margarine   1 tbs. flour

Melt the fat in a small pan, stir in the flour and cook for a minute or so.

  1 oz. (25 g.) finely chopped onion   1 tsp. grated lemon rind
  ½ oz. (15 g.) finely chopped sage   1 tsp. vinegar
  ¼ pt. (150 ml.) stock   Salt and pepper

Add to the pan and stir until the sauce boils, cover and boil gently for about ½ hr. adding more stock as needed to prevent burning. Serve hot.

SALSA VERDE

This is the well-known green sauce of Italy, served with boiled meats but suitable as an accompaniment for any meat or fish where a sharp, cold sauce is required. It is very good with grilled meat of fish and with meat fondues.

QUANTITIES FOR 8 or more.

  4 tbs. (60 ml.) olive oil   ¼ pt. (150 ml.) wine vinegar
  2 oz. (50 g.) parsley and stalks
  1 oz. (25 g.) drained and rinsed capers
  1 oz. (25 g.) pickled gherkins or cucumbers
  1 oz. (1 slice or 25 g.) bread, or 1 small boiled potato
  Pepper, salt and a pinch of sugar
  Pinch of dried garlic or ¼ clove of fresh garlic

The simplest way of making this sauce is to put all the ingredients in the blender goblet and mix until smooth. Alternatively, chop the capers, parsley, gherkins, and garlic. Crumb the bread or sieve the potato. Beat all the ingredients together thoroughly.

SAUCE GRIBICHE

To serve with cold or hot fish, hot roast or boiled meats, and cold meat.

QUANTITIES FOR 6–8.

3 hard-boiled egg yolks
¼ tsp. salt
½ tsp. sugar
1 tsp. chopped parsley
1 tsp. chopped chervil

3 tbs. olive oil
3 tbs. tarragon vinegar
1 tbs. French mustard
1 tsp. chopped chives
1 tsp. chopped tarragon

Mash the egg yolks and gradually work in the other ingredients.

3 hard-boiled egg whites

Chop finely and add to the sauce. Leave to stand a while before serving.

Alternative method: Put all ingredients except the egg whites in the electric blender, using small sprigs of the herbs. Blend until smooth and the herbs are chopped. Finally blend on/off to chop the egg whites in the sauce.

SHRIMP SAUCE

To serve with fish.

QUANTITIES FOR 4.

¾ pt. (400 ml.) Béchamel sauce (p. 113)
2 oz. (50 g.) shelled shrimps, fresh, or frozen

Anchovy sauce
Cayenne or paprika pepper
Lemon juice
Chopped dill or fennel

Make the sauce, add the shrimps and allow to heat through. Add the seasonings and herbs to taste and serve hot.

SORREL SAUCE

To serve with poultry, veal, pork, fish, or eggs.

COOKING TIME 5 mins.   QUANTITIES FOR 3–4.

2 pt. (1¼ l.) sorrel leaves, loosely packed
½ oz. (15 g.) butter

Wash the leaves and put them in a saucepan with the butter. Cook over a moderate heat, stirring frequently until the sorrel is reduced to a pulp. Rub through a sieve.

¼–½ tsp. potato flour   *¼ pt. (150 ml.) single cream or stock*

Mix the potato flour with a little of the cream or stock, add remainder and stir into the purée. Heat and stir until the sauce just boils. Remove from the heat.

Salt and pepper   *Sugar*

Add seasoning and sugar to taste and, if necessary, thin the sauce with more cream or stock. Serve hot.

SOURED CREAM SAUCE

To serve cold with grills, hot or cold meat, poultry or fish, or with meat fondues.

QUANTITIES FOR 4 or more.

½ pt. (250 ml.) soured cream
2 tbs. lemon juice
1 tsp. Worcester sauce
2 tbs. very finely chopped or grated onion (optional)

2 tbs. finely chopped fresh herbs
¼ tsp. salt
¼ tsp. freshly ground white pepper
½ tsp. dry mustard

Mix together thoroughly, cover, and store in the refrigerator until required.

SOUR SWEET CHIVES SAUCE

COOKING TIME a few mins.   QUANTITIES FOR 4.

1 egg or 2 yolks   *1 tbs. water*
2 tsp. potato flour

Mix together to a smooth paste.

¼ pt. (150 ml.) water   *1–2 tsp. sugar*
1 tbs. wine vinegar   *Salt and pepper*

Put in a small pan and bring to the boil. Pour into the egg mixture, whisking all the time. Cook over a very gentle heat until the mixture thickens and just boils. Remove from the heat.

1 tbs. wine vinegar   *2 tbs. olive oil*
3 tbs. chopped chives

Mix into the sauce and serve warm.

TARRAGON SAUCE

This is an old recipe in which the tarragon is not chopped, but the leaves added whole, infused for flavour, and then removed by straining.

COOKING TIME 20 mins.   QUANTITIES FOR 4.

  2 *oz. (50 g.) butter*   1 *tbs. flour*

Cook together in a small pan or in the top of a double boiler until the flour begins to colour. The double boiler top must be over direct heat for this.

  ½ *pt. (250 ml.) chicken or other white stock*

Add to the flour and butter and stir until the mixture thickens.

  1 *small bunch of fresh tarragon sprigs*

Add to the sauce and cook it very gently, preferably over boiling water, for about 15 mins. or until the sauce is well flavoured. Strain the sauce, rinse the pan, and return the sauce to re-heat.

  1 *egg yolk*   *Salt and pepper*

Beat the yolk to break it up, add some of the sauce, blend and add to the main sauce, stirring and heating until the egg thickens it. Season to taste and serve hot.

TOMATO SAUCE

To serve with spaghetti or other pasta.

COOKING TIME 30 mins.   QUANTITIES FOR 1 lb. (½ kg.) spaghetti.

  2 *medium-sized onions,*   2 *tbs. olive oil*
    chopped

Heat the oil and fry the onion in it for 5 mins.

  1 *small (2½ oz. or 75 g.) tin of concentrated tomato purée*

Add to the onion and stir and cook for a minute or two.

  Salt and pepper   1 *pt. (½ l.) water*
  Pinch of dried thyme   *Pinch of dried marjoram*

Add to the pan, stirring until the sauce boils. Boil gently, without a lid, for about 25 mins. or until the sauce is a creamy consistency. Season to taste.

VINAIGRETTE SAUCE

The traditional sauce to serve with boiled meats such as calf's head, tongue, and other salt meats, or with vegetables such as artichokes; but it can be used whenever an oil and vinegar sauce is required.

QUANTITIES FOR 4.

  4 *tbs. (60 ml.) oil*   *Salt and pepper*
  2 *tbs. (30 ml.) tarragon vinegar* ½ *tsp. made mustard*
  1 *tsp. each of finely chopped*
    gherkin, shallot, and parsley

Mix together and stir again before using.

YOGURT SAUCE WITH HERBS

Serve hot or cold with meat, poultry, fish, or vegetables.

COOKING TIME a few mins.   QUANTITIES FOR 4.

    1 *whole egg or 2 yolks*   ¼ *pt.* (150 *ml.*) *yogurt*

Whisk the egg in a small basin and stir in the yogurt. Put the basin over a pan of boiling water and beat the sauce with a wooden spoon as it heats. It may thin at first but will then thicken as the egg cooks. Cook until it has thickened and is really hot.

    Salt and pepper   *Chopped chives and/or parsley*
                                         or other fresh herbs

Season to taste and add herbs to taste.

Alternatives: This sauce makes a good salad dressing if it is thinned when cold with a little oil and lemon juice or vinegar; or use just as it is.

SALAD DRESSINGS

Chopped fresh or dried herbs can be added to standard dressings such as French dressing, mayonnaise, or salad cream; or these dressings can be made with herb vinegars or herb oils. When dried herbs are used they should be steeped in the oil for a while before making the dressing.

The recipes here are for a few special dressings.

DILL OR FENNEL CREAM DRESSING

QUANTITIES FOR 4.

    1 *tbs. oil*   1 *tbs. wine vinegar*
    Salt and sugar to taste   2 *tsp. finely chopped onion*
    2 *tbs. soured cream*   *Chopped fresh dill or fennel*

Combine the ingredients using plenty of the herb to give a definite flavour.

FENNEL MAYONNAISE, see p. 117.

HERB SAUCE

Also for use as a dressing, see p. 118.

SOURED CREAM AND HERB DRESSING

To use in place of mayonnaise in meat, fish, and other suitable salads.

QUANTITIES FOR 3-4.

5 *tbs.* (75 *ml.*) *soured cream*   2 *tbs. lemon juice*

Whisk these together.

1 *hard-boiled egg, chopped*   *Salt and pepper*
1-2 *tbs. finely chopped fresh*   *Sugar*
   herbs

Add to the cream, seasoning to taste. If necessary, thin with more lemon juice or with some milk or cream.

TURKISH DRESSING

QUANTITIES FOR 4 or more.

¼ *pt.* (150 *ml.*) *yogurt*   1 *tbs. lemon juice*
1 *tbs. horseradish sauce*   ½ *tsp. paprika pepper*
¼ *tsp. garlic salt*   ½ *tsp. salt*
1-2 *tbs. chopped chives or*
   mixed fresh herbs

Beat together until frothy.

YOGURT SAUCE WITH HERBS

See the alternative to the recipe on p. 126.

HERB BUTTERS

These are for serving on grilled meat or fish and hot cooked vegetables. A small pat of the butter is put on the food as it goes to table, this melts and forms a sauce. Sometimes they are served in a soft condition so that food can be dipped in the sauce, for example, a meat fondue. Herb butters make good sandwich spreads, to spread on biscuits or for canapés and other snacks. They make a first rate addition to mashed potato and cheer up the packet mashed potato no end; also very good served with baked jacket potatoes.

BASIC RECIPE

QUANTITIES FOR 4-8 depending on how it is used.

  4 *oz.* (125 *g.*) *butter*
  ¼–½ *pt.* (150–250 *ml.*) *herb leaves or* 2–4 *tbs. chopped fresh*
   herb or 1 *tsp. dried powdered herb*
  Lemon juice to taste   *Salt and pepper*

The amount of herb to use will vary with its strength and with personal taste. Add it gradually to the butter until it tastes right.

  The butter must be soft but not melted and the chopped herbs are worked in with a fork, knife, or pounded in a mortar. The butters can be made in advance and stored in the refrigerator. They can be shaped into ornamental pats or just cut a knob off as you would with ordinary butter.

SUITABLE HERBS TO USE ARE: (one or a mixture)

Basil	Marjoram	Sage
Burnet	Mint	Tarragon
Chervil	Parsley	Thyme (lemon)
Chives	Rosemary	

The following recipes are my favourites with the proportions I use.

BASIL BUTTER

  4 *oz.* (125 *g.*) *softened butter*
  1 *tsp. powdered dried basil or* 1 *tbs. finely chopped fresh basil*

This is a very strong herb and less can be used if the herb you are using is particularly strong.

MAITRE D'HOTEL SAUCE OR PARSLEY BUTTER

  4 *oz.* (125 *g.*) *softened butter*   *Lemon juice to taste*
  2 *tbs. chopped fresh parsley*

MINT BUTTER

  4 *oz.* (125 *g.*) *softened butter*   ½ *pt.* (250 *ml.*) *mint leaves*
  ½ *pt.* (250 *ml.*) *parsley sprigs*

Wash the herbs and boil them in the smallest possible amount of water until they are pulpy. Rub through a sieve, cool and then work into the butter.

MIXED HERB BUTTER No. 1

4 oz. (125 g.) softened butter
4 tbs. (60 ml.) chopped herbs in equal quantities, tarragon, chervil,
burnet, and chives
A little garlic

MIXED HERB BUTTER No. 2

4 oz. (125 g.) softened butter
4 tbs. (60 ml.) chopped herbs in equal quantities, chervil, sweet
cicely, and tarragon

This gives a decided anise flavour, very good with fish or beef
steaks.

ROSEMARY BUTTER

4 oz. (125 g.) softened butter
1 tsp. powdered dried rosemary or 1 tbs. finely chopped fresh
young rosemary leaves

This is very good on grilled fish or with lamb.

TARRAGON BUTTER (a green butter)

4 oz. (125 g.) softened butter
¼ pt. (150 ml.) tarragon leaves

Blanch the tarragon leaves by pouring boiling water over them. Then
plunge them in cold water, drain, and dry by pressing between paper
towels. Chop finely and work into the butter.

BASTING SAUCES AND MARINADES

Basting sauces are for brushing on grills or roasts during cooking,
marinades are for steeping foods (meat, game, fish, poultry), before
cooking. Some of the excess marinade is often used as a basting
sauce during the subsequent cooking; and the same recipe can usually
serve either as a basting sauce or a marinade.

Because salt tends to draw out the juices, it is not usually added
to meat marinades, but it is often included in fish marinades as

drawing out some moisture makes the flesh firmer, particularly useful for items such as kebabs.

Marinated food needs to be steeped 1–2 hrs. for small thin pieces, 24 hrs. or more for large pieces such as a joint of meat. This is to allow flavours from the marinade to penetrate the meat. Long-time marinating is best done in a covered dish in the refrigerator.

Marinades and basting sauces can be prepared well in advance, covered, and stored in the refrigerator. This allows time for dried herbs to release their flavour.

Quick marinades can be prepared by using herb oils (p. 83), or herb vinegars (p. 86). Oil is an important ingredient in basting sauces as it helps to keep the surface of the food from becoming dry.

When marinades are used for brushing food during grilling, they may need straining first to remove any larger pieces of flavourings which might burn and spoil the food being grilled.

ANISETTE MARINADE FOR GRILLED FISH

QUANTITIES FOR 4 steaks or 4 portions of fillet.

2 tbs. oil	¼ tsp. salt
2 tsp. lemon juice	Pinch of pepper
1 tbs. anisette	

Combine the ingredients. Put the fish (thawed or fresh), in a shallow dish and pour the marinade over it. Turn once or twice during marinating for about an hour. Grill in the usual way for 10–15 mins. depending on the thickness of the fish. Baste several times with the marinade.

GINGER AND LEMON MARINADE OR BASTING SAUCE

For veal, lamb, or fish.
QUANTITIES FOR 4 pieces of meat or fish.

4 tbs. oil	Pinch of ground ginger
2 tbs. vinegar	½ tsp. dried rosemary
Pinch dried garlic	¼ tsp. grated lemon rind
Pepper	½ tsp. grated horseradish

Mix, cover, and store in the refrigerator. Strain before using.

HERB BASTING SAUCE OR MARINADE

QUANTITIES FOR 4.

½–1 *tbs. dried herbs, thyme, marjoram, rosemary, sage, dill or fennel, or a mixture*
3 *tbs. oil*

Warm the oil a little, crush the herbs and add to the oil, or pound the herbs in a mortar with the warm oil.

1 *tsp. dry mustard*   2 *tbs. vinegar or lemon juice*
2 *tsp. Worcester sauce*

Mix the mustard with the sauce and vinegar and mix this with the oil. Stir before using.

MARINADE FOR BRAISED OR POT-ROASTED BEEF

This is excellent for improving the less tender cuts, preferably a fairly lean piece.

QUANTITIES FOR a 2–3 lb. (1–1½ kg.) piece.

¼ *pt.* (150 *ml.*) *wine or cider*   1 *bay leaf*
vinegar   2 *cloves*
¼ *pt.* (150 *ml.*) *water*   1 *onion, sliced*
1 *tsp. peppercorns*   1 *sprig of marjoram or savory*
1 *sprig of thyme*

Put in a pan, bring to the boil, cover and simmer for 10 mins. Cool. Put the meat in a dish just large enough to take it comfortably and pour the marinade over it. It should come about half way up. Cover the dish and store in the refrigerator from 2–4 days, turning the meat daily. Drain from the marinade and pat dry before browning in hot fat in the usual way. Then braise or pot-roast 2–3 hrs. using some of the marinating liquid to moisten the braise or make gravy for the pot roast.

MINTED ORANGE MARINADE

For lamb, pork, or veal chops or cutlets.

QUANTITIES FOR 4.

5 *tbs.* (75 *ml.*) *lemon juice*   ¼ *pt.* (150 *ml.*) *orange juice*
1 *tbs. sugar*   2 *tbs. oil*
2–3 *tbs. finely chopped fresh mint or* 1 *tbs. dried mint*

Mix together and pour over the meat, cover, and refrigerate for 2 hrs. Grill the meat, basting with some of the marinade.

SHERRY AND HERB BASTING SAUCE OR MARINADE

QUANTITIES FOR 4–6.

1 tsp. dry mustard   *1 tsp. brown sugar*
Pinch of dried garlic   *Pinch of dried thyme*
½ tsp. dried marjoram   *½ tsp. salt*
Pinch of black pepper

Mix these together in a small basin.

4 tbs. sherry   *2 tbs. oil*

Mix these gradually into the dry ingredients.

TOMATO MARINADE

For grilled meat or fish.

QUANTITIES FOR 4.

½ pt. (250 ml.) tomato juice   *½ tsp. dried rosemary*
¼ tsp. crushed white pepper-   *3 tbs. vinegar*
corns   *1 tsp. dried thyme*
Few slices of onion or a little
garlic

Mix all together and marinate the meat or fish for 1–2 hrs. Some of the marinade can be used for brushing during grilling, but only towards the end of cooking or the tomato will make the surface too dark. It is better to use oil for brushing, at least at the beginning.

CHAPTER NINE

Cheese and eggs

CHEESE

Herbs are used for flavouring cheeses made in a number of different countries. For example, caraway seeds in Dutch Kümmel cheese and Svecia cheese of Sweden; sage is used with spinach in English Sage cheese; mixtures of herbs go into Limburger cheese of Belgium, Alsace, and Germany, and the Fromage Fort of France.

Almost any herb can be used with cheese but herbs are generally most appreciated when combined with the milder soft cheeses or a mild Cheddar or Cheshire cheese.

For herbs to use with soft cheese, see p. 137.

The best for flavouring hot cheese dishes are marjoram, tarragon, basil, thyme, sage, coriander, and garlic.

For cheese sandwiches and snacks see pp. 224–32.

CHEESE FLAN WITH HERB PASTRY

COOKING TIME 30 mins.   TEMPERATURE E. 425° (220°C.) G.7
QUANTITIES FOR a 7–8 in. (18–20 cm.) flan.

4 oz. (¾ c. or 125 g.) plain   ¼ tsp. salt
   flour   1 oz. (25 g.) lard
1 oz. (25 g.) butter or
   margarine

Mix the flour and salt and rub in the fat.

About 1 tbs. finely chopped fresh herbs

The amount depends on how strongly flavoured the herbs are. Use marjoram, tarragon, chervil, or thyme or a mixture of the three. Rub the herbs into the flour to distribute them evenly.

1 egg, beaten

Use enough to make a stiff dough. Roll out and line the flan ring, prick the bottom and put the flan in the refrigerator while the filling is prepared.

> 2 *eggs, beaten, plus any left*   4 *oz.* (125 *g.*) *grated Emmental,*
> *over from mixing the pastry*   *Edam, or Gouda cheese*
> ¼ *pt.* (150 *ml.*) *single cream*   *Grated nutmeg*
> *Cayenne pepper*

Mix together and pour into the pastry case. Bake until the filling is brown and set. Serve warm or cold. The filling may rise a lot during cooking but will shrink somewhat during cooling.

CHEESE FONDUE PROVENÇALE

QUANTITIES FOR 4.

> *About a* ¼ *clove of crushed garlic or to taste*
> ½ *pt.* (250 *ml.*) *dry white wine*

Put in a cheese fondue pot and heat to boiling.

> 8 *oz.* (250 *g.*) *grated Gruyère cheese*
> 8 *oz.* (250 *g.*) *grated Emmental cheese*

Remove the wine from the heat and add the cheese. Stir and cook over a moderate heat until the cheese is completely melted.

> 2–3 *tsp. potato flour*   3 *oz.* (6 *tbs. or* 90 *ml.*) *dry French*
> *vermouth*

Mix the potato flour smooth with the vermouth, and stir it into the fondue, stirring and heating until it thickens.

> 2 *lbs. chopped green herbs which can include parsley, chives,*
> *tarragon, and marjoram; or just parsley and tarragon; or*
> *parsley and marjoram*

Add to the fondue and mix in. Serve the fondue, bubbling in the usual way, over a low heat.

> *Cubes of crusty bread*

Serve separately to be dipped in the fondue.

CHEESE SOUFFLÉ

COOKING TIME 1 hr.   TEMPERATURE E. 375° (190°C.) G.5
QUANTITIES FOR 4.

Grease a 2-pt. (1-l.) soufflé dish or other straight-sided baking dish; or use 4 small soufflé dishes.

> 2 *oz.* (50 *g.*) *butter or margarine*   2 *oz.* (6 *tbs. or* 50 *g.*) *flour*

Melt the fat in a small saucepan, stir in the flour and cook for a minute or so.

> ½ *pt.* (250 *ml.*) *milk*

Stir into the roux and stir or whisk until smooth and boiling. Cook for 3 mins. stirring frequently.

4 oz. (125 g.) *grated mature or*   *Cayenne pepper*
   well-flavoured cheese   *Mustard*
Salt   *2–4 tbs. chopped fresh herbs*

For the herbs use any of the following, or use a mixture: basil, caraway leaves, chives, parsley, sage, marjoram, thyme, chervil, or tarragon.

Add cheese, seasonings, and herbs to the sauce and mix well.

3 *large or* 4 *standard egg yolks*   1 *tbs. water*

Beat these together until thick and light and fold into the cheese mixture.

3 *large or* 4 *standard egg whites*

Beat until stiff but not dry and fold them into the other mixture as thoroughly as possible, but gently so as not to lose too much air. Put in the prepared dish and bake until the soufflé is risen and brown (½–¾ hr.). Serve at once.

GREEN CHEESE

This is fairly soft in texture, ideal to serve with bread or biscuits or to use as a sandwich spread.

4 oz. (125 g.) *grated Cheddar cheese*
2 *tbs. double cream*   3 *tbs. sherry*
3 *tbs. of the following chopped fresh herbs: parsley, sage, thyme,*
   tarragon, chives, chervil ,and savory, in equal quantities.

Beat together thoroughly and press into a small dish suitable for serving the cheese in.

CURD CHEESE AND HERB FLAN

COOKING TIME 30 mins.   TEMPERATURE E. 425° (220°C.) G.7 for
  20 mins., then E. 350° (180°C.) G.4 for 10 mins.
QUANTITIES FOR an 8 in. (20 cm.) flan.

4 oz. (¾ c. or 125 g.) *flour made into short crust pastry or use*
6 oz. (175 g.) *ready-made pastry*

Roll the pastry to line the flan, prick the bottom, and refrigerate it while the filling is being prepared.

4 oz. (125 g.) *sieved or mashed*   1–2 *tbs. chopped fresh herbs or*
   curd cheese   1–2 *tsp. dried herbs*
¼ pt. (150 ml.) *double cream*   *Salt and pepper*
                                      3 *eggs*

For the herbs use any of the following, one alone or a mixture: caraway seeds or leaves, chives, basil, mint, dill, sage, chervil.

Taste the cheese before adding salt, then beat the ingredients together to mix them well. Pour into the flan case and bake until the filling is set and lightly browned. Serve warm or cold.

Alternative: Add a little chopped fried or grilled bacon or some cooked ham, to the filling.

LIPTAUER CHEESE

This is an Austrian recipe suitable for serving with plain biscuits or for piping on canapés and similar savouries. The flavourings are added according to taste but it is meant to be strongly flavoured and pink with paprika pepper and anchovy.

QUANTITIES FOR 8 OZ. (250 g.).

4 *oz.* (125 g.) *softened butter*

4 *oz.* (125 g.) *sieved cottage or low-fat curd cheese*

Cream the butter and gradually work in the cheese. Flavour to taste with the following ingredients:

Made mustard, French or English	*Black pepper*
	Anchovy essence
Chopped chives	*Paprika pepper*
Chopped capers	*Caraway seeds*

SAGE AND CHEESE FONDUE

QUANTITIES FOR 4–6.

½ *pt.* (250 ml.) *dry cider*

Put in the cheese fondue pot and bring to the boil. Remove from the heat and add

1 *lb.* (½ kg.) *mature English Cheddar cheese, grated coarsely*

Return to a moderate heat and stir gently until the cheese is melted and the mixture bubbling.

2–3 *tsp. potato flour*   1 *tbs. lemon juice*

Blend these together and stir into the fondue, stirring until it thickens.

Pepper to taste   2 *tbs. freshly chopped sage or more to taste*

Add and serve the fondue still bubbling and with

Squares of stale bread for dipping or use bread toasted on one side and cut in squares

SAGE AND CHEESE QUICHE

COOKING TIME 40 mins.   TEMPERATURE E. 400° (200°C.) G.6
QUANTITIES FOR A 7-in. (18-cm.) flan.
Line the flan with short crust pastry, prick the bottom with a fork,
and put it in the refrigerator.

3 *oz.* (¾ *c. or 75 g.*) *strong cheese, grated*	*1 small onion, finely chopped* ¼ *pt.* (150 *ml.*) *milk*
3 *or more fresh sage leaves, finely chopped*	*Salt and pepper* *1 egg, beaten*

Mix all together and pour into the prepared flan case. Cook until the
filling is set and lightly browned. Serve warm or cold.
Alternative Method: Cut the cheese in pieces and the onion in half,
put all ingredients in the electric blender and process until the sage is
finely chopped and the cheese grated.

SOFT CHEESE WITH HERBS

Use cottage, cream, or curd cheese and freshly chopped herbs. Use
about 1 tsp. of herbs per oz. (25 g.) of cheese.

Suitable herbs are garlic (juice, powdered dry, or salt), chopped
sage, mint, marjoram, thyme, chives, basil, dill, chervil, tarragon, or
young borage leaves.

Use one herb or a mixture and combine herbs and cheese. Leave
to stand a while for the flavours to blend.

See also Liptauer cheese (p. 136).

TOMATO AND CHEESE FLAN WITH THYME OR MARJORAM

COOKING TIME 20–30 mins.   TEMPERATURE E. 400° (200°C.) G.6
QUANTITIES FOR a 7 in. (18 cm.) flan.
    4 *oz.* (¾ *c. or 125 g.*) *flour made into short pastry or use 6–8 oz.*
    (175–250 *g.*) *ready-made pastry*
Roll the pastry fairly thinly to line a flan ring or pie plate. Prick the
bottom with a fork and put the flan in the refrigerator to chill.
    14 *oz.* (400 *g.*) *can peeled whole tomatoes*
Drain and slice or cut up the tomatoes.
    1–2 *tbs. chopped fresh thyme or marjoram or use* 1–2 *tsp. dried*
    2 *oz.* (50 *g.*) *strong cheese*
Cut the cheese in small dice. Put the tomatoes in the flan case and

sprinkle them with the herbs and cheese.

1–2 oz. (25–50 *g.*) *anchovy fillets*

1–2 oz. (25–50 *g.*) *stoned black olives*

Put the anchovy fillets on top of the tomatoes and cheese in a lattice or other pattern and put the olives in between the anchovies. Bake until the pastry is lightly browned and the cheese melted. Serve warm or cold.

EGGS

Most herbs can be used for flavouring egg dishes, fresh herbs generally being more pleasant than dried ones, though the latter can be used successfully, provided they are fairly finely crushed.

Fines herbes (parsley, chives, chervil, and tarragon), are traditional in French omelets and many other egg dishes, and these herbs used individually are excellent with all egg dishes.

When cheese and tomatoes form part of the recipe, marjoram, thyme, or basil are particularly good, and with recipes including ham, sage is a good choice.

BAKED EGGS WITH HERBS

These make an excellent starter for a meal or serve two baked eggs per person as a main dish for a light meal. Individual eggs can be baked in special small dishes called cocottes or in any shallow baking dish. For a family meal you can cook all the eggs together in one large shallow dish and then portion them out. The cooking time will depend on the kind of dish used, metal takes least time to heat, thick heat-resistant glass or ceramic longest. The eggs should be served as soon as they are cooked, otherwise the heat of the dish will hard-cook them. It is a good plan to remove them from the oven before they are quite set and by the time they are served and cool enough to eat they will be set firm. The dish can be got ready in advance and put in the oven 10 mins. or so before you will want to start the meal.

COOKING TIME about 10 mins. TEMPERATURE E. 400° (200°C.) G.6

QUANTITIES FOR 2–4.

4 eggs

Salt and pepper

8 *tbs.* (120 *ml.*) *double or soured*
cream

1 *tbs. chopped fresh herbs*

Oil the baking dishes and put in the cream mixed with the herbs, or sprinkle the herbs over the cream. Best ones to use are basil, chives, tarragon, marjoram, chervil, parsley, thyme, one alone, or a mixture.

Break the eggs into the cream, season each and bake until the whites are beginning to become opaque. Serve with
Fingers of toast

EGG PATTIES WITH TARRAGON

COOKING TIME about 45 mins.
TEMPERATURE E. 425° (220°C.) G.7 for the pastry: E. 350° (190°C.) G.4 for the eggs.
QUANTITIES FOR 4.

4 *oz.* (125 *g.*) *flour made into short pastry or use 6–8 oz.* (175–250 *g.*) *ready-made pastry*

Roll the pastry thinly and line deep patty tins or small foil patty tins. Prick the bottoms and line with crumpled foil. Refrigerate for a while before baking. Then bake until the pastry is set, remove the foil and finish drying out the pastry.

While the pastry is cooking make the sauce.

1 *oz.* (25 *g.*) *butter or margarine*   2 *tbs. flour*

Heat the fat in a small pan, stir in the flour and cook until mealy.

½ *pt.* (250 *ml.*) *creamy milk*   *Salt and pepper*

Make up the half pint of milk with a little cream or use half and half. Add to the roux, stir until boiling and cook gently for 5 mins. Season to taste. Keep hot, stirring occasionally to prevent a skin from forming.

4 *eggs*

Break an egg into each cooked pastry case and bake at the lower temperature until the eggs are just set, about 20 mins.

1 *tbs. chopped parsley*   1 *tbs. chopped tarragon*

Add to the sauce, spoon over each egg, and serve hot.

HERB AND EGG QUICHE

COOKING TIME 35–40 mins.
TEMPERATURE E. 400° (200°C.) G.6 for the pastry: E. 350° (180°C.) G.4 for the filling.
QUANTITIES FOR an 8 in. (20 cm.) flan.

4 *oz.* (¾ c. or 125 *g.*) *flour made into short pastry or use 6 oz.* (175 *g.*) *ready-made pastry*

Roll the pastry fairly thinly and line the flan, prick the bottom with a fork and line the pastry with a piece of foil. Refrigerate for 20 mins.

or so before baking about 15 mins. Remove the foil before adding the filling.

    1 *shallot or ½ small onion, chopped*
    A small knob of butter

Heat the butter and cook the onion gently until it is soft but not brown. Put it in the bottom of the flan case.

    3 *eggs*   ¼ *pt. (150 ml.) single cream*
    Salt and pepper   3 *tbs. chopped fresh herbs*

For the herbs use a mixture of any of the following: parsley, tarragon, chervil, balm, thyme, savory, or mint. Beat the eggs just to break them up and mix with the cream and flavourings. Pour into the pastry case and bake until set and lightly browned (20–25 mins.). Serve hot or cold.

HARD-BOILED EGGS

Stuffed or plain, these are used cold for salads and starters, or hot, in a sauce, as a main dish. As the amount of stuffing used is comparatively small, the herbs with a strong flavour are usually more successful, or use finely crushed dried herbs of good flavour.

    Plain hard-boiled eggs are served with a sauce or salad dressing mixed with the herbs.

STUFFED EGGS WITH CHERVIL

COOKING TIME 20–30 mins.   QUANTITIES FOR 4–6.
    8 *hard-boiled eggs*   *A little cream*
    Salt and pepper   4 *sprigs of chervil*

Cut the eggs in half lengthwise. Remove the yolks and mash them with salt and pepper and enough cream to moisten. Remove the chervil leaves from the stems and scissor-chop the leaves. Mix into the egg yolks and re-fill the whites with this mixture.

    2 *oz. (50 g.) butter*   4 *tbs. flour*
    ½ *pt. (250 ml.) single cream*   ½ *pt. (250 ml.) milk*
    Salt and pepper   *Pinch of ground mace*

Melt the butter in a saucepan, add the flour and mix and cook until crumbly. Remove from the heat and stir in the cream and milk. Return to the heat and stir until the sauce boils. Simmer for 5 mins. Season to taste.

    To serve, either heat the stuffed eggs gently in the sauce or put them in a fireproof dish, pour the sauce over and heat them for 15–20 mins. in a moderate oven.

STUFFED EGGS WITH SORREL

COOKING TIME about ½–¾ hr.   TEMPERATURE E. 350° (180°C.) G.4
QUANTITIES FOR 2–4.

4 hard-boiled eggs

Shell, and cut the eggs in half lengthwise. Scoop out the yolks into a small basin and mash them with a fork.

Chopped chives or a little   *Grated nutmeg*
  chopped fried onion   *Cayenne pepper*
¼ tsp. salt   *2 tbs. cream*

Mix with the egg yolks seasoning to taste and adding more cream if necessary to make a softish mixture. Replace in the egg whites, smoothing the tops.

1–2 pts. (½–1 l.) loosely packed French sorrel leaves or the same
  amount of shredded English sorrel
A small knob of butter

Wash and drain the sorrel and stew it with the butter until the resulting pulp is no longer watery. Spread it in the bottom of a shallow baking dish or in individual dishes. Arrange the stuffed eggs on top.

2 tbs. grated Parmesan cheese

Sprinkle over the eggs and bake in a hot oven for about 20 mins. to heat through and melt the cheese. Alternatively, cook slowly under a moderate grill to heat through and brown the tops of the eggs.

HERB OMELETS

QUANTITIES FOR 1 omelet.

The following are very delicious omelets when the chopped herbs are added to the eggs before cooking. Recipes for filled omelets follow these.

CHERVIL WITH CHEESE

½ oz. (15 g.) grated cheese   *½ tbs. finely chopped chervil*

CHIVES

2 tbs. scissor-snipped chives

FINES HERBES

1 tbs. finely chopped parsley, tarragon, chervil, and chives, mixed

MARJORAM
> 1 tbs. finely chopped marjoram

PARSLEY
> 1 tbs. finely chopped fresh parsley

ROSEMARY
> ½ tsp. chopped young rosemary leaves or a pinch of dried crushed rosemary

MUSHROOM OMELET

QUANTITIES FOR 4 omelets.

> 4–6 oz. (125–175 g.) mushrooms   1 oz. (25 g.) butter

Wash, drain, and slice the mushrooms. Heat the butter in a small pan and stew the mushrooms gently for a few minutes until they are just tender.

> 2 tbs. chopped fresh herbs, tarragon, marjoram, mint, or parsley
> Salt and pepper

Add to the mushrooms and keep the mixture hot while the omelets are made. As each is made, add a portion of the mushroom mixture, fold over, and serve.

SORREL OMELET

QUANTITIES FOR 4 omelets.

> 2 pts. (1¼ l.) sorrel leaves   A little double cream or
> A small knob of butter   white sauce

If you are using English sorrel, tear the leaves in small pieces for measuring the amount. With French sorrel simply strip the leaves from the stalks. Wash and drain. Melt the butter in a small pan and stew the sorrel in it gently for just a few minutes until it is soft. Add a little cream or white sauce to bind the sorrel, and keep it hot while the omelets are made in the usual way. Spread sorrel along one side of each, fold over and serve.

Alternative: Add ½ pt. (250 ml.) scissor-snipped raw sorrel leaves to the eggs.

POTATO OMELET WITH MARJORAM

COOKING TIME about 15 mins.   QUANTITIES FOR 2–4.

   8 oz. (250 g. or 2 medium-sized) *cold boiled potatoes*
Slice the potatoes fairly thickly as for a sauté.

   2 tbs. *chopped onion*   ¼–½ *tsp. dried marjoram*
   ¼ *tsp. salt*   *Pinch of pepper*
Sprinkle over the potatoes.

   2 tbs. *oil*
Heat the oil in a frying pan 8–9 in. (20–25 cm.) size Add the
potatoes in a single layer and fry golden brown on both sides.

   3 eggs, *beaten*   ¼ *tsp. salt*   *Pinch of pepper*
Pour the eggs gently over the potatoes and continue cooking until the
eggs are almost set, and brown underneath. Put the pan in a hot oven
or under the grill to finish cooking the top. Cut in pieces for serving.

POACHED EGGS IN GREEN SAUCE

COOKING TIME about 10 mins.   QUANTITIES FOR 3–6.

   1 oz. (25 g.) *butter or margarine*   2 tbs. *flour*
Melt the butter or margarine in a small pan, stir in the flour and cook
until crumbly. Remove from the heat.

   ¼ pt. (150 ml.) *double cream*   ½ pt. (250 ml.) *milk*
   Salt and pepper
Stir in the cream and milk, return to the heat and stir until the sauce
boils. Simmer for 5 mins. and season to taste.

   While the sauce is cooking poach
   6 *eggs*
Lift out, drain, and put on hot serving dishes.

   1 tbs. *each of chopped chives, parsley, and dill*
Add to the sauce, pour it over the eggs and serve.

SCRAMBLED EGGS

QUANTITIES FOR 4 using 4–5 eggs.
Serve these hot on toast or cold for open sandwiches or sandwich fillings.

CHIVES
   Add 1–2 tbs. *scissor-snipped to the eggs*

CURRY LEAVES AND FENNEL

> *Fry 2 tsp. finely chopped onion in ½ oz. (15 g.) butter*
> *To the eggs add 1 tsp. chopped curry leaves*
> *½ tsp. chopped fennel*

Add to the onion and cook in the usual way.

FINES HERBES

> *Add 1–2 tbs. chopped mixed parsley, chives, chervil, and tarragon*

LEMON THYME

> *Sprinkle chopped lemon thyme over the eggs when they are served*

MARJORAM, THYME, OR BASIL WITH CHEESE

> *Add 1 oz. (25 g.) grated cheese to the eggs and sprinkle the chopped herbs over the eggs before serving*

MINT AND PARSLEY

> *1–2 tbs. chopped mint and parsley added to the eggs*

PARSLEY AND CHIVES

> *1–2 tbs. mixed chopped parsley and chives added to the eggs*

TOMATOES AND HERBS

> *8 oz. (250 g.) tomatoes*   *Salt and pepper*
> *1 tbs. chopped herbs (basil,*   *A knob of butter*
> *parsley, tarragon, and*
> *lemon thyme)*

Skin the tomatoes or leave the skins on according to taste. Chop them roughly. Melt the butter in a small pan, add the tomatoes and herbs and just warm through. Do not allow them to cook properly or the fresh flavour of the tomatoes and herbs will be lost. Season to taste.

Serve the scrambled eggs in a mound, surrounded by the tomatoes, and serve separately

> *Fingers of toast*

CHAPTER TEN

Fish

One of the best ways of using herbs with fish is to add them to a sauce to serve with it. Suggestions for suitable sauces will be found on pp. 110–26.

Other good ways are to sprinkle fresh or dried herbs on fish to be grilled; to add herbs to marinades and basting sauces (pp. 129–32); to use them to flavour stuffings (pp. 210–13), and to flavour the liquid used for poaching fish (p. 154).

The favourite herbs for fish cookery are usually parsley, dill, fennel, fines herbes, and tarragon. In warmer climates, where the fish has less flavour than that caught in colder waters, stronger herbs like garlic, marjoram, thyme, and basil are used. Many of these recipes are also very useful for adding flavour to frozen fish which often tends to be rather dull.

BAKED FISH STEAKS TO SERVE COLD

COOKING TIME about 1 hr.   TEMPERATURE E. 350° (180°C.) G.4
QUANTITIES FOR 4.

     2 *tomatoes skinned and chopped roughly, or use an equivalent*
        amount of canned tomato
     1 *medium-sized onion, chopped*
     1 *clove of garlic or a pinch of dried*
     4 *tbs. oil*
Heat the oil in a small pan and add the vegetables and garlic.

     2 *tsp. sugar   A pinch of fresh thyme leaves*
     Salt and pepper
Add to the pan and simmer for 15–20 mins., until the onion is tender and the sauce thick. Remove the clove of garlic when the sauce is sufficiently flavoured.

 5 *tbs.* (75 *ml.*) *white wine or dry cider*
Add and simmer for a couple of minutes.

 4 *fish steaks*   *Salt and pepper*
Put these in a shallow casserole or baking dish, pour the sauce over
the fish and cover with a lid or with foil. Bake for 30 mins. or until
the fish is cooked. Cool as quickly as possible and store in a covered
dish in the refrigerator.

 Chopped parsley
Sprinkle plenty on top before serving.

BAKED WHOLE FISH TO SERVE COLD

COOKING TIME 35–45 mins.   TEMPERATURE E. 350° (180°C.) G.4
QUANTITIES FOR 4–6.

 A whole fish weighing 2–3 lb. (1–1½ *kg.*) *or use two smaller*
  fish such as 2 large mackerel
Clean the fish and sprinkle it inside and out with salt and pepper. Cut
gashes at about 1 in. (2½ cm.) intervals on one side of the fish. Put it
in a shallow greased baking dish with the cut side uppermost.

 4 *tbs.* (60 *ml.*) *olive oil*
Pour over the fish.

 1 *dried bay leaf, crushed, or* 1 *tbs. chopped parsley*
  a good pinch of powdered 1 *sprig thyme, chopped*
  leaf   1 *tbs. chopped chives*
 1 *tbs. chopped fennel*   1 *tbs. chopped chervil*
Mix together and rub into the cuts in the fish.

 1 *tbs. lemon juice*
Sprinkle over the fish. Bake, basting occasionally with the liquid.
Allow to cool.

 4 *tbs.* (60 *ml.*) *olive oil*   1 *tbs. lemon juice*
Pour over the fish when it is almost cold. Serve cold with potato salad,
cucumber salad, or a mixed salad.

BAKED STUFFED FILLETS OF PLAICE

COOKING TIME about 30 mins. TEMPERATURE E. 375° (190°C.) G.5
QUANTITIES FOR 4.

 8 *small fillets of plaice*
Frozen plaice can be used successfully for this recipe but allow the
fillets to thaw before attempting to stuff them.

1 oz. (⅓ c. or 25 g.) fresh	½ tbs. lemon juice
breadcrumbs	1 tbs. chopped parsley
½ oz. (15 g.) melted butter	1 tsp. chopped chervil
1 tsp. chopped tarragon	Salt and pepper
¼ tsp. chopped lemon thyme	1 egg, beaten

Mix the ingredients thoroughly using enough of the egg to moisten the stuffing but keeping about half for a sauce. Spread a thin layer of stuffing on each fillet, roll up and pack them close together in a baking dish.

    White wine or dry cider   *2 tbs. lemon juice*

Add to the fillets using enough wine to moisten the fish well. Bake for about 20 mins. or until the fish seems to be cooked through. Avoid over-cooking. Lift the fish out, using a fish slice, and put it to keep hot.

    Remaining egg beaten with 2–4 tbs. double cream

Stir this into the liquid in the baking dish and stir until the sauce thickens and boils. Pour over the fish and serve. More herbs can be sprinkled on as a garnish. Any left-over fish will be very good cold.

FILLETS OF MACKEREL WITH FINES HERBES
COOKING TIME about 30 mins.   QUANTITIES FOR 4.

    4 small mackerel, filleted   *Butter*

Wash the fish. Butter a large frying or sauté pan and put the fillets in a single layer.

    Mushroom stock   *White wine*

Cover the fish with a mixture of approximately equal quantities, about 1 pt. (½ l.) in all. Bring to the boil and poach the fish for 10–15 mins. or until cooked. Lift out carefully into a heated serving dish and put to keep hot. Strain the stock.

    1 oz. (25 g.) butter   *2 tbs. flour*

Melt the butter in a small pan, add the flour and stir and cook until it looks mealy. Remove from the heat and stir in ½ pt. (250 ml.) of the strained stock. Return to the heat and stir until the sauce boils. Simmer for 5 mins.

    1 tbs. chopped fines herbes (parsley, tarragon, chervil, and chives)
    Salt and pepper

Add the herbs and season to taste. Pour over the fish and serve hot.

FISH AND FENNEL FLAMBÉ
This is suitable for small whole fish like red mullet or mackerel or

a larger whole fish like hake or haddock.

COOKING TIME 15–30 mins. depending on the size of the fish.

QUANTITIES allow ½–¾ lb. (250–375 g.) per portion.

| *Whole fish* | *Salt and pepper* |

The fish should be cleaned, scaled, washed, and drained, but the head and tail are usually left on. Cut three or four gashes in either side of the body and season with salt and pepper. Grill small fish and bake larger ones in a moderate oven. The fish should be cooked on a wire rack such as a cake cooling rack.

Dried fennel sprigs	*Melted butter*
Wedges of lemon	*Boiled potatoes*
1–2 *tbs. warmed brandy or*	
other spirit per portion	

You need enough fennel to make a bed about 2 in. (5 cm.) thick on a stainless steel serving dish or some other heat-resistant dish. When the fish is cooked, transfer it, still on the rack, to the serving dish, placing it on top of the bed of fennel. Ignite the brandy in a metal ladle or sauce warmer and pour it over the fish. This will ignite the fennel and when it has burnt out serve the fish with the melted butter, potatoes and lemon wedges handed separately.

The flambé can be done either in the kitchen immediately before serving the fish or on a side table or trolley in the dining room.

FISH CAKES WITH HERBS

QUANTITIES for 8 cakes.

8 *oz.* (250 g.) *freshly cooked mashed potato*
8 *oz.* (250 g.) *cooked or canned flaked fish*
1 *tsp. salt*   *Pinch of pepper*
1 *tsp. grated onion or a pinch of dried garlic*
A few drops of vinegar or some lemon juice
Pinch of ground mace or nutmeg
1 *tbs. chopped fresh herbs*

Use a mixture of herbs including any of the following: chives, lemon thyme, balm, fennel, dill, parsley, chervil, or tarragon.

Mix the ingredients together and shape into 8 fish cakes, or other shapes.

1 *egg, beaten*   *Breadcrumbs*

Coat the fish cakes with egg and then with breadcrumbs.

Frying oil

To deep fat fry the fish cakes heat the oil to 390° (180°C.) and fry the cakes until they are golden brown. Drain on absorbent paper.

Alternatively, fry them in shallow fat or oil until browned on both sides; or sprinkle with oil or melted fat and bake in a hot oven or grill slowly to heat through without burning the crumb coating.

Serve them with

Wedges of lemon and a sauce such as Parsley sauce (p. 121), Caper sauce (p. 113), Chives sauce (p. 114), Cucumber sauce with dill (p. 115), Remoulade sauce (p. 122).

FISH FILLETS WITH MARJORAM AND MUSHROOMS

COOKING TIME 30 mins.   QUANTITIES FOR 4.

1½ *lb.* (750 *g.*) *thick fish fillets*

Use thick fillets of coley, cod, haddock, or similar fish. Cut in four portions and poach these in salted water for about 15 mins. or until the flakes show opaque all through at the thickest ends. While the fish is cooking make the sauce.

1½ *oz.* (40 *g.*) *butter*   1 *medium-sized onion, finely chopped*

Melt the butter in a small pan and stew the onion in it until it is softened but not browned.

6 *oz.* (175 *g.*) *mushrooms, sliced*

Add to the onions and mix.

½ *pt.* (250 *ml.*) *soured cream or fresh double cream*	¼ *tsp. paprika pepper*
1½ *tbs. lemon juice or more if fresh cream is used*	1 *tbs. chopped marjoram*
	Salt and pepper
	3 *tsp. vinegar*

Stir into the onions and mushrooms and simmer very gently for 15–20 mins. If the sauce seems too thick, thin it with a little milk. Drain the fish carefully and serve it with the sauce poured over it.

FISH FILLETS WITH ONION AND TARRAGON

COOKING TIME about 45 mins.   QUANTITIES FOR 4.

Fish bones and trimmings	*A slice of onion*
½ *small carrot, sliced*	½ *bay leaf*
A few stalks of parsley	

Put the bones and trimmings in a pan, cover with cold water, add the flavourings, cover the pan and simmer for 20 mins. Strain.

4–6 *oz.* (125–175 *g.*) *sliced onion*

1 *oz.* (25 *g.*) *butter or margarine*

Stew the onion in a small pan with the fat, cooking it slowly so that it softens without browning.

2–3 *tbs. chopped tarragon and parsley, mixed*

Add to the onion and spread the mixture in the bottom of a shallow baking dish. Put to keep hot.

4 *portions of white fish fillets*

¼ *pt. (150 ml.) dry white wine or cider*

Put the fish in a large frying or sauté pan and add the wine with enough fish stock to cover. Bring to the boil and poach gently for 5–10 mins., or until the fish is cooked. Lift it out carefully and arrange the fillets on top of the onion mixture. Boil the stock and wine rapidly until there is just enough left to make a sauce for coating the fish.

1–2 *oz. (25–50 g.) butter*   *Salt and pepper*

Add to the reduced stock and allow to melt. Pour over the fish and brown under the grill. Serve with

Boiled potatoes

FISH FLAMBÉ WITH TARRAGON SAUCE

COOKING TIME 15–20 mins.   QUANTITIES FOR 4.

4 *small fish (sea or fresh-water)*

Use mackerel, trout, whiting, or any fish available. Clean the fish but leave the heads and tails on. They can be grilled, baked in the oven, or poached in simmering water with salt and a bay leaf. Avoid over-cooking. A fish weighing about 8 oz. (250 g.) will take 15 mins. to cook. While the fish is cooking, make the sauce.

5 *tbs. (75 ml.) milk*   *A good handful of fresh tarragon leaves*

Wash the leaves. Warm the milk in a small pan, add the leaves, cover, and leave to infuse.

2 *egg yolks*   5 *tbs. (75 ml.) cold milk*

1 *tsp. potato flour*   1 *oz. (25 g.) butter*

Mix these together in the top of a double boiler or in a basin to go on top of a pan of simmering water. Heat, stirring all the time until the butter melts and the sauce thickens.

1 *oz. (25 g.) butter*

Add and stir until it melts and is blended into the sauce. Strain in the tarragon milk and add

1½ *oz. (40 g.) butter in small pieces*

Mix until the butter has been blended into the sauce.

Salt and pepper   *Lemon juice*

Season the sauce to taste. If the flavour of tarragon is not strong enough, put back the tarragon leaves and infuse longer; strain before serving. The sauce should only be kept warm, otherwise it will spoil if over-heated at this stage.

When the fish are cooked, remove the skin except from over the heads and tails, and put them on a hot metal serving dish or oven-proof dish.

4 tbs. warm brandy

When serving, pour the brandy over the fish, ignite with a match and baste with the burning liquid. Serve with the sauce handed separately.

FISH IN FENNEL SAUCE

This is an unusual way of preparing fish for serving in a border of mashed or Duchess potatoes, or in a border of rice, and even for a fish pie. It can be the main course in a meal or serve a small portion as a starter.

COOKING TIME about 30 mins.   QUANTITIES FOR 4–6.

1½ lb. (750 g.) fish fillets   *A mixture of equal quantities*
A few slices of onion   *of cider, wine vinegar, and*
A good sprinkling of salt   *water, enough barely to cover*
1 bay leaf   *the fish*
4 or 5 peppercorns

Put the fish in a shallow pan or frying pan large enough to allow the fillets to be in one layer. Add the flavourings and enough liquid barely to cover. Bring to the boil, then reduce the heat to poach the fish for about 10 mins. or until a thick cut end looks opaque all through. Lift out the fish, cool a little and then flake, removing any skin and bones. Strain the liquid.

1 oz. (25 g.) butter or margarine   *1 oz. (3 tbs. or 25 g.) flour*

Melt the fat in a saucepan, add the flour and mix and cook until it looks crumbly. Remove from the heat and add ½ pt. (250 ml.) of the fish stock. Return to the heat and stir until the sauce is smooth and boiling. Simmer for 5 mins.

Salt and pepper   *2 tbs. or more chopped fresh fennel*

Season the sauce to taste, add the fish and re-heat it, then serve.

FRIED TROUT WITH ANCHOVY AND MINT

COOKING TIME about 20 mins.   QUANTITIES FOR 4.

4 *trout*   *Salt and pepper*
Flour

Clean and dry the fish, season it well, and sprinkle with flour.

4 *tbs. (60 ml.) olive oil*

Heat in a frying pan and cook the trout for 5 mins. each side. When the fish is cooked, drain and keep hot. While it is cooking, begin making the sauce.

1 *oz. (25 g.) butter*

Heat in a small pan.

4 *fillets canned anchovy, rinsed and chopped*

Add to the butter and cook slowly for 5 mins.

¼ *pt. (150 ml.) dry sherry*

Add to the pan and cook for a minute.

2 *tsp. chopped fresh mint*   2 *tsp. chopped parsley*

Add and cook for 5 mins.

2 *tbs. lemon juice*

Add to the sauce, mix, and pour over the fish.

GRILLED FISH STEAKS OR FILLETS

COOKING TIME 15–20 mins.

METHOD 1

Use one of the Herb Marinades (pp. 129–32), and steep the fish in it for not less than ½ hr. There is no need to have sufficient marinade to cover the fish, but turn it over once or twice during the marinating process. Use any spare marinade as a basting sauce to brush over the fish during cooking.

METHOD 2

Season the fish with salt and pepper and either brush it with oil before grilling, or brush it both before and during grilling with a salt solution made by dissolving 1 tbs. salt in 4 tbs. cold water.

Serve the cooked fish with a sauce containing herbs (see Sauces, pp. 110–26), or with a Herb Butter (pp. 127–9).

METHOD 3

Brush the fish with oil and sprinkle with chopped fresh or crushed dried herbs, for example, marjoram, dill, or fennel. Serve with lemon wedges.

FISH KEBABS WITH BAY LEAVES

COOKING TIME 15 mins. after ½ hr. marinating.
QUANTITIES FOR 4.

1½ *lb.* (750 g.) *fillet of halibut or other firm fish*

Wash and drain the fish leaving any skin on. Cut it into pieces about the size of a walnut. Put the fish in a shallow dish.

1 *tbs. oil*   2 *tsp. salt*   1 *tbs. chopped parsley*
¼ *tsp. freshly ground pepper*   2 *tbs. lemon juice*

Mix together and pour over the fish. Cover and refrigerate for ½ hr. or so. This helps to make the fish firmer and to flavour it.

Fresh bay leaves

Wash, drain, and cut large leaves in half. Thread the fish on skewers with a piece of bay leaf between each pair of pieces. Brush the kebabs with the remaining oil and lemon mixture and brush again once during cooking. Grill slowly until the fish looks opaque Avoid over-cooking or it will be dry and lacking in flavour and will be inclined to fall off the skewers. Serve with

A green salad   *A sauce such as Bearnaise* (p. 112)
French bread or rolls   *or Melted Butter Sauce* (p. 119)

POACHED FISH WITH BALM SAUCE

COOKING TIME about 20 mins.   QUANTITIES FOR 4.
  1 *small carrot, sliced*   1 *small onion, sliced*
  1 *sprig parsley*   ½ *bay leaf*
  2 *peppercorns*   1 *tsp. salt*
  ½ *tbs. vinegar*   1 *pt.* (½ *l.*) *water*
  1 *sprig lemon thyme*

Put in a large frying or sauté pan and bring to the boil.

4 *fish steaks or portions of fillet*

Put in the liquid and poach gently for 10–15 mins. or until just cooked through. Drain from the liquid and keep hot. Strain the liquid.

1 *oz.* (25 g.) *butter*   2 *tbs. flour*

Melt the butter in a small pan, stir in the flour and cook for a minute. Remove from the heat and whisk in ½ pt. (250 ml.) of the strained stock. Heat until boiling, whisking all the time, and boil gently for 5 mins.

Salt and pepper   ½ *pt.* (250 *ml.*) *balm leaves*

Chop the leaves, season the sauce, and add the balm. Pour over the fish and serve.

POACHED FISH WITH MUSHROOMS AND HERB SAUCE

COOKING TIME about ½ hr. QUANTITIES FOR 4.

1½ *lb.* (750 *g.*) *fillets of white fish*

Cut the fish in portions and poach it gently in boiling salted water to cover. Cook until a thick cut end looks opaque all through (about 10–15 mins.). Drain the fish and keep it hot. While the fish is cooking, begin making the sauce.

1 *small onion finely chopped* 1 *oz.* (25 *g.*) *butter*

Heat the butter in a small saucepan and fry the onion until it just begins to colour.

6 *oz.* (175 *g.*) *mushrooms,*   1–2 *tbs. chopped fresh*
 sliced   *marjoram or 2 tsp. dried*
½ *pt.* (250 *ml.*) *soured cream* 2 *tbs. lemon juice*
 or use fresh double cream ½ *tsp. paprika pepper*
Salt and pepper

Add to the onions, mix, and simmer gently for 15 mins. or until the sauce begins to thicken. Pour over the fish.

POACHED HERRINGS

This method of cooking, plus the mixture of herbs, gives the herrings a special delicate flavour which is quite different from that of grilled or fried herrings. The same method can be used for cooking other small fish.

COOKING TIME 15–20 mins. QUANTITIES FOR 4.

4 *herrings* *Salt* ½ *oz.* (15 *g.*) *butter*

Clean, scale, and remove heads from the herrings. Drain well and sprinkle inside and out with salt. Grease the bottom of a stewpan with the butter and put in the herrings.

2 *tbs. chopped parsley*   2 *tbs. chopped chives*
2 *tbs. chopped dill*   ½ *oz.* (15 *g.*) *butter*

Sprinkle the herbs over the fish and dot with butter. Add ¼–½ pt. (150–250 ml.) water or just enough to make a thin layer in the pan. Cover and cook gently until the fish is tender. Lift out onto a serving

dish and pour the liquid over it as a sauce. Serve hot with
  Boiled potatoes

SALMON WITH HERBS

GRILLED STEAKS   COOKING TIME 20–25 mins.
Brush the steaks with oil and grill, turning once. The times given
are for steaks about 1 in. (2 cm.) thick.

Serve with a herb sauce such as Cucumber Sauce with Dill (p. 115),
Dill or Fennel Cream Dressing (p. 126), Fennel Mayonnaise (p. 117),
Remoulade sauce (p. 122), Soured cream Sauce (p. 124), or a Herb
Butter (p. 127).

Alternatively serve with a vegetable dish containing herbs, for
example, New Potatoes with Cream and Herbs (p. 206), or Cucumber
Salad with Dill and Chives (p. 118).

POACHED OR BOILED SALMON

COOKING TIMES:
  Whole fish: 10 mins. per lb. (½ kg.) for the first 6 lb. (3 kg.); 5
mins. per lb. for the next 6 lb.; 3 mins. per lb. for the next 6 lb.; 2
mins. per lb. for each lb. over 18 lb. (8 kg.).
  Slices: 35 mins. for slices 1 in. (2½ cm.) thick; 45 mins. for slices
1½ in. (4 cm.) thick; 50 mins. for slices 2 in. (5 cm.) thick.
QUANTITIES ½–¾ lb. (250–375 g.) per person.
  1½ oz. (40 g.) salt per 4 pt.   *2 sprigs dill or fennel*
    (2 l.) water   *3 slices lemon*
Use enough water to cover the fish but first bring the water and
flavourings to the boil. Lower the fish into it and reduce the heat to
simmering so that the fish poaches rather than boils. Drain the fish
carefully and serve with any of the herb sauces listed for grilled
salmon.

SMOKED HADDOCK WITH HORSERADISH AND APPLE SAUCE

COOKING TIME 10–20 mins.   QUANTITIES FOR 4.
Make the sauce before cooking the haddock. It will keep for ½ hr.
or so without discolouration of the apple.
  ¼ pt. (150 ml.) horseradish   *A little vinegar or lemon juice*
    sauce   *Pinch of sugar*
  2 medium-sized apples, peeled
    and grated

Use either bottled, or home-made horseradish sauce (see p. 119). Mix the apple into the sauce as soon as it has been grated. Add vinegar or lemon, and sugar, to taste; the sugar will probably not be needed if you use sweet dessert apples. Put the sauce in a small bowl or sauce boat.

4 portions smoked haddock or other smoked fish

Allow 1½ lb. (750 g.) of fillet or 4 small whole haddocks on the bone. Put the fish in a wide shallow pan and cover with cold water. Bring to the boil and simmer until the fish is cooked. Test fish on the bone by seeing if the flesh parts easily from the bone; thick fillets should be opaque all through at a cut end. Drain well and serve with the sauce handed separately.

Any left-over fish and sauce will make a good mixture for a sandwich or other snack.

CHAPTER ELEVEN

Meat, poultry and game

BEEF

Casseroles and Stews: Most herbs are suitable, including frozen and dried, but some are better if added at the end of cooking rather than at the beginning (see p. 78). It is a good plan to use some of each, for example, a bouquet garni at the beginning of cooking and some fresh chopped herbs such as chives, parsley, chervil, or tarragon, stirred in at the end or sprinkled over the top.

Some prefer to use just two or three herbs in a dish, others like to combine many different flavours so that none predominates. It is really a question of personal taste and the herbs available. Even with dried herbs I think it is always better to make your own mixtures rather than use the ready-made commercial blends; this way you get variety because you can vary the proportions of each herb in a mixture and thus avoid the monotony of a standardised flavour.

BEEF CASSEROLE WITH GARLIC AND THYME

COOKING TIME 1½–2 hrs.   TEMPERATURE E. 300° (150°C.) G.2
QUANTITIES FOR 4.

1½ *lb.* (750 g.) *stewing steak*   1 *clove garlic, skinned*
1 *oz.* (25 g.) *fat or 2 tbs. oil*

Heat the fat or oil in a casserole or frying pan and fry the garlic for a couple of minutes. Lift out the garlic, discard it. Add the meat, cut in small pieces, and fry it until brown.

3 *oz.* (75 g.) *stuffed olives, sliced*   1 *tsp. salt*
½ *a red or green pepper, fresh or canned, sliced*
About ½ *pt.* (250 ml.) *canned tomato juice*
2 *sprigs fresh thyme or* 1 *tsp. dried thyme*

Add to the meat. If sprigs of thyme are used, tie together with thread and remove before serving the casserole. Use enough tomato juice almost to cover the meat. Put on the lid and cook gently until the meat is tender.

BEEF CASSEROLE WITH BASIL, BAY, AND MARJORAM

COOKING TIME 2¼ hrs.   QUANTITIES FOR 4.

   1 oz. (25 g.) *butter or 2 tbs. olive oil*   3 *rashers bacon*
   1 *medium-sized onion, sliced*

Remove the rinds and cut the bacon in small pieces. Heat the butter or oil in a casserole or saucepan and fry the onion and bacon gently until brown.

   1½ lb. (750 g.) *stewing beef*

Cut in small pieces. Remove the bacon and onion from the pan, using a perforated spoon. Add the meat and fry until it is brown.

   2 *tbs. flour*

Sprinkle over the meat and cook until the flour browns.

   ¼ pt. (150 ml.) *stock*   1 *sprig marjoram or* ¼ *tsp. dried*
   2 oz. (50 g.) *mushrooms, sliced* ¼ pt. (150 ml.) *red wine*
   Pepper   1 *tsp. salt*
   1 *sprig basil or* ¼ *tsp. dried* 1 *bay leaf*

Add to the meat together with the bacon and onion. Tie the herbs together with thread or in a muslin bag. Bring to the boil, cover and cook slowly for at least 2 hrs. This may be done on top or in a slow oven (E. 325–350° (125–180°C.) G.3–4). Remove the herbs before serving the casserole.

BEEF CASSEROLE WITH SEVEN HERBS

COOKING TIME 3 hrs. or longer
TEMPERATURE E. 250–300° (125–150°C.) G.½–1.   QUANTITIES FOR 4.

   1 lb. (½ kg.) *lean stewing steak cut in pieces*
   3 *tbs. flour*   1 *tsp. salt*   *Pepper*

Mix flour and seasonings and toss the meat in this to coat well. Set aside.

   2 oz. (50 g.) *fat or 4 tbs. oil*   1 *clove garlic, skinned*

Heat the fat or oil in a casserole if this is suitable to use for frying, or heat in a frying pan and transfer later to the casserole. Fry the garlic for a minute or two, remove, and discard it. Add the meat and fry until it is well browned all over.

1 *lb.* (½ *kg.*) *mixed vegetables*

This can be made up with any vegetables available, carrots, onions, turnips (not too much), celery, sweet peppers, mushrooms, fresh peas or beans, to mention some possibilities. The vegetables should be cleaned, peeled when necessary, and cut up small, slicing or dicing according to the kind. Add to the meat and fry for a minute longer, turning all the time.

½–¾ *pt.* (250–375 *ml.*) *stock or water or use some beer, wine, or*
  cider with water or stock
1 *bay leaf* (*small, or half a large one*)
1 *sprig each of thyme, parsley, and marjoram*

Stir in the stock or other liquid adding just enough to moisten well, remembering that some liquid will come from the vegetables during cooking. Tie the herbs in a bunch or in muslin and add to the centre of the mixture. Bring the casserole to the boil, cover and cook slowly on top or in the oven until the meat is tender. The longer the cooking the better the flavour. If you are going to cook the casserole in the oven for more than 3 hrs., use the lower temperature.

Chopped parsley or chervil
Chopped lemon balm or lovage leaves

Mix the chosen herbs and sprinkle over the top of the casserole at serving time. If you are using dried herbs, stir them into the casserole a little while before serving, to allow them to soften and release their flavours. Remove the herb sprigs before serving the casserole.

BEEF GOULASH WITH HERB DUMPLINGS

COOKING TIME 2–3 hrs.   QUANTITIES FOR 4.

1 *lb.* (½ *kg.*) *lean stewing beef*
1 *oz.* (25 *g.*) *fat or 2 tbs. oil*

Cut the meat in ½–1 in. (1–2 cm.) cubes and fry it brown in the hot fat or oil, in a saucepan or casserole.

2 *onions, sliced*

Add to the meat towards the end of browning and continue cooking until the onions begin to brown.

¼ *pt.* (150 *ml.*) *stock*   2 *tsp. or more paprika pepper*
1 *tsp. salt*   ¼ *tsp. caraway seeds*
2 *tbs. concentrated tomato*
  purée or 2 tomatoes

Add to the meat, cover and simmer for 2–3 hrs. adding a little more stock if necessary.

Herb dumplings (see recipe, p. 240)
Add to the goulash for the last 20–30 mins. of cooking, replace the lid and continue cooking. Serve the goulash and dumplings on a hot dish in a border of
Freshly boiled cabbage

Beef Steaks with Herbs: Use herbs for flavouring fried or grilled steaks, steak kebabs, and in sauces with beef fondue (Bourguignonne).

RECOMMENDED HERBS:

Chervil	Garlic	Parsley
Chives	Horseradish	Tarragon
Dill	Marjoram	

FRIED STEAKS

Fry the steaks in the usual way and then add chopped fresh herbs to the pan juices to pour over the steak; or add herbs to the accompanying salads or vegetables (see pp. 191–209).

GRILLED STEAKS

These can be steeped in a marinade before grilling (see p. 000 for marinade recipes); or rub the steaks with finely chopped fresh, or powdered dried, herbs before grilling; or serve them with a Herb Butter (see pp. 127–9); or with a sauce like Bearnaise (p. 112); or just plain grated fresh horseradish, or a horseradish sauce (p. 119); or add herbs to accompanying salads or vegetables (pp. 191–209).

STEAK KEBABS

Either steep the meat in a marinade (p. 119) and/or baste with a marinade or basting sauce during grilling; or sprinkle chopped herbs over the meat before cooking it.

FONDUE BOURGUIGNONNE

Serve with sauces containing herbs (see pp. 110–26), for example, Bearnaise, Chives, Cold Tomato, Dill, Fennel Mayonnaise, Horseradish, Herb Sauce, or Remoulade sauce.

ROAST BEEF WITH HERBS

The traditional herb accompaniment is horseradish, fresh grated, or in a sauce (see p. 119).

The cheaper cuts of beef such as those suitable for slow roasting, pot-roasting, or braising, benefit from the addition of herbs during cooking.

For a roast, rub a cut clove of garlic or fresh, chopped or powdered dried herbs, into the surface of the meat before cooking.

RECOMMENDED HERBS:

Basil	Marjoram	Rosemary
Bay	Parsley	Thyme
Garlic		

BRAISED BEEF WITH HERBS

Use this recipe for cooking the less tender joints of beef and pieces too small to roast satisfactorily.

COOKING TIME: Pieces less than 3 lb. (1½ kg.) 2 hrs.; 3 lb. and over, 20 mins. per lb. (½ kg.) and 20 mins. over.
TEMPERATURE E. 350° (180°C.) G.4.
QUANTITIES without bone, allow 4–6 oz. (125–175 g.) per portion, with bone, allow 6–8 oz. (175–250 g.) per portion.

Beef in one piece
Fat or oil for frying
Stock or half stock and half
  wine or beer
Herbs: a bouquet garni, garlic,
  basil, rosemary, or thyme
Mixed vegetables in season
Salt and pepper

Choose a pan or casserole just large enough to take the joint comfortably. Slice or chop enough vegetables to make about a 2 in. (5 cm.) layer in the pan. Use just one vegetable or any mixture you have at hand.

Wash the herbs, using sprigs of fresh herbs or crushed leaves of dried herbs (1–2 small sprigs or 1 tsp. dried is sufficient). Use just one herb or a mixture.

Heat a little fat or oil in the pan and brown the meat well all over. Lift out the meat and pour off surplus fat or oil. Add the bed of vegetables with the herbs and put the meat on top of this. Add just enough liquid to come almost to the top of the vegetables. Season with salt and pepper. Cover and cook slowly on top or in the oven, turning the meat once during cooking.

When the meat is cooked, lift it out, slice, and arrange on a hot serving dish. Either rub the juices and vegetables through a sieve to make a sauce or put them in the blender. Reheat the sauce, season and thicken with a little potato flour if necessary. Serve with the meat.

BRAISED OR POT-ROASTED MARINATED BEEF

See Marinades (p. 131)

LAMB AND MUTTON

RECOMMENDED HERBS:

Basil	Garlic	Sage
Bay	Marjoram	Savory
Coriander	Mint	Tarragon
Dill	Rosemary	Thyme
Fennel		

Casseroles and Stews: For methods of adding herbs to casseroles and stews see p. 157.

LAMB CASSEROLE WITH BAY AND MINT

COOKING TIME 1–1 ½ hrs.   TEMPERATURE E. 350° (180°C.) G.4
QUANTITIES FOR 4.

  8 *best end of neck cutlets*
  1 *oz.* (25 *g.*) *fat or 2 tbs. oil*

Trim surplus fat from the cutlets and brown them in the hot fat or oil. Transfer to a casserole.

  1 *onion, sliced or a whole clove of garlic, skinned*
  1 *rasher bacon, chopped*

Add to the fat in the frying pan and cook for a few minutes. Remove the clove of garlic if used. Discard it.

  8 *oz.* (250 *g.*) *canned tomatoes*   *Salt and pepper*
  ½ *fresh or canned sweet*
    pepper, sliced

Add to the frying pan and bring to the boil. Pour over the meat.

  1 *bay leaf*   2 *tbs. chopped mint*

Add to the casserole. Cover and cook until the meat is tender. Remove the bay leaf and serve.

LAMB RAGOUT WITH SAGE AND HYSSOP

COOKING TIME 2 hrs.   TEMPERATURE E. 350° (180°C.) G.4
QUANTITIES FOR 4.

3 *lb.* (1½ *kg.*) *middle neck*	2 *medium onions, sliced*
of lamb cut in pieces	2 *oz.* (50 *g.*) *lard*

Heat the lard in a casserole or frying pan and fry the meat until it begins to brown. Add the onions and continue frying.

4 *tbs. flour*	*Salt and pepper*

Sprinkle over the meat and mix well.

¾ *pt.* (400 *ml.*) *beef stock*	1 *small sprig hyssop*
1 *sprig parsley*	*A pinch each of ground ginger,*
1 *sprig sage*	*cloves, and nutmeg*
4 *tbs. lemon juice*	

Tie the herbs together in a bunch and add to the meat with the other ingredients. Cover and cook until the meat is tender. Remove the bunch of herbs before serving the casserole.

GRILLED CHOPS OR CUTLETS AND KEBABS

The three best ways of using herbs with these are:
1. Rub the meat with fresh chopped, or dried herbs before grilling (see Grilled Lamb Chops with Herbs, below).
2. Brush the meat with a herb basting sauce during grilling, or marinate the meat (see pp. 129–32).
3. Serve the grill or kebabs with a herb butter (see pp. 127–9).

GRILLED LAMB CHOPS WITH HERBS

COOKING TIME 15–20 mins. after 1 hr. marinating.
QUANTITIES FOR 4.

4 *loin chops*	1 *tsp. salt*
1 *tsp. dried rosemary*	1 *tsp. dried marjoram*
1 *tsp. dried thyme*	

If powdered herbs are used, simply mix them with the salt. Other dried herbs should be pounded in a mortar to make a fine mixture with the salt. Rub both sides of the chops with this mixture and put them in a covered dish in the refrigerator for an hour.

Pre-heat the grill and turn the chops frequently during grilling so that browning and cooking finish together. Cooking time depends on the grill and on the thickness of the meat. It should still look plump and should be pink near the bone. If you are not sure about the timing, cut one to see.

Alternative: Use any of the herbs recommended (see p. 162); or use spiced salt (p. 92).

LAMB FONDUES

Serve these with herb butters (p. 127), or other sauces (pp. 110–26). Herbs can also be added to accompanying salads (pp. 191–209) or to boiled rice (p. 214) to serve with the chops.

ROAST LAMB OR MUTTON

TRADITIONAL HERB: plain roast with Mint Sauce (p. 120).

WITH GARLIC: either rub the meat all over with a cut clove of garlic before roasting it, or cut a small slit by the bone and insert slivers of garlic. I think the first method is the better one as nobody runs the risk of getting unwanted pieces of garlic to eat.

WITH A MARINADE: see Roast Shoulder in Herb Marinade (below). For other marinades to use, see pp. 129–32.

WITH POWDERED HERBS: cut small slits through the skin of the joint and rub in powdered herbs, with garlic, if liked, or use crushed coriander seeds with garlic.

WITH SPRIGS OF FRESH HERBS: put a good sized sprig of rosemary, fennel, or tarragon under the joint and baste during cooking with the aromatic drippings. Remove the herbs before making the gravy.

WITH HERB STUFFINGS: bone the meat and stuff it with any of the following: Cheese and Rosemary Stuffing (p. 210), Mint Stuffing (p. 212), Rice Stuffing with Rosemary (p. 212).

ROAST SHOULDER OF LAMB WITH HERB MARINADE

COOKING TIME 45 mins. per lb. (½ kg.), after marinating over-night.

TEMPERATURE E. 350° (180°C.) G.4   QUANTITIES FOR 4-6.

1 *small shoulder of lamb*

Put the meat in a shallow dish choosing one just large enough to take the joint. Alternatively, you can bone it and tie the meat in a more compact shape.

1½ *tsp. chopped (or ½ tsp. dried) rosemary*
1½ *tsp. chopped fresh (or ½ tsp. dried) thyme*
1½ *tsp. chopped fresh tarragon*
8 *tbs. (120 ml.) olive oil*

Heat these together but not enough to fry the herbs, just to bring out the flavours, then cool the mixture.

¼ *pt. (150 ml.) lemon juice*

Add to the cold oil and herbs and pour the marinade over the meat. Cover, and either keep it at room temperature for a few hours, or refrigerate it over-night. Lift the meat out of the marinade and roast it in the usual way, using surplus marinade to baste the joint during cooking.

The resulting gravy will be quite sharp with lemon juice so you may prefer to dilute it with some lamb or chicken stock.

BRAISED LAMB SHANK WITH TARRAGON, THYME, AND CAPERS

COOKING TIME 2¼ hrs.   TEMPERATURE E. 300° (150°C.) G.2
QUANTITIES FOR 4.

2 *oz. (50 g.) fat or 3-4 tbs. oil*
The shank end of a leg of lamb

A large casserole in which you can both fry and cook the meat is ideal for this recipe. Heat the fat or oil and brown the meat all over. Lift it out and pour off any remaining fat or oil.

1 *onion, sliced*   1 *tsp. chopped tarragon*
1 *tsp. chopped thyme*   Salt and pepper
¼–½ *pt. (150–250 ml.) white*
   wine or dry cider

Put the onion in the bottom of the casserole with the meat on top. Sprinkle the meat with herbs and seasonings. Pour in the wine or cider to a depth of about ½ in. (1 cm.). Cover the casserole and cook for 2 hrs. or until the meat is tender. Remove the meat and carve it, arranging the slices on a hot dish. Put to keep hot. Carefully pour off the fat from the onion and juices in the casserole.

¼ *pt. (150 ml.) yogurt*   2 *tbs. capers*

Rinse the capers and add them with the yogurt, stirring with the onion and juices and heat until boiling. Pour the sauce over the meat and serve. If preferred, the onion may be strained out before adding the other ingredients to the sauce.

BOILED LAMB OR MUTTON WITH DILL SAUCE

This somewhat plain sauce served with the meat may sound dull but it is in fact more palatable with this rather fatty meat than a more elaborate sauce would be. If, however, you prefer a richer sauce you can use one of the dill sauces given on pp. 115–16.

COOKING TIME about 2 hrs. QUANTITIES FOR 6 or more.

3 *lb.* (1½ *kg.*) *shoulder of*	1½ *tbs. salt*
mutton or lamb	2 *or* 3 *sprigs dill*

Use a pan just large enough to take the meat comfortably. Boil enough water to cover the meat, add the salt, dill, and meat, bring to the boil and then cook very slowly on top or in the oven until the meat is tender. Remove the meat and put it to keep hot. Strain the stock.

4 *tbs. flour*   1 *pt.* (½ *l.*) *strained stock*

Mix the flour to a smooth cream with a little cold water. Heat the stock and pour some into the flour mixture, stir well and add to the pan stirring until the sauce thickens and comes to the boil. Simmer for 5 mins.

1 *tbs. sugar*	1½–2 *tbs. vinegar*
Plenty of chopped dill, about	
4 *sprigs*	

Add the sugar to the sauce, and vinegar to taste, leaving the addition of the dill until just before serving. Slice the meat, put it in a deep hot serving dish, and pour the sauce over it.

LAMB PIE WITH MINT

COOKING TIME about 45 mins.   TEMPERATURE E. 425° (220°C.) G.7
QUANTITIES FOR a 7 in. (18 cm.) flan ring or pie plate.

6 *oz.* (1¼ *c. or* 175 *g.*) *flour made into short crust pastry*

Roll the pastry to line the flan ring or pie plate and roll another piece for a lid. Refrigerate these while the filling is being prepared.

6 *oz.* (175 *g.*) *cold cooked lean lamb*

Cut the meat in dice or thin slices.

1 tbs. chopped fresh mint   *Salt and pepper*
6 oz. (175 g.) *cottage cheese*

Put a layer of cottage cheese in the bottom of the pie, then the meat, seasoning it and adding the mint. Cover with another layer of the cheese.

2 tbs. *cream*   *Milk or egg for brushing the top*

Pour the cream over the filling. Cover with the pastry lid, sealing the edges together. Cut a slit in the centre top and brush the top with milk or egg. Bake the pie until the pastry is brown. Serve hot or cold.

Variation: Substitute any other meat for the lamb and change the herbs to suit the type of meat you are using. Or the meat can be flavoured with ground cumin and the brushed pie sprinkled with sesame seeds before baking it.

PORK, HAM, AND BACON

RECOMMENDED HERBS:

Basil	Fennel	Sage
Capers	Garlic	Tarragon
Coriander	Marjoram	Thyme
Dill	Rosemary	

Sorrel purée to serve with pork

Grilled or Fried Chops or Cutlets: Before grilling, pork can be marinated with a herb mixture (see p. 129), or rub dried powdered herbs into the meat before grilling it.

With fried meat, it is best to add chopped fresh herbs to the juices left in the pan, or to add herbs to an accompanying sauce, see Sauté of Pork Chops (below) or Pork Fillet (p. 168).

A good mixture of herbs to add to the sauté pan for 4 chops consists of 2 tbs. capers and 2 tbs. chopped parsley, with a little red wine for the liquid and some sliced onion cooked with the chops.

SAUTÉ OF PORK CHOPS WITH HERBS

COOKING TIME ½–¾ hr.   QUANTITIES FOR 4.
    4 *pork chops*   1 oz. (25 g.) *lard*

Trim surplus fat from the chops. Heat the lard in a sauté or frying pan and cook the chops until brown on both sides. Reduce the heat, cover, and continue cooking for about 20 mins. or until the chops are cooked through. Remove them from the pan and put to keep hot. Pour off any fat in excess of about 2 tbs.

    1 *small onion, finely chopped*

Add to the pan and fry until golden.

    ½ *tbs. flour*

Sprinkle in and blend with the onions.

    ¼ *pt.* (150 *ml.*) *stock or wine*

Blend with the onions and flour and stir until it boils.

| 1 *tbs. finely chopped fresh fennel, marjoram, sage, or tarragon, or a mixture* | ¼ *pt.* (150 *ml.*) *double cream or thick yogurt*
Salt and pepper
1 *tsp. dry mustard* |

Mix these together and add to the pan. Stir and heat. Then return the chops and make sure they are well heated before serving.

SAUTÉ OF PORK FILLET WITH SAGE

COOKING TIME 20–30 mins.   QUANTITIES FOR 4.

    1 *lb.* (½ *kg.*) *pork fillet or tenderloin*
    ½ *oz.* (15 *g.*) *lard*

Cut the fillet into pieces about ¾ in. (2 cm.) thick. Heat the lard in a frying or sauté pan. There should be just enough to make a thin coating on the pan. Add the slices of pork and fry until brown on both sides and cooked through. Remove and keep hot.

    1 *small onion, chopped*

Add more lard to the pan if necessary and fry the onion until almost tender.

| 6 *sage leaves, finely chopped* | *Salt and pepper* |
| ½ *pt.* (250 *ml.*) *dry cider* | 1 *tbs. concentrated tomato purée* |

Add to the onions and stir and cook until the sauce has thickened a little. Return the pork, re-heat, and serve with

    Boiled rice or noodles and green beans or a salad

Roast Pork: Dried herbs are usually the most satisfactory for rubbing into the cuts in the scored skin and into exposed surfaces. The herbs can first be mixed with dry mustard, salt and pepper, or use a herb salt (p. 92).

    Crushed coriander seeds with dried garlic or garlic salt are good, and for those who like an anise flavour, sprinkle caraway seeds into the cuts.

For stuffed roast meat use Sage and Onion Stuffing (p. 213), or Prune and Rosemary Stuffing (p. 212).

ROAST SPARE RIBS OF PORK WITH SAGE AND GINGER

COOKING TIME 35 mins. per lb.   TEMPERATURE E. 375° (190°C.) G.5
QUANTITIES FOR 4–6.

2–3 *lb.* (1–1½ *kg.*) *spare ribs*   ¼ *tsp. ground ginger*
¼–½ *tsp. salt*   *Pinch of pepper*
2 *tsp. crushed dried sage*

Mix the flavourings together and rub well into the joint on the non-bony parts of the meat. Put it on a rack in or above the roasting pan, meaty side up, and cook without basting.

Lift out the meat and make gravy in the pan in the usual way. This meat has an excellent flavour when cold as well as when hot.

Alternative: Instead of the above flavourings, use ½–1 tbs. Spiced Salt (p. 92).

SOUSE OF COLD PORK

This is a delicious way of serving cold roast pork either as part of an hors d'oeuvre or as cold meat with salad.

Trim the slices of pork to remove untidy bits and excess fat. Arrange the slices in a shallow serving dish. Sprinkle them liberally with fresh lemon juice, salt, and freshly ground pepper. Cover the dish and store for several hours in the refrigerator for the meat to marinate.

Sprinkle with chopped fresh herbs and serve with potato, beetroot, or cucumber salad.

For the herbs, choose from the following, using one herb or a mixture: marjoram, caraway leaves, sage, rosemary (soft tips), chives, fennel, or tarragon.

BOILED HAM, BACON, OR PICKLED PORK

Add sprigs of herbs (for example, bay, marjoram, basil, tarragon, or fennel) to the cooking liquid and then use some of this stock to make a sauce containing chopped fresh herbs. See Piquant Sauce (p. 121), Tarragon Sauce (p. 124), Fennel Sauce (p. 117), or Caper Sauce (p. 113).

FRIED OR GRILLED BACON WITH POTATOES AND HERB SAUCE

COOKING TIME 20–30 mins.   QUANTITIES FOR 4.

   1 ½ *lb. (750 g.) potatoes*
Peel, and put to boil in a little salted water.
   1 *oz. (25 g.) butter or margarine*   ½ *oz. (1½ tbs. or 15 g.) flour*
   ½ *pt. (250 ml.) creamy milk*
Heat the fat in a saucepan, add the flour and mix and cook for a
few minutes. Remove from the heat and add the milk, return and
stir until the sauce boils and thickens. Cook gently for 5 mins.
   Salt and pepper   2 *tbs. chopped fresh parsley or dill*
Season to taste and add the herbs just before serving the sauce. If
you want a sharper sauce, add a little lemon juice or tarragon vinegar.
Serve with 8 rashers fried or grilled bacon.

GAMMON RASHERS WITH CREAM AND HERBS

COOKING TIME 20–30 mins.   QUANTITIES FOR 4.

   4 *thick slices of raw gammon*
Remove the rind and snip the fat at intervals. Put the gammon in
a frying or sauté pan.
   1 *small onion, finely chopped*   *Pepper*
   ½ *pt. (250 ml.) soured cream*
Sprinkle the onion over the gammon, add pepper to taste and then
the cream. If this is not enough to cover the meat, add a little white
wine, cider, or stock. Bring to the boil and simmer until the bacon
is cooked.
   1 *hard-boiled egg, chopped*
   Chopped fresh herbs, basil, marjoram, or dill, or mixed
Sprinkle egg and herbs over the bacon and serve with the cream
sauce. Serve with
   Boiled potatoes   *Green salad or cooked spinach*

HAM AND EGG PIE

COOKING TIME ½–¾ hr.   TEMPERATURE E. 425° (220°C.) G.7
QUANTITIES FOR 4.

   4 *oz. (125 g.) flour made into short pastry or use*
   6–8 *oz. (175–250 g.) ready-made puff or short pastry*
Make the pastry or thaw frozen pastry.

1 oz. (25 g.) *butter or margarine*
1 oz. (3 tbs. or 25 g.) *flour*

Melt the fat in a small pan and stir in the flour. Cook gently until crumbly.

½ pt. (250 ml.) *chicken stock*

Add to the pan and whisk until smooth, thickened, and boiling. Boil for about 3 mins.

Salt and pepper   *Pinch of ground mace or nutmeg*
1 tsp. chopped marjoram 1 tsp. chopped tarragon

Add to the sauce and set aside to cool.

8 oz. (250 g.) *cold cooked ham* 3 *hard-boiled eggs*
10 oz. (284 g.) *can broad beans*
 or other vegetables, for
 example, corn kernels

Remove fat from the ham and cut the meat into small cubes. Shell the eggs and cut in quarters. Drain the vegetables and remove tough skins from broad beans, easy to do by gently pinching the bean at one end. Mix the sauce with the ham and vegetables and put in a flat pie plate, 1 pt. (½ l.) size. Press the eggs into the surface. Cover with pastry, brush with egg or milk and bake until the pastry is brown and the filling bubbling. Serve hot.

VEAL

Being one of the meats rather lacking in natural flavour, veal is very much improved by the addition of herbs during cooking or in accompanying sauces.

RECOMMENDED HERBS:

Fines Herbes (chervil, parsley, tarragon, and chives)
Basil   Marjoram   Sage
Costmary   Rosemary   Thyme
Fennel   Savory
Sorrel purée to serve with the cooked meat

Veal Casseroles: Any herbs can be used, either sprigs cooked with the meat and then removed before serving, and/or chopped fresh herbs added at the end of cooking.

For notes on using herbs in casseroles (see p. 157).

VEAL CASSEROLE WITH ROSEMARY OR THYME

COOKING TIME about 1½ hrs.   TEMPERATURE E. 300° (150°C.) G.2
QUANTITIES FOR 4.

1–1½ *lb.* (500–750 *g.*) *pie veal*   1 *tbs. flour*
1 *tsp. salt*

Trim the meat and cut it in small pieces. Toss in the flour and salt to coat it well.

1 *tbs. olive oil*

Heat in a casserole or pan and brown the meat well. Remove the meat.

1 *tbs. olive oil*   1 *medium onion, finely chopped*

Add the oil to the pan and fry the onion until it just begins to brown.

8 *oz.* (250 *g.*) *canned tomatoes*   *Pinch of pepper*
2 *oz.* (50 *g.*) *sliced mushrooms*   ¼ *pt.* (150 *ml.*) *white wine or*
½ *tsp. dried rosemary or*   *cider*
  thyme or 1 *tsp. chopped*
  fresh

Add to the pan, mix to dissolve any sediment, return the meat, cover and cook in the oven until the meat is tender.

1 *tbs. flour*
¼ *pt.* (150 *ml.*) *soured cream or fresh double cream*

Mix the cream gradually into the flour and then stir into the casserole. Stir until it thickens and simmer for 1–2 mins.

VEAL CHOPS, CUTLETS, AND ESCALOPES

As these are most often fried, the best way of using herbs is to add fresh chopped ones to the pan drippings or to an accompanying sauce, for example, Yogurt sauce with Herbs (p. 126), Cucumber sauce with Dill (p. 115), Chives sauce (pp. 114–15).

If the veal is grilled, use a basting sauce to add flavour and keep the surface moist (see pp. 129–32).

ROAST VEAL

Adding a well-flavoured stuffing or serving forcemeat balls with the cooked meat is one of the best ways for roast veal. For example, stuffed breast of veal or boned and rolled stuffed shoulder. For suitable stuffings, see Cheese and Rosemary stuffing (p. 210), Chicken stuffing (p. 211), and Rice stuffing with Rosemary or Thyme (p. 212).

Using a marinade (p. 129), adds flavour to the meat, and basting sauces also help to keep the surface moist during roasting. For basting sauces, see pp. 129–32.

VEAL AND HAM PIES

The traditional pie contains forcemeat balls, flavoured with herbs, among the pieces of veal and ham; but chopped herbs can be used without the forcemeat.

OFFAL

Any herbs can be used, those with a stronger flavour generally being the more successful. Straight fried kidneys or liver and bacon can have fresh, chopped herbs added to the pan drippings while grilled kidneys and liver are improved by being brushed with a herb basting sauce (see pp. 129–32).

Ox liver and tripe are both improved by the addition of herbs, as in the two recipes I have included in this section.

KIDNEY RAGOUT WITH SAGE

COOKING TIME 20 mins.　　QUANTITIES FOR 4.

6 lamb's or 4 pig's kidneys　　*Salt and pepper*

Wash, remove skins, slice the kidneys, and remove the hard core. Sprinkle with salt and pepper.

1 oz. (25 g.) lard or 2 tbs. oil

Heat in a frying pan or small saucepan and fry the kidneys for 5 mins., turning them once. Lift them out, using a perforated spoon, and put them to keep hot.

1 rasher bacon, chopped　　*1 oz. (3 tbs. or 25 g.) flour*

Add the bacon to the pan and fry until the fat runs. Add the flour and mix and cook for a few minutes.

¾ pt. (400 ml.) stock or use some red wine and some stock

Stir in gradually and bring to the boil.

2 oz. (50 g.) sliced mushrooms　　*Salt and pepper*

Add the mushrooms, return the pieces of kidney, and simmer the ragout gently for a few minutes. Taste for seasoning.

1 tbs. or more of chopped sage

Add just before serving. Serve the ragout in a border of

Boiled rice or mashed potato

CHICKEN LIVER KEBABS WITH ROSEMARY OR THYME

COOKING TIME about 15 mins.   QUANTITIES FOR 4.

8 *oz.* (250 *g.*) *chicken livers*   1 *oz.* (25 *g.*) *butter*

Wash and drain the livers and remove any fat or fibres. Heat the butter in a frying pan and cook the livers for a minute or two just to stiffen them. Remove from the pan and cut each liver into three or four pieces, depending on its size. Keep any butter left in the pan and use it for basting the kebabs.

8 *big, plump prunes*

Remove the stones, cutting the prunes in half. If they are not plump ones, soak the prunes in water for a while to soften them a little.

4 *rashers streaky bacon*   Salt and pepper
Cayenne pepper   Powdered dried rosemary or
                                    thyme

Remove the bacon rinds and stretch out the rashers by stroking them with the back of a knife. Cut each in four pieces.

Thread the liver, prunes, and bacon, alternating them, on the kebab skewers. Season well and sprinkle them generously with the herbs and any butter left from the frying pan. Grill until the bacon is crisp. Serve with

Rice with Herbs (p. 214), *Saffron Rice* (p. 217), *or green beans or a salad. For a sauce, use a Herb Butter* (pp. 127–9) *or Bearnaise sauce* (p. 112).

LIVER KEBABS WITH BAY OR SAGE LEAVES

COOKING TIME 10–15 mins., after ½ hr. marinating.
QUANTITIES FOR 4.

1 *lb.* (½ *kg.*) *liver in one piece, calf's, lamb's, or pig's liver is suitable*

Wash the liver thoroughly and remove the skin. Drain the liver and pat with paper towels to dry the outside. Cut it in approximately 1½-in. (4-cm.) cubes, removing any coarse tubes.

2 *medium-sized onions*   8 *oz.* (250 *g.*) *mushrooms*
8 *medium sized tomatoes,*   *Fresh bay or sage leaves*
firm-ripe

Peel and quarter the onions, wash tomatoes and cut them in quarters. Wash the mushrooms and, if they are very large, cut in halves. Wash the bay or sage leaves.

Take 8 long, thin skewers or brochettes and thread the ingredients on them in the following order; bay or sage leaf, liver, mushroom, tomato, onion; repeating these until all are used up. Put in a large flat dish.

Oil, vinegar, salt and pepper, or use a basting sauce (see pp. 129–132)

Brush the kebabs with oil and sprinkle with vinegar and seasoning or brush with a basting sauce. Leave to marinate for ½ hr. Grill until beads of blood begin to appear on the surface of the pieces of liver. Remove the kebabs to a hot dish.

Chopped parsley	2 *tbs. lemon juice*

Add a little water or stock to the drippings from the kebabs. Mix to dissolve any sediment, transfer to a small pan and boil hard to reduce the quantity. Add parsley and lemon juice and pour over the kebabs.

Serve them on a bed of
Boiled rice

LIVER PATÉ WITH HERBS

This is a soft kind of pâté, not meant for slicing. Serve portions with a spoon, to be spread on toast, or use for sandwiches, for stuffing tomatoes and eggs, or other similar purposes. It is best made in the electric blender but can be finely minced or rubbed through a sieve.

COOKING TIME 5–10 mins.   QUANTITIES FOR 8 or more.

8 *oz.* (250 *g.*) *liver, calf's, lamb's, or pig's*

Remove any skin and tubes, cut the liver in small pieces about an inch cube (2½ cm.), wash thoroughly and drain.

1 *oz.* (25 *g.*) *butter or* *margarine*	6–8 *oz.* (175–250 *g.*) *mild fat* *bacon*
2–3 *tbs. chopped fresh sage or* *fennel*	

Remove rinds and cut the bacon in pieces. Heat the fat in a frying pan and cook the bacon for a few minutes. Add the liver and cook it slowly until just done (beads of blood begin to appear on the surface). Avoid over-cooking as this makes the pâté granular in texture instead of creamy. Add the herbs towards the end of cooking.

2 *anchovy fillets or* 1 *tsp.* *anchovy essence*	*Pinch of pepper* ¼ *pt.* (150 *ml.*) *red wine*

Put in the blender in one or more lots with the fried ingredients and any juices in the pan. Blend until smooth. Tip into a dish and leave to become quite cold before covering it and storing the pâté in the refrigerator.

LIVER VENEZIANA

This should be made with fresh calf's liver but quite a palatable substitute is either lamb's or pig's liver, or even frozen lamb's liver if a bit more sage is added to help the flavour.

COOKING TIME about 10 mins.   QUANTITIES FOR 4–6.

   1 *lb.* (½ *kg.*) *liver cut in very thin slices*
Wash and dry the liver and remove any stringy bits. Cut the thin slices in pieces about 1 in. (2½ cm.) square.

   4 *medium-sized onions*
Skin, and slice them very finely. This is most important.

   4 *tbs.* (60 *ml.*) *olive oil*
Heat in a frying pan or sauté pan and fry the onions until brown. Add the pieces of liver and cook for 2 mins., stirring and tossing to cook them on both sides.

   Salt and pepper   1 *tbs. chopped parsley*
   6 *or more large sage leaves*
      chopped finely
Add to the pan and cook for ½ min. longer.

   3–4 *tbs. red wine, stock, or lemon juice plus stock or water*
Add enough just to moisten and dissolve the sediment in the pan. It is meant to be a dry dish. Serve at once with

   Boiled or sauté potatoes and a salad
Alternative herbs:

1. Replace the sage by 2 tbs. chopped fennel and use some lemon juice in the liquid.
2. Replace the sage and parsley by 2 tbs. mixed chopped parsley, chervil, and tarragon, with a pinch of dried garlic.
3. Replace the sage with 1 tsp. dried powdered rosemary.

OX LIVER CASSEROLE

COOKING TIME 1¼ hrs.   TEMPERATURE E. 350° (180°C.) G.4
QUANTITIES FOR 4–6.

   1 *lb.* (½ *kg.*) *thinly sliced ox liver*   *Seasoned flour*
Wash and drain the liver. Remove any coarse tubes and dust the liver with seasoned flour.

   1 *oz.* (25 *g.*) *butter or 2 tbs. olive oil*
Heat in a frying pan and brown the liver quickly on both sides, lift out, and set aside.

2 *rashers streaky bacon, diced*   1 *small onion, finely chopped*

Add to the pan and fry until the onion begins to colour.

2 *tbs. chopped fresh herbs, sage, tarragon, or fennel; or use* 1
    tsp. dried powdered sage or rosemary
Salt and pepper   2 *tbs. lemon juice*
5 *tbs. (75 ml.) stock or water*   *Pinch of garlic salt*

Add to the pan and just bring to the boil. Put half of the sauce in
a shallow casserole, add the slices of liver and pour the rest of the
sauce over it. Cover and cook slowly until the liver is tender, about
1 hr.

CASSEROLE OF TRIPE

COOKING TIME 2–3 hrs.   TEMPERATURE E. 300° (150°C.) G.2
QUANTITIES FOR 4.

1 *oz. lard (25 g.) or 2 tbs. oil*   ½ *pt. (250 ml.) stock*
1 *oz. (3 tbs. or 25 g.) flour*

Heat the fat or oil in a casserole or stewpan, add the flour and cook
until it turns yellow. Remove from the heat and stir in the stock.
Return to the heat and stir until it boils.

1 *onion, sliced*   ¼ *tsp. each of ground ginger,*
2 *carrots, sliced*   *nutmeg, and cloves*
½ *tsp. mixed dried herbs or*   2 *small turnips, sliced*
   1 *tbs. chopped fresh sage*   2 *sticks celery, sliced*
Pinch of cayenne pepper   2 *tsp. salt*
1 *lb. (½ kg.) tripe cut in small*
   pieces

Add to the pan, cover, and cook gently in the oven, the longer the
better.

1 *tsp. chopped fresh marjoram*   ½ *oz. (15 g.) grated Parmesan*
                                     cheese

Mix these and sprinkle on top of the tripe just before serving it.

MINCED MEAT

Whether using raw minced meat or left-over cooked meat, all need
to be well flavoured to make them interesting. The mere fact of
mincing meat reduces its natural flavour, the finer the mincing, the
less flavour.

Either fresh chopped, or dried herbs are ideal for flavouring all minced meat dishes, using just one herb with onion and seasonings, or a mixture of herbs. Some of the blends of herbs (p. 85) or Spiced Salt (p. 92), are specially useful here.

The other ways in which herbs can help these dishes is by serving the meat with a sauce containing herbs or with salad or vegetables containing herbs.

Fresh herbs can either be chopped separately or minced with the meat, onion, and other ingredients; or chopped in the electric blender using as moisture a little liquid or an egg from the recipe.

RECIPES USING RAW MINCED MEAT

MEAT BALL KEBABS WITH CHEESE AND HERBS

COOKING TIME about 15 mins.   QUANTITIES FOR 4.

1 *lb.* (½ *kg.*) *lean raw minced beef or use three parts beef to one part pork*

2 *oz.* (50 *g.*) *grated cheese*   8 *oz.* (250 *g.*) *mashed potato*

1 *tsp. salt*   *Pinch of pepper*

A little garlic salt   4–8 *tbs.* (60–120 *ml.*) *milk or cream*

1 *tbs. chopped thyme, basil, sage, or a mixture*

Mix all the ingredients together using enough of the liquid to moisten the mixture but avoid making it too soft to handle. Shape into about 24 small balls.

4 *medium-sized tomatoes*   2–4 *oz.* (50–125 *g.*) *mushrooms*

Cut the tomatoes in half and thread the meat balls on kebab skewers alternating with tomato halves and mushrooms. Grill until the meat balls are well browned and cooked through. Serve with

Fried potatoes or a rice dish and salad

Alternative: Instead of cooking the meat balls as kebabs, fry them in a little shallow fat or oil, shaking the pan frequently to keep them round.

MINCED BEEF SAUSAGE (for serving cold)

COOKING TIME 2 hrs.   QUANTITIES FOR 8–10.

1 *small onion, minced or finely chopped*

8 *oz.* (250 *g.*) *streaky bacon, minced or finely chopped*

1 *lb.* (½ *kg.*) *lean minced beef*

The meat should be finely minced, otherwise the roll will fall apart

when sliced. For home mincing, put it through twice. Put the
ingredients in a bowl.

4 oz. (1 c. or 125 g.) *rolled oats*   1 *tbs. Worcester sauce*
1 *egg, beaten*   1 *tsp. salt, less if the bacon is*
Pinch of pepper   *salty*
1 *tbs. chopped marjoram, dill,*
and basil, mixed

Add to the meat and mix thoroughly. Shape it into a long sausage
about the thickness of a breakfast sausage. Wrap it carefully in foil,
sealing the ends carefully. Put the roll in boiling water to cover and
simmer for 2 hrs.

Dried breadcrumbs

Remove the foil and, while the roll is still hot, coat it with crumbs.
Allow to become quite cold and then wrap and store in the
refrigerator

STUFFED MINCED BEEF LOAF

COOKING TIME 1 hr.   TEMPERATURE E. 375° (190°C.) G.5
QUANTITIES FOR 4.

2 *oz.* (50 *g.*) *prunes*

Wash the prunes and soak them for a few hours until they are soft
enough to remove the stones.

1 *small onion, chopped*   *Fat or oil*

Fry the onion in very little fat or oil until it is softened but not
browned. Leave to cool.

1 *lb.* (½ *kg.*) *lean minced beef*   ½ *tsp. crushed coriander seeds*
1½ *oz.* (½ *c. or* 40 *g.*) *fresh*   2 *tsp. chopped thyme or* ½ *tsp.*
breadcrumbs, or 6 *tbs. rolled*   *dried*
oats   1 *tsp. salt*
¼ *tsp. ground mace or nutmeg*   1 *egg, beaten*
A little garlic juice or salt   *Pinch of pepper*

Mix all the ingredients together with the fried onion. Turn the
mixture onto a floured board and pat it out to a rectangle about
1 in. (2½ cm.) thick. Put the stoned prunes in a line parallel with
the short side of the meat and mould the meat over to enclose the
prunes, finally patting it to a loaf about 2 in. (5 cm.) thick.

Fat or oil

Heat a little in a roasting pan, add the meat loaf and cover the top
with a piece of foil. Bake, removing the foil for the last 10 mins.
to allow the loaf to brown. Serve on a hot dish. Make gravy in the

pan, or serve the loaf with a sauce such as tomato. Cut the loaf in slices.

Alternative: Serve the loaf cold with salad.

MINCED LAMB PATTIES

COOKING TIME 20–25 mins. QUANTITIES FOR 4.

1 *lb.* (½ *kg.*) *lean lamb or 2*	½ *tsp. powdered rosemary*
lb. (1 *kg.*) *with fat and bone*	*Pinch of pepper*
½ *tsp. salt*	

Mince the meat finely with the seasonings. Shape into four flat cakes about 1 in. (2½ cm.) thick.

4 *rashers streaky bacon*

Remove rinds and wrap a rasher round the sides of each patty, securing the ends with a wooden cocktail stick. Grill slowly under a medium heat, turning once during cooking. Serve with

Rosemary Butter (p. 129), *Garlic Butter* (p. 127), *or Maître d'Hôtel Butter* (p. 128).

RECIPES USING COOKED MINCED MEAT

BEEF FRICADELLES

COOKING TIME 10–15 mins. QUANTITIES FOR 4.

8 *oz.* (250 g.) *cold cooked beef*   1 *oz.* (25 g.) *onion*

Remove any skin or gristle from the meat and mince meat and onion finely.

4 *oz.* (½ *c. or* 125 g.) *mashed*	*Salt and pepper*
potatoes	½ *tsp. crushed coriander seeds*
1 *egg. beaten*	*Wine or bottled sauce*
2 *tbs. chopped parsley*	

Mix all these with the meat and onion, adding a little wine or bottled sauce if it seems necessary to bind the mixture which should be soft enough to mould easily. Turn the mixture onto a floured board and divide it into four pieces. Shape each into a large round flat cake.

Oil or butter

Heat in a frying pan and fry the fricadelles until they are brown on both sides. Serve hot with

A Sauce such as Piquant (p. 121) *or Tomato* (p. 125) *Salad*

Alternative: Use lamb instead of beef and flavour with a pinch of dried garlic and 1 tbs. chopped fresh marjoram.

CHICKEN AND HAM MOULD WITH TARRAGON

QUANTITIES FOR 4–6.

½ *pt.* (250 *ml.*) *chicken stock*   ½ *oz.* (1½ *tbs. or* 15 *g.*) *gelatine*
Heat the stock and dissolve the gelatine in it. Pour a little of it into a 1 pt. (½ l.) mould and leave to set.

   8 *oz.* (250 *g.*) *minced cooked chicken and ham, mixed*
   2 *tsp. chopped fresh tarragon, or to taste*
   Grated nutmeg or mace   1 *tsp. Worcester sauce*
   Salt and pepper
Mix all together with the remaining stock and gelatine.

   1 *hard-boiled egg, sliced*
Use this to decorate the layer of jelly set in the mould. Carefully spoon in the chicken and ham mixture and refrigerate until set. Unmould and serve with salad.

CHICKEN AND HAM TURNOVERS WITH FINES HERBES

COOKING TIME 25–30 mins.   TEMPERATURE E. 450° (230°C.) G.8
QUANTITIES FOR 4 large turnovers.

   1 *oz.* (25 *g.*) *butter or margarine*   1 *oz.* (3 *tbs. or* 25 *g.*) *flour*
   ½ *pt.* (250 *ml.*) *milk or chicken*
     stock, or a mixture
Melt the butter or margarine in a small saucepan, add the flour and stir and cook until it looks mealy. Remove from the heat and stir in the liquid. Return to the heat, stir until the sauce boils and simmer for 5 mins. Set aside to cool.

   4 *oz.* (125 *g.*) *minced or finely chopped cooked chicken*
   4 *oz.* (125 *g.*) *minced or finely chopped cooked ham*
   Salt and pepper
   1 *tbs. chopped mixed parsley, tarragon, chives, and chervil*
Add to the cold sauce, seasoning to taste.

   12 *oz.* (375 *g.*) *puff pastry*
Roll the pastry into an oblong not more than ⅛ in. (3 mm.) thick. Cut it into four pieces and put some of the mixture on one half of each piece. Moisten the edges of the pastry with water or milk, fold in half and seal the edges. Put on a baking tray, brush with egg and water or with milk, and cut a small slit in the top of each turn-

over. Bake until the pastry is crisp and brown. Serve hot or cold.

CHICKEN OR RABBIT TIMBALES WITH TARRAGON

Suitable for a starter or a light meal.

COOKING TIME ½–¾ hr.   TEMPERATURE E. 350° (180°C.) G.4
QUANTITIES FOR three 8 fl. oz. (200 ml.) pudding moulds or 4–6
timbale moulds.

1 oz. (⅓ c. or 25 g.) *fresh*
breadcrumbs
1 oz. (25 g.) *melted butter or*
margarine
2 *eggs, beaten*
¼ *pt.* (150 ml.) *stock*

6 oz. (175 g.) *finely minced*
cooked chicken or rabbit
1 *tbs. chopped tarragon*
1 *tsp. salt*
Pepper

Mix all together and put in oiled moulds. Stand the moulds in a
shallow pan of hot water and bake until the mixture is firm. Remove
from the water and leave the moulds to stand for a few minutes to
settle. Loosen the edges and turn them out on a hot dish. Serve with
Tarragon sauce (p. 124), *Parsley sauce* (p. 121), *or Chives sauce*
(pp. 114–15).
Alternative method: Process the ingredients together in the electric
blender until the meat is finely broken up.

POULTRY: CHICKEN

No flavourings are more useful than herbs for making the somewhat
tasteless modern chicken into an appetising dish. Herbs are not
only used in the traditional stuffings for roast chicken but in all
kinds of other recipes as well, for example, marinades for grilled
chicken, in casseroles, sautés, chicken pies, and so on.

RECOMMENDED HERBS:

Balm	Garlic	Rosemary
Basil	Lemon Thyme	Sage
Bay	Lovage	Savory
Capers	Marjoram	Sorrel purée
Dill	Parsley	Tarragon
Horseradish		

DUCK AND GOOSE

These are best with fairly strongly flavoured herbs such as:
    Caraway seeds sprinkled over before roasting
    Costmary   Rosemary   Sorrel
    Mint   Sage   Thyme

TURKEY

The same herbs as for chicken.

CHICKEN CASSEROLE WITH BASIL AND MARJORAM

COOKING TIME 1–1 ½ hrs.   TEMPERATURE E. 350° (180°C.) G.4
QUANTITIES FOR 4.

    4 portions of roasting chicken   *4 tbs. (60 ml.) oil*

Wash and dry the chicken. Heat the oil in a large casserole or frying pan and brown the chicken pieces on both sides. If a frying pan has been used transfer the chicken to a casserole.

    1½ tsp. salt   *1 tsp. paprika pepper*
    Pinch of pepper   *1 tsp. dried basil or 2 tsp. chopped*
    2 tbs. chopped parsley   *fresh*
    ¼ tsp. garlic powder   *2 tbs. concentrated tomato purée*
    1 tsp. dried marjoram   *Wine to moisten*

Combine the seasonings and sprinkle them over the chicken. Add the tomato purée and enough wine just to moisten the chicken. Cover and cook until the chicken is tender. Turn the chicken over once during cooking.

CHICKEN GOULASH

COOKING TIME 1 hr. or longer, according to the type of chicken used
QUANTITIES FOR 4.

    1 oz (25 g.) lard   *1 medium-sized onion, finely chopped*

Heat the lard in a saucepan or casserole and stew the onion in it until it begins to soften.

    4 portions of chicken   *2 tbs. paprika pepper*

Mix the pepper with the onion and then add the chicken, turning it over to coat it.

1 *large tomato, fresh or canned,*	¼ *tsp. or more of caraway*
or use 1–2 tsp. concentrated	*seeds*
tomato purée	½ *pt. (20 ml.) chicken stock*
	Salt

Cut up the tomato and add it with the other ingredients. Cover the pan and cook gently on top or in a moderate oven until the chicken is tender. Remove the chicken and keep it hot.

2 *tbs. flour*   ¼ *pt. (150 ml.) soured cream or yogurt*

Blend the flour to a smooth paste with the cream or yogurt and stir this into the chicken liquid. Stir until it boils and boil gently for a few minutes. Return the chicken and make sure it is hot before serving.

CHICKEN SAUTÉ WITH TARRAGON SAUCE

COOKING TIME ¾–1 hr.   QUANTITIES FOR 4.

Begin by making the sauce in a small pan.

½ *oz. (15 g.) fat*   1 *small onion, chopped*
1 *rasher bacon, chopped*

Heat the fat and fry the bacon and onion until just beginning to brown.

1 *tbs. flour*

Add, mix, and cook until the flour is just beginning to brown.

½ *pt. (250 ml.) chicken stock*   *Salt and pepper*
2 *tsp. concentrated tomato*
purée

Add to the pan and stir until boiling. Put to simmer while the chicken is cooked.

4 *portions of frying chicken (breast or leg are the easiest to handle)*
1 *oz. (25 g.) butter*

Heat the butter in a deep frying or sauté pan. Fry the chicken until golden brown on both sides. Reduce the heat, cover the pan with a lid or foil, and cook gently for about 30 mins. or until the chicken is tender.

2 *tbs. chopped fresh tarragon*

Remove the chicken and put it to keep hot. Add the tarragon to the sauce and continue to keep it hot.

¼ *pt. (150 ml.) white wine*

Add to the frying pan and stir until it boils. Turn up the heat and boil rapidly to reduce it by about half. Add the sauce and mix well. Return the pieces of chicken and turn them over in the sauce to coat them. Make sure they are hot before serving chicken and sauce.

SAUTÉ OF CHICKEN WITH HERBS AND OLIVES

COOKING TIME 45 mins.   QUANTITIES FOR 4.
   4 *portions of frying or*   1 *clove garlic*
      roasting chicken   4 *tbs. (60 ml.) olive oil*

Heat the oil in a sauté pan or deep frying pan. Add the garlic and
chicken and fry until brown. Remove the chicken. Discard the garlic.
   2 *tbs. flour*

Add to the oil remaining in the pan and mix well. Cook for 2–3
mins.
   1 *tbs. each chopped fennel, chives, and parsley*

Add to the pan and cook for a minute longer.
   ½ *pt. (250 ml.) white wine or dry cider*

Stir into the pan and stir until it boils.
   ¼ *pt. (150 ml.) soured cream*   1 *doz. stoned black olives*
      or thick yogurt   *Salt and pepper*

Add to the pan, mix, and return the chicken; cover the pan and
cook slowly until the chicken is tender.

SAUTÉ OF COOKED CHICKEN WITH THYME AND WALNUTS

COOKING TIME about ½ hr.   QUANTITIES FOR 4.
   1 *onion, finely chopped*   1 *stick of celery, chopped*
   Oil

Heat enough oil to make a thin coating on the bottom of a frying
or sauté pan. Add the onion and celery and cook for a few minutes.
   4 *oz. (125 g.) sliced mushrooms*   2 *tbs. chopped fresh thyme*
   ¾–1 *lb. (375–500 g.) diced*
      cooked chicken

Add to the pan and cook for 10 mins. over a gentle heat.
   1 *tbs. potato flour*   ¼ *pt. (150 ml.) white wine or cider*
   Chicken stock

Mix the potato flour to a smooth paste with the wine and pour this
over the chicken mixture, adding chicken stock if more moisture
seems necessary. Stir until it thickens and boils.
   2 *tbs. soy sauce*   *Salt and pepper*
   3 *oz. (75 g.) chopped walnuts*

Add to the chicken and continue cooking gently for about 10 mins.
Serve hot.
   Brussels sprouts make a very good accompaniment for this, or
serve a green salad.

CHICKEN ROASTED WITH BAY LEAVES

COOKING TIME 1½–2 hrs.   TEMPERATURE E. 375° (190°C.) G.5
QUANTITIES FOR 4.

2½–3 lb. (1–1½ kg.) roasting chicken   5 fresh bay leaves
Wash and dry the chicken. Put one bay leaf inside it and tie the
other four leaves over the breast, using coarse white cotton.

½ oz. (15 g.) melted butter
Brush exposed parts of the chicken with butter. Put it in a pan
and roast 1–1½ hrs., depending on the size. Remove the chicken and
cut it into portions. Put it in a serving dish and keep hot.

*2 oz. (50 g.) butter   6 tbs. (90 ml.) or more of thick
1 tsp. potato flour   yogurt
                                     Salt and pepper*

Melt the butter in a small pan. Mix the flour with a little cold
water or stock and add the yogurt. Stir this into the melted butter
and stir until it boils. Season to taste and add more yogurt if needed
to thin the sauce. Pour over the chicken pieces and serve.

DUCK WITH MINT

COOKING TIME 1½ hrs. for the duck; ¼–½ hr. for the sauce.
TEMPERATURE E. 425° (220°C.) G.7   QUANTITIES FOR 4–6.

*4 lb. (2 kg.) duck, trussed weight   Salt
1 oz. (25 g.) softened butter   1 tsp. chopped mint*
Begin cooking the duck about 2 hrs. before serving time. If the skin
is damp pat it dry with paper towels, then sprinkle with salt and
rub it in. Work the mint into the softened butter and spread this
over the breast of the duck.

*2 small carrots, chopped   2 medium-sized onions,
2 sticks celery, chopped   chopped
1 sprig thyme   1 rasher bacon, chopped
1 oz. (25 g.) butter   ½ bay leaf, crushed
                                 2 tbs. madeira or sherry*

Use a covered roasting pan or a large casserole for cooking the duck.
Melt the butter in it and add the wine, bacon, vegetables, and herbs.
Put the duck on top of the vegetables, breast up. Cover and cook
for 1½ hrs. or until the duck is tender when tested in the thick part
of the thigh. By this time the lower half of the duck will be surrounded by melted fat, and juices from duck and vegetables, the
upper half will be brown like roast duck. Remove the duck, put it in

a baking tin or oven dish and return it to the oven to dry and crisp the skin, then keep hot. Meanwhile, prepare the sauce.

¼ *pt.* (150 *ml.*) *stock from the giblets, or use chicken stock*
Add to the vegetables and liquid in the pan and boil for 5 mins. If more convenient, do this in a saucepan. Strain the sauce into a basin and use a spoon or ladle to remove as much of the fat as possible. Return the sauce to the pan and re-heat, adding more stock if you want more sauce.

1–2 *tbs. lemon juice*   2 *tbs. chopped mint*
Pepper
Add to the sauce, taste for seasoning and serve in a sauce boat. Alternatively, carve the duck and pour the sauce over it.

TURKEY PAPRIKA WITH CARAWAY SEEDS

A good way of using up cooked turkey. The mixture can be used as a flan or pie filling, to make a potato pie, to serve in a border of mashed potatoes, or with rice or pasta.

COOKING TIME about 30 mins.   QUANTITIES FOR 4.
  1 *medium-sized onion, chopped*   3 *tbs. oil*
  1 *small green pepper or 2*
    sticks celery, chopped
Heat the oil in a saucepan and fry the vegetables slowly until they are soft. Remove from the heat.

  1 *tbs. flour*   1 *tbs. or more of paprika pepper*
  1 *tbs. concentrated tomato*   1 *tsp. sugar*
    purée
Add to the pan and mix in.

  ½ *pt.* (250 *ml.*) *turkey stock*
Blend in, return to the heat, and stir until it boils.

  ½ *tsp. salt*   ½ *tsp. or more of caraway seeds*
Add, cover the pan, and simmer for 15 mins.

  12 *oz.* (375 *g.*) *cooked turkey, cut in small pieces*
  ¼ *pt.* (150 *ml.*) *yogurt, beaten smooth*
Add to the sauce and boil gently for 5 mins. longer. Serve straight away.

GAME

Any game, but specially that which has not been hung for a long time, is improved by the use of herbs during cooking. These can be added to a stuffing for roast game, in casseroles, game pies, terrines, and any other recipes.

The following is a list of recommended herbs for different kinds of game but others can be used as well and a combination of herbs and spices is very good.

GAME BIRDS

Grouse—thyme, sage, parsley
Partridge—basil, rosemary
Pheasant—basil, bay, marjoram, thyme
Pigeon—sage, thyme

HARE AND RABBIT

Sage, bay, lemon or common thyme

VENISON

Lemon or common thyme, basil, marjoram, bay

JUGGED HARE

COOKING TIME 3–4 hrs.   TEMPERATURE E. 300° (150°C.) G.2
QUANTITIES FOR 6–8.

    1 *hare or 6–8 portions of cut hare*
    1 *oz. (25 g.) dripping or 2 tbs. oil*

Heat the fat or oil and fry the pieces of hare until they are well browned all over. Put them in a deep casserole.

    2 *onions, sliced*   2 *tsp. salt*
    ½ *tsp. freshly ground black*   1 *apple, sliced*
        pepper   6 *cloves*
    1 *tsp. grated lemon rind*   3 *whole allspice*
    2 *oz. (50 g.) mushrooms, sliced*
    A bouquet garni of thyme, bay, parsley, and marjoram

The allspice and cloves should be tied loosely in a muslin bag with the bouquet garni herbs. Add all the flavourings to the hare.

    1 *oz. (25 g.) butter or*   ¼ *pt. (150 ml.) wine vinegar*
        margarine   ½ *pt. (250 ml.) stock*
    1 *oz. (3 tbs. or 25 g.) flour*
    ½ *pt. (250 ml.) red wine*

Melt the butter or margarine in a small pan, add the flour and stir and cook for a few minutes. Add the liquid gradually and stir until it boils. Pour the sauce over the hare, cover and cook very slowly until the meat is quite tender.

Forcemeat balls made with Chicken Stuffing recipe (p. 211), *using lemon thyme for flavouring*

Fat or oil

Roll the stuffing into small balls and fry these in hot fat or oil until they are well browned. Drain on absorbent paper and keep hot. Remove the bag of herbs from the hare and either serve the hare in the casserole or transfer it to a heated serving dish. Put the forcemeat balls on top and serve with

Red currant jelly   Baked jacket, or boiled potatoes

RABBIT PIE

COOKING TIME 1½–2 hrs.

TEMPERATURE E. 450° (230°C.) G.8 for 10 mins., then E. 350° (180°C.) G.4

QUANTITIES FOR 4–6.

Flaky or short pastry using 8 oz. (250 g.) flour or use 12 oz. (375 g.) ready-made pastry

1 rabbit or 6 portions of cut rabbit

Make the pastry and refrigerate it while the filling is being prepared.

Divide a whole rabbit into joints and boil the trimmings for stock, preferably in the pressure cooker. If there are no trimmings, use chicken stock instead.

12 oz. (375 g.) bacon or salt pork

Forcemeat balls made with Sage and Onion stuffing (p. 213), *or Chicken stuffing* (p. 211)

Remove any rind and cut the bacon or pork in small dice. Roll the stuffing into small balls. Pack the rabbit, bacon or pork, and the forcemeat balls in layers in a 1½–2 pt. (1 l.) pie-dish.

Salt and pepper   Stock

Season well with salt and pepper and add enough stock to three-quarters fill the dish. Cover with pastry and bake until the meat is tender. Should the pastry become well-browned before the meat is tender, cover the top loosely with a piece of foil. Serve the pie hot or cold.

ROAST PHEASANT WITH HERBS

COOKING TIME 1½ hrs.   TEMPERATURE E. 350° (180°C.) G.4

QUANTITIES: 1 bird will serve 2–4 people depending on its size: a brace will serve 5–6 people.

STUFFINGS

> *Use Walnut stuffing (p. 213), and for variation substitute basil or marjoram for the thyme in the recipe. Alternatively, put a large knob of Herb Butter inside (see pp. 127–9), using either basil, marjoram, or thyme, or a mixture*

Put the prepared bird on a rack in the roasting pan with the giblets round or underneath the bird.

> *Slice of fat pork or a rasher of mild bacon*

Put this over the breast and roast, removing the pork or bacon for the last 10 mins. to allow the breast to brown. Make gravy in the pan. Other optional accompaniments are

> *Bread sauce   Watercress*

CHAPTER TWELVE

Vegetables and salads

There are three main ways of using herbs to add extra flavour to
vegetables. These are: to add sprigs of herbs to the cooking water,
for example, a bay leaf or a sprig of mint; to add chopped herbs to
cooked vegetables, for example, chopped chives in mashed potatoes;
to add herbs to a sauce to be served with the vegetable, for example,
parsley sauce with carrots. Herb Butters (p. 127) are particularly suitable for dressing cooked vegetables, including baked jacket potatoes.

For salads, any fresh scissor-snipped, chopped herbs or whole leaves
can be added—one herb or a mixture of many. Dried herbs can be
added to dressings (see p. 126).

For herb flowers to use as garnishes for salads see p. 81.

ARTICHOKES

Dill and parsley are particularly good in dressings or sauces with globe
artichoke hearts or bottoms. Use the same herbs in sauces for Jeru-
salem artichokes.

ASPARAGUS

Add chervil, dill, parsley, or tarragon to recipes using asparagus as
an ingredient, in mayonnaise or other sauce to serve with fresh cooked
asparagus, hot or cold.

ASPARAGUS FLAN WITH CHERVIL

This can be made either by adding chervil to the pastry (see Herb pastry, p. 238), or by adding it to the filling as in the following recipe. Alternative herbs could be dill or tarragon.

COOKING TIME 40 mins.

TEMPERATURE E. 400° (200°C.) G.6 for 10 mins., then E. 350° (180°C.) G.4 for 25–30 mins.

QUANTITIES FOR an 8–in. (20 cm.) flan ring or pie plate.

> 6 oz. (175 g.) *flour made into short pastry or use 8 oz. (250 g.) ready-made pastry*

Roll the pastry thinly and line the flan ring or pie plate with it. Prick the bottom with a fork and put the pastry to refrigerate while the filling is prepared.

> 4 *small rashers bacon*

Grill or fry until crisp. Leave to cool and then chop.

> 15 oz. (425 g.) *can of asparagus or 12 oz. (375 g.) cooked fresh or frozen asparagus*

Drain the asparagus and cut it in pieces about 1 in. (2½ cm.).

2 *eggs, beaten*	1 *tbs. finely chopped onion*
¼ *pt. (150 ml.) single cream*	1 *tsp. sugar*
2 *oz. (50 g.) finely grated strong cheese*	½ *tsp. salt*
Pepper	1 *tbs. chopped chervil*

Mix these together in a basin. Strew the chopped bacon in the pastry flan and add asparagus to make a good layer. Keep surplus asparagus for a garnish. Pour the egg mixture carefully over the asparagus and bake the flan until the filling is set and browned. Serve warm or cold.

AUBERGINES

Mint, basil, and marjoram are specially good in baked stuffed aubergines, or any recipe containing aubergines as an ingredient.

AVOCADO PEARS

Marjoram is good added to a vinaigrette dressing for avocados served plain, or add it to cocktails or salads containing avocados.

BEANS

For broad beans use fennel, parsley, savory, lemon thyme.

For *green beans* use marjoram, basil, dill.
For *dried beans* (butter, etc.) use parsley, thyme, sage, basil, mint.

BOILED BROAD BEANS WITH SAVORY

Boil the beans in a little salted water for 10–20 mins. until tender.
Drain and then toss in butter and finally in chopped savory.

BROAD BEANS IN FENNEL SAUCE

To serve with bacon, ham, pork, veal, lamb, or chicken.
COOKING TIME 20–30 mins.   QUANTITIES FOR 4.
  2–4 lb. (1–2 kg.) beans depending on the fullness of the pods; or
  1 lb. (½ kg.) shelled or frozen beans
Shell the beans and put them in a little lightly salted water. Boil until
tender, 10–20 mins, depending on their age. Drain, keeping the liquid.
Put the beans to keep hot.
  ½ oz. (15 g.) butter or margarine
  ½ oz. (1½ tbs. or 15 g.) flour
  ½ pt. (250 ml.) bean stock or stock plus milk or single cream
Melt the butter or margarine in a saucepan large enough to take the
beans. Stir in the flour and cook a minute or so. Remove from the
heat and whisk in the liquid. Return to the heat, bring to the boil and
simmer for 5 mins.
  Salt and pepper   2 or more tbs. chopped fennel
Season the sauce, add the fennel, return the beans and allow them to
become hot before serving.

ITALIAN BEANS WITH SAGE

COOKING TIME 2 hrs. boiling, 25–30 mins. pressure cooking, or use
  canned beans.
QUANTITIES FOR 4.
  8 oz. (1 c. or 250 g.) haricot or butter beans, or 1 lb. (½ kg.)
    cooked or canned
  1 onion stuck with 3 or 4 cloves, or a few bacon rinds
  2 pt. (1½ l.) water
Boil the water and add the uncooked beans and onion or bacon rinds.
Boil very gently until the beans are tender when tested with a fork.
When using a pressure cooker be sure it is not more than ⅓–½ full
of beans and water. Drain the beans. Drain canned beans if used.

    4 tbs. (60 ml.) oil   2 tbs. concentrated tomato purée
    2 or more fresh sage leaves   Salt and pepper

Chop the sage leaves, heat oil and sage together and, when hot, add the beans and cook gently until the oil is absorbed. Add the tomato and season to taste. Serve hot as a vegetable or cold as part of a hors d'oeuvre.

WHITE BEAN SALAD

QUANTITIES FOR 4.

    1 lb. (½ kg.) cooked or canned butter beans or other white beans

Drain well.

    4 tbs. (60 ml.) olive oil   1 tbs. lemon juice
    Salt and pepper

Put the beans in a serving dish. Mix the oil, lemon juice, and seasoning and pour over the beans.

    Chopped fresh mint or dill

Sprinkle liberally over the beans and serve.

BEETROOT

In sauces for hot cooked beetroot, use fennel, caraway, dill, or parsley. In dressings for cold cooked beetroot, use horseradish, coriander, tarragon, basil, savory, capers, sorrel, mint, or parsley.

BEETROOT, APPLE AND POTATO SALAD

QUANTITIES FOR 3–4.

    4 oz. (125 g.) sliced pickled   Pinch each of ground coriander
       beetroot   seeds and caraway seeds
    4 oz. (125 g.) boiled potatoes,   1 small apple, sliced
       sliced   1 tsp. grated horseradish
                                                   3–4 tbs. French dressing

Add the horseradish and herb seeds to the dressing. Use this to mix with the salad ingredients. Leave to stand for about ½ hr. to allow the flavours to blend. Garnish with

    Sprigs of watercress or other salad greens

BEETROOT AND MINT SALAD

QUANTITIES FOR 4.

4 *medium-sized beetroot*   2 *tbs. chopped fresh mint*
3–4 *tbs. French dressing*   1 *small lettuce*

Skin and slice the beetroot. Wash and dry the lettuce and arrange nests of the lettuce on each plate or in one serving dish. Put the sliced beetroot in the centre of the lettuce, cover with dressing and sprinkle with the mint.

Alternative: Instead of lettuce use a bed of shredded chicory or sprigs of watercress. For beetroot salad as part of an hors d'oeuvre, serve just the dressed beetroot sprinkled with chopped fresh mint.

Chopped savory can be used instead of the mint.

BEETROOT IN DILL OR FENNEL SAUCE

COOKING TIME 5–10 mins.   QUANTITIES FOR 4.

1 *lb.* (½ *kg.*) *cooked beetroot*

Skin and chop coarsely.

1 *oz.* (25 *g.*) *butter*   1 *medium-sized onion, finely chopped*

Fry the onion in the butter until it is soft; add the beetroot.

Salt and pepper   Sugar

Season to taste.

½ *pt.* (250 *ml.*) *soured cream*

Stir in gently and heat to boiling.

2–4 *tbs. chopped dill or fennel*

Mix in and serve with hot meat dishes such as grilled gammon, pork chops, veal escalopes, or fish.

BEETROOT SALAD WITH HORSERADISH AND FENNEL

To serve with hot boiled meat, fried or grilled fish, or cold meat.

QUANTITIES FOR 4–6.

1 *lb.* (½ *kg.*) *cooked beetroot*

Skin the beetroot and slice it thinly. Arrange in a serving dish.

¼ *pt.* (150 *ml.*) *wine vinegar*   ¼ *pt.* (150 *ml.*) *water*
1 *tsp. salt*   2 *tbs. oil*
2 *oz.* (4 *tbs. or* 50 *g.*) *sugar*

Mix to dissolve the sugar

2 *oz.* (50 *g.*) *grated horseradish*   2 *tsp. chopped fresh fennel*

Sprinkle the horseradish and fennel over the beetroot and add the vinegar mixture.

BRUSSELS SPROUTS

See Cabbage. Use the same herbs as for fresh cabbage.

CABBAGE

Herb seeds are particularly good cooked with cabbage; also with sauerkraut. Use dill, fennel or caraway seeds. Fresh herbs to add to cooked cabbage are fennel, marjoram, and mint.

For cole slaw and other cabbage salads use chives, caraway leaves, dill, marjoram, nasturtium leaves, lovage, or sorrel.

COLE SLAW

Mix very finely sliced white cabbage with mayonnaise or other salad dressing and plenty of chopped fresh marjoram and chives. Serve plain or garnished with hard-boiled eggs cut in slices or coarsely chopped.

SAUERKRAUT SALAD WITH CAPERS

To serve with cold ham, pork, or sausages.
QUANTITIES FOR 4.

8 *oz.* (250 *g.*) *sauerkraut*

Put in a sieve or colander and squeeze gently to extract as much moisture as possible. Chop finely and put in a bowl.

2 *or more tbs. mayonnaise or*   Lemon juice
   salad oil   *Pinch of sugar*
   Salt

Mix with the sauerkraut, seasoning to taste. Put in a serving dish.

1–2 *tbs. capers*

Sprinkle over the salad and serve.

SAUERKRAUT WITH CARAWAY OR CAPERS

Serve this hot, with sausages, ham, or bacon.
COOKING TIME ½–1 hr.   QUANTITIES FOR 4.

1 oz. (25 g.) *lard*   1 *onion, chopped*

Heat the lard in a saucepan and cook the onion in it until it begins to colour.

1 *lb.* (½ *kg.*) *sauerkraut*

Add and cook for a few minutes.

¼ *pt.* (150 *ml.*) *white wine*   ¼ *pt.* (150 *ml.*) *water*

Add to the pan, bring to the boil, cover and boil gently until the sauerkraut is tender.

1 *tsp. potato flour blended*   ½ *tsp. sugar*
  with a little cold water   1 *tsp. caraway seeds or* 1 *tbs.*
Salt and pepper   *capers, or to taste*

Thicken the liquid in the pan with the blended potato flour and add seasonings to taste. Serve hot.

WHITE CABBAGE WITH CARAWAY SEEDS

COOKING TIME about 15 mins.   QUANTITIES FOR 4.
1 *lb.* (½ *kg.*) *finely sliced*   1 *oz.* (25 *g.*) *lard*
  white cabbage   1 *onion, finely chopped*

Put in a saucepan with just enough boiling water to moisten. Cover and cook gently until the cabbage is tender.

2 *tbs. lemon juice*   1 *tsp. caraway seeds*
Salt and pepper

Stir into the cabbage.

1 *tsp. flour*

Sprinkle over the cabbage, mix in and cook for a few minutes longer. Serve hot.

Alternative: Use dill or fennel seeds in place of caraway.

CARROTS

Parsley is the traditional herb for carrots: carrots with parsely sauce, Vichy carrots dressed with parsley.

Either of these can be adapted for using other herbs which have an affinity with the flavour of carrots, for example, instead of adding parsley to the sauce for boiled carrots, use marjoram, basil, savory, thyme, or even the green leaves of anise or caraway. All these herbs are also suitable for salads containing carrots.

Vichy carrots can be sprinkled with chopped marjoram, mint (very good when serving them with lamb), basil, savory, or thyme.

VICHY CARROTS

COOKING TIME 15–20 mins.   QUANTITIES FOR 4.

1 *lb.* (½ *kg.*) *young carrots*

Wash and, if necessary, scrape the carrots. Remove the tops and cut large carrots in pieces, leave small ones whole.

1 *oz.* (25 *g.*) *butter*   1 *tsp. sugar*
½ *tsp. salt*

Melt the butter in a saucepan or casserole and add the other ingredients with the carrots. Cover and cook until the carrots are tender. Do this on top or in a moderately hot oven.

1 *tbs. chopped fresh herbs* (see above)

Sprinkle over the carrots and serve hot.

CARROT, APPLE, AND CELERY SALAD

QUANTITIES FOR 4.

2 *c.* (½ *l.*) *raw grated carrot*   2 *c.* (½ *l.*) *raw grated apple*
½ *c.* (150 *ml.*) *chopped celery*   *French dressing*
1 *tbs. chopped chives*   1 *tbs. chopped marjoram*

Combine the ingredients with enough dressing to moisten. Serve plain or on a bed of salad greens.

CAULIFLOWER

To cook with it, use dill leaves or seeds, caraway seeds or sorrel leaves. To sprinkle over the cauliflower when cooked, or to add to a sauce, use marjoram, savory, parsley, chervil. The same herbs are good with raw or cooked cauliflower salads.

CAULIFLOWER SALAD

Boil cauliflower sprigs in a little salted water until they are barely tender. Drain well and leave to become cold.

Make a mayonnaise using lemon juice instead of vinegar, add enough chopped fresh fennel or dill to give a good flavour. Arrange the cauliflower in a serving dish and mask it with the mayonnaise.

CAULIFLOWER, CHEESE, AND CHERVIL SALAD

Serve this as part of an hors d'oeuvre or as a salad on its own.

COOKING TIME 5–10 mins.   QUANTITIES FOR 4.

1 *medium-sized cauliflower*
Wash, break into sprigs, and put in a little boiling salted water. Boil until barely tender as the salad is not pleasant if the cauliflower is too soft. Drain and cool. Arrange in a shallow dish.

4 *oz.* (125 g.) *sieved cottage cheese*   2 *egg yolks*
Beat together thoroughly in a small basin, using a whisk or wooden spoon.

3–4 *tbs. oil*
Beat in gradually adding as much as needed to produce the desired consistency, like a thick mayonnaise.

2 *tsp. lemon juice or* 1 *tsp.*   *Plenty of chopped fresh chervil*
 vinegar   ½ *tsp. French mustard*
Salt and pepper   *A pinch of sugar*
Beat into the cottage cheese and refrigerate the dressing until ready to serve the salad.

Anchovy fillets and sprigs of chervil to garnish
Mask the cauliflower with the dressing and garnish to taste.

CELERY

To flavour celery during cooking, add whole bay leaves. Use chives or parsley to sprinkle over cooked celery or in a sauce.

CELERY, APPLE, AND BEETROOT SALAD WITH FENNEL

QUANTITIES FOR 4.
2 *sticks celery, chopped*   2 *apples, peeled and chopped*
1 *medium-sized beetroot, diced*   1 *tbs. chopped fennel*
French dressing
Combine the salad ingredients with dressing and sprinkle with the chopped fennel.

CHICORY

For cooked or raw chicory use chopped chives, parsley, marjoram, or tarragon.

CHICORY, CHICKEN, AND CHEESE SALAD WITH TARRAGON

QUANTITIES FOR 4.

4 oz. (125 g.) *cottage cheese*   *Cream or top of milk*
Salt and pepper   *Lemon juice*
Horseradish sauce

Mash the cheese with enough cream or top of milk to make it soft and smooth but not runny. Season it very well.

8 oz. (250 g.) *cold, cooked chicken, diced*

Mix into the cottage cheese just before you are ready to serve the salad.

2 *large pieces of chicory*   1–2 *tbs. French dressing*

Separate the chicory pieces into leaves and dress them. Either put individual portions on plates or put it all in a shallow serving dish. Put the chicken and cheese mixture in a heap in the middle.

1 *large orange*   *Chopped fresh tarragon*

Peel the orange and cut it in very thin slices. Use this as a garnish, finally sprinkling the salad generously with the fresh tarragon.

COURGETTES OR MARROW

Having little flavour of their own, these vegetables are improved by the addition of any herbs, especially good being basil, caraway, marjoram, mint, and thyme.

COURGETTES WITH MINT

COOKING TIME 15–20 mins.   QUANTITIES FOR 4.
1 *lb.* (½ *kg.*) *courgettes*   1 oz. (25 g.) *butter*
Salt and pepper

Wash the courgettes. Cut off the stems. If they are 3 in. (8 cm.) or less in length leave them whole, but cut longer ones in pieces. Melt the butter in a saucepan, add the courgettes and seasoning, cover and stew gently until they are just tender. Shake the pan occasionally to turn the courgettes in the butter.

Chopped fresh mint

Sprinkle on generously just before serving.

Alternative: Instead of mint use marjoram, thyme, or basil.

COURGETTES OR MARROW WITH TOMATOES

COOKING TIME 35 mins.   QUANTITIES FOR 4.

2 lb. (1 kg.) marrow or 1 lb. (½ kg.) courgettes

Wash courgettes, trim the ends, and cut in slices about 1 in. (2½ cm.) thick. Peel marrow and remove the seeds before cutting the flesh in small pieces.

8 oz. (250 g.) tomatoes   *1 oz. (25 g.) fat or 2 tbs. oil*
1 medium onion, chopped

Wash and slice the tomatoes. Heat the fat or oil in a saucepan and fry the onion and tomatoes for about 5 mins. If oil is used the dish is suitable for serving cold as a salad or hors d'oeuvre.

Salt and pepper   *½ tsp. sugar*
¼ pt. (150 ml.) stock   *2 tsp. chopped basil, marjoram,*
A little crushed or powdered   *or thyme*
garlic

Add to the pan together with the prepared marrow or courgettes, cover and cook gently until the vegetables are just tender.

Chopped parsley or some more of the herbs used in cooking
Serve garnished with chopped herbs.

COURGETTE SALAD WITH MINT AND CHIVES

COOKING TIME 20 mins.   QUANTITIES FOR 4–6.

1 lb. (½ kg.) courgettes

Wash, trim the ends, and boil the courgettes in a little salted water until they are only just tender. Drain and allow to become cold. Cut diagonally in ¼-in. (½-cm.) slices. Arrange in a shallow serving dish.

4 tbs. olive oil   *3 tbs. lemon juice*
1 tsp. sugar   *½ tsp. salt*
Pepper   *1 tbs. chopped mint*
1 tbs. chopped chives

Mix together and pour over the courgettes.

MARROW WITH CARAWAY

COOKING TIME 20–30 mins.   QUANTITIES FOR 3–4.

1 medium-sized onion, chopped   *2 tbs. oil*

Heat the oil in a saucepan and fry the onion in it until it just begins to brown.

1 lb. (½ kg.) marrow   Salt
Pinch of caraway seeds

Peel the marrow, remove the seeds, and cut the flesh in about 1-in. (2½-cm.) pieces. Add to the pan, with salt and caraway seeds and fry for 5 mins.

2 tbs. flour   ¼ pt. (150 ml.) water

Sprinkle the flour over the marrow, stir in, and then stir in the water to make a sauce. Simmer until the marrow is tender.

1 tsp. vinegar   1 tsp. sugar
Chopped parsley

Add the vinegar and sugar and serve garnished with parsley.
Alternative: Garnish with chopped grilled or fried bacon.

CUCUMBER

To chop and sprinkle over cucumber salads, use chervil, dill, chives, fennel, nasturtium leaves, or parsley. The same herbs are suitable for adding to dishes of cooked cucumber, for example, stuffed cucumber, or in sauces or soups.

CUCUMBER AND MELON SALAD

QUANTITIES FOR 4–6.

1 pt. (½ l.) peeled, diced cucumber
1 pt. (½ l.) peeled, diced melon
4 tbs. (60 ml.) French dressing made with lemon juice
A sprinkling of caster sugar
4 tbs. chopped mixed dill, mint, and tarragon in equal quantities.

Combine the cucumber and melon with the dressing and sugar. Sprinkle the salad with the chopped herbs.

CUCUMBER AND NASTURTIUM SALAD

This salad is pretty to look at and very refreshing to eat, including the flowers.

Cucumber, peeled and sliced very thinly
French dressing made with a herb vinegar

Put the cucumber in a shallow serving dish and add a generous quantity of dressing. Leave to marinate for at least ½ hr.

Nasturtium flowers and small leaves

Be sure to wash the flowers well under a running tap, or soak in cold water to draw out any insects. Wash the leaves gently under running water. Drain both well.

Just before serving, put flowers and leaves in a garland round the cucumber.

LEEKS

Use the same herbs as those recommended for onions (p. 204).

LEEKS VINAIGRETTE WITH THYME

To serve as a salad with hot or cold meat, or as a starter.
COOKING TIME 10–20 mins.

8 *small to medium-sized leeks*

Trim off all the green tops and the roots and wash the leeks very thoroughly bending back the tops and holding them under running water. Boil in a little salted water until they are just tender. Drain well and dress and serve before they become quite cold.

3–4 *tbs. French dressing   Chopped fresh thyme*

Spoon the dressing over the leeks while they are still warm and sprinkle them generously with chopped thyme. If you only have dried thyme soak this in the dressing for $\frac{1}{2}$ hr. or so before pouring it over the leeks. Alternatively, use a herb oil or vinegar for making the dressing.

LETTUCE

For salads use any fresh chopped herbs or herb leaves; or flavour dressings with dried herbs (see p. 126).

MARROW

See Courgettes (pp. 200–201).

MUSHROOMS

Chopped or dried herbs can be sprinkled on mushrooms before grilling, added to fried mushrooms, or to a mushroom sauce or soup. Alternatively, sprinkle fresh chopped herbs on the mushrooms after grilling or frying. Recommended herbs: marjoram, mint, and tarragon.

ONIONS AND LEEKS

Herbs with a fairly strong flavour are the best for these vegetables, for example, basil, sage, tarragon, or thyme.

BAKED STUFFED ONIONS WITH SAGE

Serve these as a dish on their own or to accompany meat, for example, roast lamb or pork.

COOKING TIME about 20 mins. to boil the onions, then 40–50 mins. for baking. TEMPERATURE E. 400° (200°C.) G.6

QUANTITIES FOR 4.

4 large Spanish onions

Remove the outer skins and boil the onions in salted water until they are almost tender but still firm enough to keep their shape. Drain and cool.

Using a small pointed knife, remove most of the centre of the onion, keeping just enough of the original to hold the shape. Put the onions in a baking dish. Chop the rest of the onion and put it in a basin.

1 oz. (⅓ c. or 25 g.) *fresh breadcrumbs*	*Salt and pepper* ½ *tsp. paprika pepper*
2 oz. (½ c. or 50 g.) *grated strong cheese*	8–10 *large sage leaves, finely chopped*
¼ *tsp. ground mace*	

Add to the chopped onions and mix well.

½ *pt. (250 ml.) soured cream or use fresh double cream with a squeeze of lemon*

Use a little of the cream to bind the stuffing together. Fill the onions, piling up the tops. Pour remaining cream round and over the onions and bake until they are quite tender. Serve with the cream.

ORANGE SALAD WITH TARRAGON AND CHERVIL

QUANTITIES FOR 4.

  4 *oranges*

Peel the oranges and remove all pith. Slice into thin rounds removing the pips.

  Chopped fresh tarragon and chervil

Sprinkle generously over the oranges.

  2 *tbs. olive oil*   1 *tbs. vinegar*
  2 *tsp. lemon juice*

Mix these and pour over the oranges. Leave to marinate for a while.

  Watercress or other green garnish

Serve the salad on individual plates, and garnish with greenery.

PARSNIPS

Fennel is one of the best herbs for this vegetable, used generously. Also suitable are any of the other herbs with a strong flavour, such as basil, thyme, marjoram.

PEAS

Sprigs of mint are traditional for cooking with green peas but other herbs can be used in the same way: dill, tarragon, basil, or savory. Fresh chopped herbs are best of all, added when the cooked peas are tossed in butter just before serving them.

PEPPERS (sweet)

Recommended herbs for recipes made with peppers are basil, marjoram, or rosemary. Use them in cooked dishes or salads.

ITALIAN DISH OF GREEN PEPPERS

COOKING TIME ½–¾ hr.   QUANTITIES FOR 4.

   1 *medium onion, chopped*   2 *tbs. olive oil*

Heat the oil in a sauté pan or saucepan and cook the onions in it gently until they are just beginning to colour.

   4 *large green peppers*   1 *lb.* (½ *kg.*) *tomatoes*
   Garlic to taste   *Salt and pepper*
   1 *tbs. finely chopped fresh*
     rosemary

Cut the peppers in half, remove seeds and white pith and cut the halves in pieces about 1 in. (2½ cm.) square. Add all these ingredients to the onions, cover and cook gently until the peppers are just tender. Serve hot or cold.

POTATOES

Boiling sprigs of mint with new potatoes is traditional; bay leaves and sprigs of dill or fennel are good cooked with new or old potatoes. To sprinkle on cooked potatoes, or mix with mashed potatoes use chives, parsley, dill, fennel, mint, basil, or tarragon.

For baked jacket potatoes, plain or stuffed, use either chopped fresh herbs or one of the Herb butters (pp. 127–9).

Mashed potato powder is vastly improved if a good knob of butter is added and enough finely chopped chives to make it look green. Alternatively add a generous knob of herb butter. The same treatment can be given to freshly cooked mashed potatoes; or add herb sprigs when boiling the potatoes and then mash together.

Herbs are also a great improvement in potato salads; add to salads dressed in the usual way with French or other dressing, or use one of the recipes given below.

POTATO SALAD WITH CARAWAY AND MINT

QUANTITIES FOR 4.

   1 *lb.* (½ *kg.*) *cooked diced potatoes*

The salad is better if the potatoes are freshly cooked.

   ½ *pt.* (250 *ml.*) *thick yogurt*   1 *tsp. caraway seeds*
   1 *tsp. curry powder or to taste*   1 *tsp. salt*
   2 *tbs. finely chopped onion*   2 *tbs. scissor-snipped mint*

Combine thoroughly and pour over the potatoes. Mix gently and then refrigerate until the potatoes are well chilled.

POTATO SALAD WITH CHIVES AND BAY

COOKING TIME about 20 mins.　　　QUANTITIES FOR 4.

　1 *lb.* (½ *kg.*) *new potatoes*

Scrub the potatoes removing some, but not all of the skin. This is to allow the flavour of the onion and herbs to penetrate.

　1 *large or 2 small bay leaves*　1 *small onion, skinned*

Boil the potatoes, with bay leaves and onion, in salted water until they are just tender. Drain and allow to cool enough to handle. Skin and cut in slices. Include the onion but discard the bay.

　2-3 *tbs. French dressing*　　*Chopped chives or other herbs*

Dress the still warm potatoes and combine with the chopped herbs. Allow to become cold before serving.

POTATO AND FISH SALAD WITH CHERVIL

COOKING TIME about 15 mins.　　　QUANTITIES FOR 4-6.

　1 *lb.* (½ *kg.*) *fish fillets*

Poach the fish in a court bouillon or in salted water. Drain, remove skin, and flake the fish. Leave to become cold.

　8 *oz.* (250 *g.*) *dessert apples,*　*French dressing or mayonnaise*
　　peeled and diced　　　　　2 *tbs. chopped parsley*
　8 *oz.* (250 *g.*) *cold, boiled*　　2 *tbs. chopped chervil*
　　potatoes, diced　　　　　2 *tbs. finely chopped onion*

Combine these with the fish using enough dressing to moisten well.

PAPRIKA POTATOES

To serve with frankfurters or other sausages, or with pork.

COOKING TIME 40–50 mins.　　　QUANTITIES FOR 4.

　1 *oz.* (25 *g.*) *fat or 2 tbs. oil*　1 *medium onion, chopped*

Heat the fat or oil in a saucepan and fry the onion gently until it begins to brown.

　3 *tbs. flour*　　　　　　　1 *tsp. paprika pepper*

Add and mix well, stirring and cooking for a minute or so.

　1 *tbs. wine vinegar*　　　　2 *tsp. salt*
　½ *pt.* (250 *ml.*) *stock or water*　¼ *tsp. caraway seeds*
　1 *tbs. fresh chopped marjoram*
　　or 1 tsp. dried

Add to the pan, stir until boiling.

1 ½ *lb. (750 g.) potatoes*

Peel and cut in pieces about half the size of an egg. Add to the pan, mix, cover, and cook very gently until the potatoes are tender but not broken.

If frankfurters or other cooked sausages are being served with the potatoes, add them towards the end of the cooking time and let them heat through on top of the potatoes.

SORREL

A few leaves cooked with other vegetables add a refreshing sharp flavour, likewise when added to a mixed salad. Sorrel purée is served as a vegetable in small amounts as an accompaniment for meat and egg dishes.

SORREL PURÉE

See Sorrel Omelet (p. 142).

SORREL AND LETTUCE SALAD

Use equal quantities of sorrel leaves and lettuce leaves
French dressing, 3–4 tbs. for a salad for 4
Fines herbs, 1–2 tbs. for a salad for 4

Wash and drain the sorrel and lettuce. Pick French sorrel leaves from the stalks, shred English sorrel or tear the leaves in small pieces.

Tear the lettuce leaves in small pieces and combine with the sorrel. Dress the salad just before serving, adding the herbs at the same time.

SPINACH

For flavouring cooked spinach, leaf or purée, use either chopped fresh marjoram or mint.

TOMATOES

For adding to cooked tomato dishes including sprinkling on tomatoes before grilling, use chopped basil, marjoram, sage, or thyme. For adding to tomato salads use basil, chervil, parsley, savory, tarragon, or a mixture. These salads are nicest if the tomatoes are just dressed with salt, pepper, and olive oil before sprinkling on the fresh herbs, omit vinegar or lemon juice, but add a sprinkling of sugar, if liked.

TURNIPS

Recommended for sprinkling on cooked turnips are fresh chopped chives or fennel.

Very good are young turnips stewed gently in a little butter until just tender (about 20 mins.), seasoned with salt and pepper and sprinkled with chopped fresh fennel, about 1 tbs. to 1 lb. (½ kg.) turnips.

CHAPTER THIRTEEN

Stuffings, rice, pasta and pancakes

STUFFINGS

RECOMMENDED HERBS FOR FISH STUFFINGS:

Balm (generously)	Mint	Sorrel
Chervil	Parsley	Tarragon
Fennel	Savory	Thyme (lemon)

RECOMMENDED HERBS FOR LAMB, MUTTON, OR PORK STUFFINGS:

Coriander	Rosemary	Savory
Mint	Sage	Thyme
Parsley		

RECOMMENDED HERBS FOR POULTRY STUFFINGS:

Balm (generously)	Mint	Savory
Curry leaf (a little)	Parsley	Tarragon
Marjoram	Rosemary	Thyme (lemon)

RECOMMENDED HERBS FOR VEAL STUFFINGS:

Balm (generously)	Mint
Marjoram	Rosemary

CHEESE AND ROSEMARY STUFFING

For roast lamb, mutton, veal, or chicken
Quantities for a medium-sized shoulder of lamb or a small chicken.

2 oz. (⅔ c. or 50 g.) fresh breadcrumbs
1 oz. (¼ c. or 25 g.) grated strong cheese
2 oz. (50 g.) very finely chopped onion
1 tsp. concentrated tomato purée
1–2 tsp. finely chopped fresh rosemary, or ½ tsp. dried
½ oz. (15 g.) melted butter
1 egg, beaten
Pinch of pepper
2 tbs. white wine
½ tsp. salt

Combine the ingredients thoroughly, adding more wine if it is needed to bind the mixture together. Stuff the meat just before cooking it.

If preferred, the onion can be par-boiled before chopping it. This gives a milder flavour and ensures that it will be cooked.

CHICKEN STUFFING

QUANTITIES FOR a small chicken.

2 oz. (⅔ c. or 50 g.) *fresh breadcrumbs*

2 oz. (6 *tbs.* or 50 g.) *grated suet*

½ *tsp. grated lemon rind*

Pinch of ground mace or nutmeg

2 *tsp. fresh chopped thyme or savory or* 1 *tsp. dried*

1 *egg, beaten*

½ *tsp. salt*

1 *tbs. chopped parsley*

Pinch of pepper

Milk to mix

Mix all the ingredients together.

Alternative: Fry the chicken liver in a little fat, then chop it and mix with the stuffing.

FISH STUFFING WITH TARRAGON OR SAVORY

This can be used to stuff a whole large fish or small one. It is very good as a stuffing for rolled fillets of plaice or sole. Pack the rolls in a flat baking dish, pour in a little white wine to moisten, and bake.

QUANTITIES FOR 4.

1 oz. (⅓ c. or 25 g.) *breadcrumbs*

1 oz. (¼ c. or 25 g.) *finely chopped hazel nuts*

Prepare and put in a basin.

1 *rasher bacon, chopped*   1 *slice onion, finely chopped*

Heat the bacon in a small pan and when the fat runs, add the onion and fry until it begins to brown. Add to the crumbs.

1 *tbs. chopped parsley*

¼ *tsp. celery salt*

1 *egg, beaten*

½ *tbs. lemon juice*

Pinch of pepper

1 *tsp. chopped savory or tarragon, or to taste*

Combine thoroughly with the other ingredients.

MINT STUFFING

Use to stuff lamb or mutton for roasting, or chicken or pork.
QUANTITIES to stuff a boned shoulder of lamb or a small chicken.

 4 tbs. finely chopped onion   1½ oz. (40 g.) butter or
                margarine

Fry the onion in a little of the fat. When it is soft, add the rest of
the fat and leave to melt.

 4 oz. (1½ c. or 125 g.) fresh   1 tsp. salt
  breadcrumbs   1 tbs. sugar
 3 tbs. chopped parsley   ¼ pt. (150 ml.) chopped fresh
 Pinch of pepper   mint

Mix all these with the melted fat and onion and allow to become
cold before using.

PRUNE AND ROSEMARY STUFFING

Suitable for pork or poultry.

 6 prunes

Soak in cold water for an hour or until soft enough for the stones
to be removed. Chop the flesh and put it in a mixing bowl.

 1 medium-sized onion, sliced   1½ oz. (40 g.) margarine

Heat the margarine in a small pan and stew the onion in it until
tender but not brown. Add to the prunes.

 3 oz. (1 c. or 75 g.) fresh   Salt and pepper
  breadcrumbs   1 egg, beaten
 1 tsp. chopped fresh rosemary
  leaves

Add to the prunes and onion and mix thoroughly.

RICE STUFFING WITH ROSEMARY

This is very good for stuffing lamb or mutton when roasted or
braised, but it is also suitable for stuffed hearts, liver, poultry, or
veal.

QUANTITIES FOR a medium-sized shoulder of lamb.

 3 oz. (6 tbs. or 75 g.) rice

Boil the rice according to the directions on the packet (or see
p. 214).

4 *rashers bacon, chopped*	½ *tsp. grated lemon rind*
1 *lamb's kidney*	*Salt and pepper*
2 *oz. (⅓ c. or 50 g.) sultanas*	1 *egg or 2 yolks*
½ *tsp. chopped fresh rosemary*	
or ¼ *dried*	

Remove the core and skin and chop the kidney. Mix all the ingredients with the cooked rice and stuff the meat just before cooking it. If the stuffing is prepared in advance, cover and refrigerate.

SAGE AND ONION STUFFING

For goose, duck, or pork.
QUANTITIES FOR 1 small goose or 2 ducks.

4 *large onions*

Skin, and boil in a little salted water for 5 mins. Drain and allow to cool.

10 *fresh sage leaves or* 1 *tsp. dried*

Dip fresh sage leaves in boiling water for a minute. Dry. Chop or mince the sage and onion.

1 *oz. (25 g.) melted butter or*	2 *tsp. salt*
margarine	¼ *tsp. pepper*
4 *oz. (1*½ *c. or 125 g.) fresh*	
breadcrumbs	

Mix all the ingredients together. This may be prepared in advance but do not stuff the bird or pork until just before cooking it.
Alternative: Shape the stuffing into small balls and cook these under or round the meat, or in a separate pan.

WALNUT STUFFING

Specially good with pheasant but also suitable for poultry or pork.
QUANTITIES FOR 1–2 pheasants or a small to medium-sized chicken.

8 *oz. (250 g.) chopped or coarsely minced lean pork*
1½ *oz. (40 g.) butter*

Melt the butter and fry the pork in it until it is cooked through.

1 *oz. (⅓ c. or 25 g.)*	*Pinch of pepper*
breadcrumbs	1 *tsp. chopped thyme*
2 *oz. (¼ c. or 50 g.) chopped*	1 *tsp. salt*
walnuts	2 *tbs. red wine*
2 *tbs. chopped parsley*	½ *egg or* 1 *yolk, beaten*

Mix all these together with the pork and butter. Use straight away or cool and then refrigerate until required. Do not stuff the bird or meat until just before it is to be cooked.

RICE

BOILED RICE WITH HERBS

To serve hot with any meat, poultry, or fish.

COOKING TIME about 15 mins.   QUANTITIES FOR 4.

    8 *oz. (250 g.) long grain rice*   1 *tsp. salt*
    1 *pt. (½ l.) cold water*

Wash the rice by putting it in a sieve and letting cold water run through it. Put in a pan with the water and salt. Bring to the boil, stir once, cover and simmer for 15 mins. without lifting the lid. Test a few grains to see if it is cooked. Fluff it up with a fork, cover, and put in a warm place for a few minutes.

    2 *or more tbs. chopped fresh herbs (thyme, parsley, chives, marjoram)*

Add plenty of the herbs to give a good flavour, using just one herb or a mixture according to the dish it will accompany.

FRIED RICE WITH HERBS

To serve with meat, poultry, or fish. Rice can be boiled in advance and kept covered, in the refrigerator.

COOKING TIME a few mins.   QUANTITIES FOR 4.

    1 *lb. (2 c. or ½ kg.) dry*   4 *tbs. mixed chopped herbs*
    cooked rice (8 oz. (250 g.)   *Salt and pepper*
    raw rice)   1 *small onion, finely chopped*
    2 *tbs. olive oil or* 1 *oz. (25 g.)*
    butter

Heat the oil or butter in a pan and fry the onion until it softens. Add the rice and stir and heat until all the oil or butter is absorbed and the rice is beginning to brown. Season to taste and add the herbs.

This is specially good served with lamb. Use olive oil for frying and for the herbs, dill, rosemary, tarragon, and thyme, mixed.

LAMB PILAU WITH FENNEL

COOKING TIME about 1 hr.   QUANTITIES FOR 4–6.

8 *oz.* (250 *g.*) *rice*
Wash and drain.

1½ *lb.* (750 *g.*) *leg lamb,*   2 *tbs. lemon juice*
  boneless

Cut the meat in small pieces and sprinkle it with lemon juice.

2 *oz.* (50 *g.*) *butter*

Heat in a large heavy saucepan, add the rice and cook gently for about 10 mins., without browning. Stir frequently.

¼ *pt.* (150 *ml.*) *double cream*   ¼ *pt.* (150 *ml.*) *thick yogurt*
½ *pt.* (250 *ml.*) *lamb or*   *Pinch of ground cloves*
  chicken stock   *Pinch of ground cinnamon*
1 *tbs. chopped fennel*   *Salt and pepper*
Pinch of ground cumin seeds

Add to the rice, mix, cover and cook gently for 15 mins. on top or in the oven E. 350° (180°C.) G.4.

2 *oz.* (50 *g.*) *butter*

Heat in a frying pan, drain any liquid from the meat and fry the meat in the butter until it changes colour. Add it and the drained liquid to the rice, mix and continue cooking until the meat is tender (about ½ hr.). Remove the lid and let the rice dry for a few minutes before serving.

LIVER PILAFF WITH HERBS

In this recipe the herbs are used to flavour the rice during cooking. As an alternative, sprinkle the finished pilaff with chopped fresh herbs.

COOKING TIME 45 mins.   QUANTITIES FOR 4–6.

2 *oz.* (50 *g.*) *butter*   1 *or* 2 *bay leaves or* 1–2 *sprigs*
1 *pt.* (½ *l.*) *chicken stock*   *fennel or sage*

Put in a large pan and bring to the boil.

8 *oz.* (1 *c. or* 250 *g.*) *long grain rice*

Add to the stock, stir, and then cook very slowly. This can be done in a slow oven E. 350° (180°C.) G.4. Cook until the rice is quite tender, 20–30 mins., and the stock all absorbed.

Salt and pepper

Remove the herbs, season the rice to taste and mound it on a hot serving dish or pack into a border mould or individual moulds. Keep hot.

8–12 *oz.* (250–375 *g.*) *liver*   1–2 *oz.* (25–50 *g.*) *butter*
Salt and pepper

Cut the liver in small cubes. Chicken livers can be left whole or cut in two or three pieces, according to their size. Heat the butter and fry the liver in it until lightly browned and beads of blood begin to appear on the surface. Season and pile on top of the rice. Serve with

Grilled tomatoes   Salad or green peas

RICE WITH EGG AND MINT

This makes a delicious rice dish to eat on its own with an accompanying salad or to serve with meat, for example, chicken, lamb, pork, or veal.

COOKING TIME 20 mins. QUANTITIES FOR 2–4.

 8 *oz.* (1 *c. or* 250 *g.*) *long grain rice* 1 *pt.* (½ *l.*) *water*
 1 *tsp. salt*

Put in a pan, bring to the boil, stir, cover and cook over a gentle heat for 15 mins. Then test. It should be tender and the water all absorbed. If necessary remove the lid and allow the rice to dry.

 2 *eggs, beaten*   1 *tbs. lemon juice*
 1 *oz.* (25 *g.*) *grated Parmesan*
  cheese

Combine and stir into the hot rice.

 2 *tsp. chopped mint, or more to taste*

Stir in gently and serve.

RICE SALAD

COOKING TIME 15 mins. QUANTITIES FOR 4.

 4 *oz.* (125 *g.*) *rice*   ½ *tsp. salt*
 ½ *pt.* (250 *ml.*) *water*

Put in a pan, bring to the boil, stir once, cover and reduce the heat to simmering, cooking until all the water is absorbed. Stir with a fork to fluff up the rice.

 3 *tbs. French dressing*

Dress the rice while it is still hot and then put it aside to become cold.

 8 *oz.* (250 *g.*) *of cooked chicken or shellfish or a mixture of these*
  with some hard-boiled eggs; or a mixture of chicken, ham
  and egg.
 Diced cucumber   *A few raisins*
 Chopped green pepper or *Chopped tomato*
  celery   *Plenty of chopped fresh herbs*

The ingredients can be varied according to what is available and the herbs can be just one kind or a mixture. Mix the ingredients with the rice.

Lettuce leaves

Line the salad bowl with washed and dried leaves and pile the rice mixture in the centre.

RISOTTO WITH HERBS

COOKING TIME 20–30 mins.   QUANTITIES FOR 4–6.

4 *oz.* (125 *g.*) *fat or* 8 *tbs.* (120 *ml.*) *oil*
6 *oz.* (175 *g.*) *onions, chopped*

Heat the fat or oil in a heavy frying pan or sauté pan (about 9–10 in. (23–25 cm.)). Fry the onions in the fat until they begin to brown.

12 *oz.* (1½ *c. or* 375 *g.*) *rice*

Add the raw rice to the pan and cook for a few minutes longer, stirring all the time.

2 *pt.* (1 *l.*) *chicken or other white stock*

Add about a quarter of the stock to the rice and cook gently for 15–20 mins., adding the rest of the stock gradually. By the time the rice is cooked all the stock should be absorbed.

4 *tbs.* (60 *ml.*) *chopped fresh*   8 *oz.* (250 *g.*) *meat or fish*
   herbs, one kind or a   *Fat for frying*
   mixture, as available   *Salt and pepper*

For the meat use small pieces of liver, kidney, chicken, veal, or pork and fry the meat brown in a little fat. Otherwise use shellfish or mushrooms, or a mixture of ingredients. Just before serving, season the rice well, add the herbs and the cooked meat or fish and serve hot.

2 *oz.* (50 *g.*) *grated cheese*

Serve the cheese separately to be sprinkled on the risotto at table.

SAFFRON RICE

COOKING TIME 20–25 mins.   QUANTITIES FOR 4.

8 *oz.* (1 *c. or* 250 *g.*) *long grain*   2 *bay leaves*
   rice   *A good pinch of ground cloves*
1 *pt.* (½ *l.*) *white stock or*   *and cinnamon*
   water   *Pepper*
1 *tsp. salt*   *Pinch of saffron shreds*

Put the saffron in a small basin, pour boiling water over it and leave to become cold. Strain, and add to the stock to make it yellow.

Put all the ingredients in a pan, bring to the boil, stir and cover. Reduce the heat to simmering or put the pan in a moderate oven. Test the rice after 15 mins. (no hard core in the middle when a few grains are squeezed). All the water should be absorbed by this time. To dry it, fluff with a fork, cover, stand the pan in a warm place for 5–10 mins. Do not keep it hot enough to continue cooking or it will become a sticky mess. Remove the bay leaves before serving.

Alternative: Infusing marigold petals in hot stock is quite a good substitute for saffron, though not as bright a yellow, nor the same flavour (see p. 46).

PASTA

Spaghetti, macaroni, and noodles can all be flavoured with herbs simply by boiling the pasta in water containing sprigs of the chosen herb. Bay leaves are the best for this method as other herbs tend to disintegrate and you may not like having bits of herb among the pasta.

An alternative method is to cook the pasta in plain water and salt and add chopped herbs after draining and before serving it. The choice of herbs will depend on the dish which the pasta will accompany, for example, rosemary is very good with pasta to serve with pork or beef, basil for veal or beef, and marjoram for any meat.

When the pasta is to be served with a meat sauce the herbs can either be cooked with the pasta or added to the sauce, or both.

BUTTERED NOODLES WITH BAY LEAVES

To serve with meat or poultry in place of potatoes.

COOKING TIME about 10 mins.   QUANTITIES FOR 4.

8 oz. (250 g.) *egg noodles*   Salt
2 *bay leaves*

Boil about 3 pt. (1½ l.) water in a large pan with ½ tbs. salt and the bay leaves. Add the noodles and boil rapidly with the lid off until they are just tender. If the noodle packet gives a cooking time, follow this. Remove the bay leaves.

1–2 oz. (25–50 g.) *butter*

Melt in the pan and toss the noodles in the butter to coat well. Serve as soon as possible.

NOODLES WITH HAM, CHEESE, AND HERBS

To serve as a main dish.

COOKING TIME about 15 mins.   QUANTITIES FOR 4.

1 *lb.* (½ *kg.*) *egg noodles*

Boil these according to directions on the packet or boil them in plenty of salted water until they are just tender, usually about 8–10 mins. Avoid over-cooking or the noodles will clump together. Drain the noodles and rinse the pan.

4–6 *oz.* (125–175 g.) *butter*   8 *oz.* (250 g.) *diced cooked ham*

1 *tbs. chopped marjoram, tarragon, basil, or thyme, or mixed*

Melt the butter in the pan and add the ham, heating for a minute, then return the noodles and mix them well with the butter and ham. Add the herbs and mix them in.

2 *oz.* (50 g.) *grated Parmesan or other strong cheese*

Mix with the noodles or serve separately, according to taste. Serve hot.

Alternative: Prepare macaroni in the same way with or without the ham.

SPAGHETTI WITH MEAT SAUCE

COOKING TIME 1 hr.   QUANTITIES FOR 4.

8 *oz.* (250 g.) *minced lean*   4 *tbs. olive oil*
  beef   1 *medium-sized onion, chopped*
½ *clove crushed garlic or a*
  pinch of dried garlic

Heat the oil and fry the meat, garlic, and onion in it until the meat loses its red colour.

1 *oz.* (25 g.) *mushrooms, chopped*

Add to the meat and fry for about 10 mins.

1 *lb.* (½ kg.) *can of whole tomatoes*   *Salt and pepper*
2 *tbs. concentrated tomato purée*

Add to the meat and simmer for about ½ hr. or until the sauce is thick.

½–1 *tbs. chopped marjoram or basil or* 1–2 *tsp. dried*

Add herbs to taste.

½–1 *lb.* (¼–½ kg.) *spaghetti*

Boil the spaghetti according to the directions on the packet, or in plenty of boiling salted water for about 10 mins. Drain and serve with the sauce on top or mixed with the spaghetti.

SPAGHETTI WITH TOMATO SAUCE AND MARJORAM

COOKING TIME 20–30 mins.   QUANTITIES FOR 2–3.

1 *small onion, sliced*   ½ *clove garlic*
2 *tbs. oil*

Fry together in a saucepan for 5 mins. without browning. Remove the garlic.

1 *lb. (454 g.) can tomatoes*

Add and cook rapidly for 5 mins. to evaporate some of the liquid.

2 *pieces of canned anchovy fillet, chopped*

Add and cook for 10 mins. or until the sauce is thick.

Salt and pepper
½–1 *tsp. chopped fresh marjoram or* ¼–½ *tsp. dried, or to taste*

Add and keep the sauce warm.

8 *oz. (250 g.) spaghetti*

Boil according to the directions on the packet or for 10 mins. in plenty of boiling salted water. Drain and serve with the sauce on top and serve separately

Plenty of grated Parmesan or other dry cheese.

PANCAKES

PANCAKE BATTER WITH HERBS

COOKING TIME 1–2 mins. per pancake.   QUANTITIES FOR 8 pancakes.

4 *oz.* (¾ *c. or 125 g.) plain flour*   ½ *tsp. salt*

Put in a basin and make a well in the centre.

2 *eggs*   ½ *pt. (250 ml.) milk*

Break the eggs into the well in the flour and begin mixing with a wooden spoon working from the centre and gradually bringing in the flour. Add milk as it becomes thick, until half the milk has been added. Then beat the batter very thoroughly before adding the rest of the milk.

1–2 *tbs. chopped fresh herbs, one kind or a mixture*

Stir into the batter and pour into a jug.

Alternative method: Put all except the herbs in the goblet of an electric blender and process for 1 min. Add unchopped herbs and process just long enough to chop them finely; or process longer to give a green batter.

Lard

Use a 7–8-in. (18–20-cm.) frying pan and add a knob of lard. When this is very hot tip out any surplus and pour in a thin layer of the batter. Cook until brown underneath, turn or toss and cook the other side. Tip the pancake onto a piece of greaseproof paper. Either fill and roll up or put the pancakes in a pile as they are made and fill them at the end.

CHICKEN FILLING WITH TARRAGON

COOKING TIME 20–30 mins.

1 oz. (25 g.) *butter*   2 oz. (50 g.) *finely chopped mushrooms*

Melt the butter in a small pan, add the mushrooms, cover and stew gently for 3–4 mins.

2 tbs. *flour*   ¼ pt. (150 ml.) *stock*

Add to the mushrooms and mix well, then stir in the stock and stir until it boils.

4 oz. (125 g.) *diced cooked chicken*   1 tbs. *cream*
2 *finely chopped hard-boiled eggs*   1 tsp. *chopped parsley*
    1 tsp. *chopped tarragon*
    Salt and pepper

Add to the mushrooms, seasoning to taste. Bring to the boil and then put the mixture to keep hot while the pancakes are made. As each is made, fill with some of the chicken mixture, roll up and put to keep hot. Serve as they are or crisp the tops in a hot oven or under the grill. Alternatively, pour a little cream over the finished pancakes, sprinkle with grated cheese, and heat as before to melt the cheese.

FISH FILLING WITH DILL OR FENNEL

COOKING TIME a few mins.

8 oz. (250 g.) *cooked flaked white fish*
¼ pt. (150 ml.) *soured cream or use fresh double cream with a squeeze of lemon*
1 tbs. *chopped dill or ½ tbs. fennel   Salt and pepper*

Heat these together in a small pan and keep the mixture hot while the pancakes are being made. Pile the pancakes flat on a hot plate and, when all are made, fill each in turn, roll up and place close together in a shallow baking dish.

A few spoons of cream   *Grated Parmesan cheese*

Spoon a thin layer of cream over each pancake and sprinkle with cheese. Brown and crisp under the grill or in a hot oven.

HAM AND CHEESE FILLING

COOKING TIME about 5 mins.

¼ *pt. (150 ml.) evaporated milk*   4 *oz. (125 g.) cheese*

Grate the cheese coarsely or dice it finely. Put in a pan with the milk and heat gently until the cheese melts. Stir frequently to keep the sauce smooth, beating if necessary.

8 *oz. (250 g.) chopped or minced lean cooked ham*	*Chopped fresh herbs such as marjoram, basil, chervil, or dill*
French mustard	
Salt and pepper	*Wine or evaporated milk as required*

Add the ham to the cheese sauce, bring to the boil, simmer for a few minutes and season to taste. Add wine or milk as needed to thin the mixture but it should not be sloppy. Keep the filling hot while the pancakes are made.

As each is made put a little filling on it, roll up and put to keep hot in a shallow fireproof dish. When all are made, either heat them under the grill or in a moderate oven to crisp the outsides. Serve at once.

PORK AND APPLE FILLING WITH SAGE

COOKING TIME a few mins.

8 *oz. (250 g.) cold, cooked pork*

Trim off skin, gristle, and surplus fat and cut the pork in tiny pieces, or mince it.

½ *pt. (250 ml.) apple sauce*	*Pinch of ground nutmeg*
2 *sage leaves finely chopped or use a pinch of dried sage*	1 *tbs. finely chopped onion*
	Pepper
1 *tsp. salt*	1–2 *tbs. wine or bottled sauce*

Heat together in a small pan and simmer for a few minutes, adding more wine or sauce if it seems too thick. Add the meat and simmer for a few minutes longer. Keep hot while making the pancakes. Put a little of the filling on each, roll up and keep hot. When all are finished put the dish in a moderate oven or under a grill to crisp the outsides.

CHAPTER FOURTEEN

Sandwiches and snacks on toast

To add Herbs is an easy way of giving fresh interest and variety to favourite sandwiches and snacks.

One of the simplest methods is to substitute a Herb butter (see pp. 127–9), for plain butter normally used for spreading bread or toast or for cooking the ingredients. Supplies of herb butters will keep several days in the refrigerator.

When this is not suitable, a good alternative is to use a Herb mustard (see p. 84), especially for cold meat sandwiches and with cheese.

To use Herb bread (p. 233) instead of plain bread, for sandwiches, is another interesting possibility.

Some other ideas for using herbs in sandwiches and snacks are given in the recipes which follow.

SANDWICH FILLINGS

For open or closed sandwiches.

BACON AND CHEESE WITH BASIL

4 rashers bacon
Remove the rinds and fry or grill the bacon until crisp. Leave to cool.
8 oz. (250 g.) curd or cream cheese *Pepper*
Finely chopped fresh or dried basil
Crumble the cold bacon and mix with the cheese. Add pepper and basil to taste.

BEEF

Slices of cold roast beef with horseradish sauce or a herb mustard.

Corned beef, mashed or chopped and mixed with plenty of chopped chives and with horseradish sauce to moisten.

CHEESE AND SAGE

8 oz. (250 g.) *sieved or mashed cottage cheese*	*Salt and pepper* *Milk or cream*
4 oz. (1 c. or 125 g.) *grated strong cheese*	*Finely chopped fresh sage* *1 tsp. French mustard*

Combine the ingredients adding enough milk or cream to give the consistency you want. Add sage to taste.

CHEESE, SOFT, AND HERBS see Cheese p. 137.

CHEESE AND HORSERADISH

8 oz. (250 g.) *cottage cheese*	*Salt*
2–3 tbs. *horseradish sauce*	2 oz. (50 g.) *melted butter*
1–2 tbs. *chopped parsley*	

Mash the cheese with the other ingredients to give a smooth spread. Leave to stand for the butter to set, when the spread will thicken a little.

CHICKEN

Mix finely chopped or minced cooked chicken with mayonnaise to bind, and flavour with some chopped sweet pepper and finely chopped fresh herbs: lemon thyme, balm, curry leaves, dill, marjoram, savory, or tarragon. Use just one or a mixture.

CRAB MEAT

Fresh or canned crab meet mixed with mayonnaise to moisten and flavoured with chopped fresh sage, lemon thyme, chervil, or tarragon.

CUCUMBER

Thinly sliced, sprinkled with salt and pepper and chopped chives, chervil, dill, nasturtium leaves, or fennel.

CUCUMBER AND CHEESE WITH FENNEL

4 oz. (125 g.) cottage or curd cheese
2 tbs. chopped pickled cucumber
1 tsp. or more of finely chopped fennel
Salt and pepper

Sieve or mash the cheese to make it smooth. Mix it with the other ingredients, seasoning to taste. When used for an open sandwich garnish with
Small sprigs of fennel

HAM

Use thin slices spread with a herb mustard or make the following mixture:

2 oz. (50 g.) finely chopped or minced ham
1 medium-sized apple, grated   2 tbs. mayonnaise
1–2 tbs. chopped basil, dill, or marjoram

HERRING

½ oz. (15 g.) butter or margarine   ½ tbs. finely chopped onion

Heat the fat in a small pan and fry the onion until it begins to brown.

6 oz. (175 g.) cooked, flaked   2 tsp. vinegar
    herring   Pinch of pepper
1 tsp. salt
1 tbs. chopped capers, dill,
    fennel, or parsley, or
    mixed

The herring can be grilled, boiled, or fried. Mix all the ingredients to a smooth paste with the onion.

LIVER SAUSAGE

2 rashers bacon

Remove the rinds and grill or fry the bacon until crisp. Cool and then chop it finely.

4 oz. (125 g.) *soft liver sausage*   1 *tsp. French mustard*
4 *tbs. mayonnaise*   1 *oz.* (25 g.) *melted bacon fat or*
A little garlic (optional)   *lard*
Finely chopped fennel or sage
    to taste

Mix all together with the bacon.

MINT AND RAISIN

Mince together or chop finely, equal quantities of raisins and fresh
mint, adding a little hot water to make the mixture a spreading consistency. Use as a filling for either white or brown bread sandwiches.
See also, Mint Chutney (uncooked) (p. 90).

PORK

For an open sandwich garnish slices of cold roast pork with apple
sauce and plenty of chopped fresh sage, basil, dill, or marjoram.

For a closed sandwich either spread the meat with a herb mustard
or use a herb butter for spreading the bread.

PRAWN AND CHEESE WITH FENNEL OR DILL

QUANTITIES FOR 4 open sandwiches.

4 oz. (125 g.) *cottage cheese*   *A little cream or milk*
Lemon juice   *Chopped fresh fennel or dill*
Salt and pepper

Mash together, seasoning to taste and adding milk or cream as needed.

4 *slices buttered bread, prefer-*   *Cucumber or other salad vege-*
    ably wholemeal or rye   *tables to garnish*
4 oz. (125 g.) *cooked shelled*   *Sprigs of fennel or dill to garnish*
    prawns

Spread the cheese mixture on the bread, put a row of prawns along
the middle, and garnish to taste.

SALMON AND EGG

2 *hard-boiled eggs*   2 *tbs. mayonnaise*
3½–4 oz. (100 g.) *can salmon,*   *Chopped dill, fennel, marjoram,*
    including oil and bones   *parsley, tarragon, or mixed*
2 *slices green pepper, chopped*   *herbs*

Shell the eggs and separate the yolks. Put them in a small bowl and mash with the mayonnaise. Add the salmon and mash together thoroughly. Add the chopped pepper and the finely chopped egg whites. Add freshly chopped herbs to taste, just one kind or a mixture of two or three.

SMOKED HADDOCK OR OTHER SMOKED FISH

Flake cooked cold fish carefully removing bones and skin. Bind it with a thick white sauce containing herbs or any other thick herb sauce, for example, Green Dutch sauce (p. 117) or Sauce Gribiche (p. 123).

Use plenty of herbs in the white sauce, parsley, chives, dill, or fennel or, in place of a white sauce use horseradish sauce.

TOMATO

Thinly sliced and seasoned tomato sprinkled generously with finely chopped fresh chervil, dill, chives, basil, or fennel.

TOASTED SANDWICHES AND SNACKS ON TOAST

BEANS AND MUSHROOMS

COOKING TIME 10 mins. QUANTITIES FOR 3–4.

2 tbs. finely chopped onion
8 oz. (250 g.) sliced mushrooms
1 ½ *oz. (40 g.) butter or margarine*

Heat the fat in a large frying pan. Fry the onion and mushrooms until the onion begins to brown.

16 oz. (454 g.) can baked beans in tomato sauce
1 tbs. Worcester sauce
Salt to taste
1 tsp. soy sauce
1–2 tbs. chopped fresh marjoram or ½–1 tbs. dried

Add to the pan and simmer until well heated. Taste for seasoning.

Chopped parsley or marjoram　　*Toast*

Either serve on toast or hand the toast separately. Sprinkle with the herbs.

CHEESE ON TOAST WITH HERBS

COOKING TIME a few mins.   QUANTITIES FOR 4.
   4 *slices toast*
   4 *thick slices of cheese the same size as the toast*
   2 *tsp. chopped fresh herbs or to taste*
For the herbs use thyme, sage, savory, or tarragon.
Cover the toast with cheese and grill fairly slowly until the cheese
melts and bubbles. Serve hot, sprinkled generously with herbs.

CHEESE, TOMATO, AND BACON

Use the previous recipe but this time add
   2 *sliced tomatoes*
   4 *small rashers bacon, diced or cut in strips*
Put the tomatoes on top of the cheese and herbs, the bacon on top of
the tomatoes, and grill until the bacon is cooked.

CRAB AND CHEESE

COOKING TIME about 5 mins.   QUANTITIES FOR 4.
   4 *slices bread toasted on one side*   *Chopped fresh sage, chervil,*
   4 *oz. (125 g.) cooked or canned*   *thyme or tarragon, or dried*
      crab meat
   Mayonnaise or salad dressing
      to moisten
Mix the crab meat with mayonnaise or salad dressing and plenty of
herbs. Spread it on the untoasted side of the bread.
   4 *thin slices of cheese*
Put on top of the crab and grill slowly until the cheese is melted.

CROQUE MONSIEUR WITH HERBS

COOKING TIME 10–15 mins.   QUANTITIES FOR 4.
   8 *thin slices of bread*
   4 *slices Emmental cheese a little smaller than the bread*
   4 *slices cooked ham the same size as the cheese*
   Softened Herb butter (see pp. 127–9).
For cooking the Croque Monsieur use either an electric frypan, a
griddle, or a heavy frying pan over a moderate heat.
   Spread one side of four pieces of bread, using any of the herb

butters, or mix a soft margarine with finely chopped herbs, sage, marjoram, dill, or basil being particularly suitable. Put the spread side of the bread downwards on the griddle or pan. Put on the cheese and then the ham, then cover with the remaining bread and spread the top with herb butter. Cook until the underneath is brown, turn, and cook the other side by which time the cheese should be softened but not really melted. Serve hot.

EGG, CHEESE, AND BACON

QUANTITIES FOR 4.

2 *eggs, beaten*
1 *tsp. Worcester sauce*
½ *tsp. dry mustard*
1–2 *tbs. chopped tarragon, chervil, dill, or marjoram*

8 *oz. (250 g.) grated cheese*
1 *tsp. paprika pepper*
A little garlic salt or dried garlic

Combine the ingredients thoroughly.

4 *thick slices bread toasted on one side*

Spread the mixture in a thick layer on the untoasted side.

2 *rashers bacon, diced*

Cover the filling with the bacon and grill until it is crisp.

EGG AND HADDOCK

COOKING TIME about 10 mins.

4 *eggs, beaten*
8 *oz. (250 g.) cooked, flaked smoked haddock*
1 *tbs. lemon juice*

QUANTITIES FOR 4.

2 *tbs. grated horseradish or horseradish sauce*
2 *tbs. milk*
Pepper

Combine all the ingredients.

½ *oz. (15 g.) butter or margarine*

Melt in a small pan and scramble the egg and fish mixture.

4 *slices bread*   4 *thin slices of cheese*

Toast the bread on one side and put the filling on the untoasted side. Cover with the cheese. Grill slowly until the cheese has melted and begun to brown.

FISH RAREBIT

COOKING TIME 10 mins.

1 *oz. (25 g.) butter*
2 *tbs. cornflour*

QUANTITIES FOR 4.

Pinch of paprika pepper

Melt the butter in a small pan, add the paprika and cornflour. Mix well.

½ pt. (250 ml.) milk   *1 tsp. finely chopped onion*

Gradually stir in the milk and add the onion. Bring to the boil and cook for 5 mins.

3 oz. (1 c. or 75 g.) grated cheese   *8 oz. (250 g.) flaked cooked fish*

Add to the sauce and heat without boiling. As soon as the cheese melts add

1 egg, beaten   *1–2 tbs. chopped dill, fennel, tar-*
1 tbs. lemon juice   *ragon, chervil, or marjoram*
Salt and pepper

Heat until it thickens, tasting for seasoning. Serve on
Toast

ONIONS AND CHEESE ON TOAST

COOKING TIME 20 mins.   QUANTITIES FOR 4.

4 medium-sized onions, sliced   *1 oz. (25 g.) fat*

Heat the fat in a frying pan and cook the onions slowly until they are tender. Stir frequently.

1–2 tbs. chopped sage, tarragon, marjoram, or basil, or use ½–1
tbs. dried   *Salt and pepper*

Mix into the onions, seasoning to taste.

4 slices hot buttered toast

Spread the onions on the toast.

4 slices cheese   *French or Herb mustard*

Spread the cheese with mustard and place on top of the onions. Grill until the cheese melts.

RAREBIT WITH HERBS

This will keep for a week in the refrigerator and makes a useful emergency snack.

COOKING TIME about 5–10 mins.   QUANTITIES FOR 4.

8 oz. (250 g.) grated Cheshire or   *1 tbs. cornflour*
Cheddar cheese   *1 tbs. fresh chopped herbs or*
2 tsp. made mustard or Wor-   *1 tsp. dried (basil, chives,*
cester sauce   *parsley, and thyme are a*
4 tbs. milk, ale, or stout   *good mixture)*

Mix all the ingredients to a smooth paste, cover and store until required.

4 *slices toast*

Spread the cheese mixture on the hot toast and brown under the grill.

CHAPTER FIFTEEN

Breads, pastry, biscuits, cakes and desserts

BREADS

In general, herb seeds are the most satisfactory to use as they lose less flavour during cooking. Dried herbs I put next and fresh herbs probably as the least satisfactory, though it does, of course, depend on the herb. Those with a strong flavour which stand up well to cooking (see p. 78) are the best herbs to use fresh.

Herbs can be added to any bread recipe in the proportions of about 1 tbs. of seeds, or 1 tsp. dried crushed herbs, or 1 tbs. chopped fresh herbs to 1 lb. (½ kg.) flour.

Another way of enjoying the flavour of herbs with bread is to use herb butters for spreading on plain bread or to use as sandwich fillings. This is in some ways more practical than adding herbs to the bread mixture as you may not want a whole loaf flavoured with herbs. For Herb butter recipes, see pp. 127–9, and for Herbed loaf using them, p. 236.

Or try sprinkling herb seeds on buttered bread, especially good if you like the flavour of small seeds like caraway. Larger seeds can be used either crushed or ground.

I have included here a few recipes for breads, including baking powder breads and scones. Cheese bread with herbs is particularly good.

YEAST BREADS

FENNEL SEED PLAITS

COOKING TIME about 20 mins. TEMPERATURE E. 425° (220°C.) G.7
QUANTITIES FOR 2 loaves.

1 *tsp. sugar* ½ *oz.* (15 *g.*) *fresh yeast or* 2
¼ *pt.* (150 *ml.*) *luke-warm* *tsp. dried*
  milk 1 *tsp. flour*

Put in a small basin and whisk together to mix well. Put in a warm place for the yeast to begin to work and the mixture to become frothy.

1 *lb.* (3 *c. or* ½ *kg.*) *plain bread flour* 1 *tsp. salt*
1 *tbs. fennel seeds*

Put in a mixing bowl.

2 *oz.* (50 *g.*) *melted butter* *About* ¼ *pt.* (150 *ml.*) *luke-warm*
1 *egg, beaten* *milk*

The butter should not be hot. Add butter, egg, and yeast mixture to the flour with enough milk to make a sticky dough. Beat thoroughly until the mixture leaves the sides of the bowl. If you have a suitable electric mixer, use the dough hook for mixing and beating. Cover the bowl with a polythene bag and put it in a warm place for the dough to rise to double its bulk (about 1 hr.).

Turn the dough out on a lightly floured board, cut in half, and then cut each half in three equal portions. Roll each of these into a long, thin sausage, about 1 in. (2½ cm.) thick. Press three pieces together at one end and then make a plait, pressing the other ends together. Do this with the other half of the mixture. Put the plaits on oiled baking trays leaving room for them to double in size. Put the trays in a warm place until this happens and then bake them until they are firm and brown.

Cool them on a wire rack and then store in polythene bags. The loaves freeze very well.

SOFT DINNER ROLLS WITH DRIED HERBS

COOKING TIME 15 mins. TEMPERATURE E. 425° (220°C.) G.7
QUANTITIES FOR 20 rolls.

1 *tsp. sugar* ½ *oz.* (15 *g.*) *fresh yeast or* 2 *tsp. dried*
1 *tsp. flour* ¼ *pt.* (150 *ml.*) *luke-warm milk*

Whisk together in a small bowl. Put in a warm place to become frothy.

12 *oz.* (2½ *c. or* 375 *g.*) *plain bread flour* ½ *tsp. salt*
1 *oz.* (25 *g.*) *butter or margarine*

Put the flour and salt in a mixing bowl and rub in the fat.

1 *egg, beaten*   ½–1 *tsp. mixed crushed herbs*

For the herbs use fennel seeds, coriander seeds, marjoram, and thyme, or use the herb mixture on p. 85. Pound the herbs well in a mortar to give a fine mixture; or use crushed herbs as purchased.

Add egg and herbs to the flour, together with the yeast mixture, to make a sticky dough. Beat well until the dough leaves the sides of the bowl clean. Put the bowl in a large polythene bag. Leave to rise until double in bulk (about 1 hr.). Turn the dough onto a floured board and knead lightly. Shape into rolls and put them on greased trays, leaving room for rising. Put in a warm place to rise to double in bulk. Brush with a little milk or beaten egg and bake until brown and firm to the touch.

WHOLEMEAL BREAD WITH HERBS

COOKING TIME 40–45 mins.   TEMPERATURE E. 425° (220°C.) G.7
QUANTITIES FOR two 1 lb. (½ kg.) loaves.

¼ *pt.* (150 *ml.*) *luke-warm*   1 *tsp. flour*
   water   1 *tsp. sugar*
½ *oz.* (15 *g.*) *fresh yeast or* 1
   tsp. dried

Put in a small bowl and whisk together. Put in a warm place until the mixture begins to work and becomes frothy.

1½ *lb.* (4 *c. or* 750 *g.*) *plain* 100% *wholemeal flour*
1 *tbs. salt*   ½ *oz.* (15 *g.*) *lard*

Put flour and salt in a mixing bowl and rub in the lard.

1½ *tbs. caraway, dill, or fennel seeds*
About ½ *pt.* (250 *ml.*) *luke-warm water*

Mix the seeds into the flour. If you would prefer to have one loaf plain or to use a different herb for each loaf, the seeds can be kneaded in after the dough has been divided into loaves.

Use the water to mix the flour, with the yeast mixture, to a soft dough, using more or less water as required. Knead the dough thoroughly, by hand or machine, until it is smooth and elastic to the touch. Put the bowl in a large polythene bag and put this in a warm place for the dough to double in bulk (about 1 hr.).

Turn the dough onto a floured board and knead lightly. Divide in half and shape each into a loaf. Put in oiled loaf tins and put to rise to double in bulk or almost to the tops of the tins. Bake until brown and producing a hollow sound when tapped. Cool on wire racks. Store in polythene bags. The loaves freeze very well.

HERBED LOAF

This is a variation on the well-known garlic bread.

1 *stale French or Vienna loaf, or a similar shape*

3–4 oz. (75–125 g.) *mixed herb butter* (p. 129)

Cut the loaf almost through diagonally in ½-in. (1-cm.) slices and spread both sides of each cut with the herb butter. Press the loaf back into shape, wrap it loosely in foil, and put it in a hot oven (E. 425° 220°C.) G.7), for 12–15 mins. Serve hot, separating the slices with a bread knife.

BAKING POWDER BREADS OR QUICK BREADS

CHEESE LOAF

COOKING TIME 1 hr.   TEMPERATURE E. 350° (180°C.) G.4

QUANTITIES FOR a 1 lb. (½ kg.) loaf. Grease the tin.

8 oz. (1½ c. or 250 g.) self-raising flour	½ tsp. *dried herbs or* ½ tbs. *herb seeds or chopped fresh*
3 oz. (1 c. or 75 g.) grated strong cheese	*herbs*
	½ tsp. *salt*

For the herbs use basil, marjoram, thyme, savory, dill, or fennel. Put the ingredients in a mixing bowl.

1 *egg, beaten*   ¼–½ pt. (150–250 ml.) *milk*

Use these to mix the dry ingredients to a soft cake consistency. Turn the mixture into the prepared tin, smooth the top, and bake until a skewer inserted in the middle comes out clean. Turn out of the tin and leave to become cold. Store in a polythene bag and leave for 24 hrs. before slicing the loaf.

Alternative Method: Instead of grating the cheese, cut it in small pieces and put it in the blender goblet with the unbeaten egg and about ¼ pt. (150 ml.) of the milk. Blend to make smooth and use this to mix the dry ingredients as before, adding more milk as needed.

FRUIT LOAF WITH MARJORAM, BASIL, AND THYME

COOKING TIME 1 hr.   TEMPERATURE E. 350° (180°C.) G.4

QUANTITIES FOR a 1 lb. (½ kg.) loaf. Grease the tin.

8 oz. (1½ c. or 250 g.) *self-raising flour*   ½ tsp. *salt*

2 oz. (50 g.) *butter or margarine*

Put flour and salt in a mixing bowl and rub in the fat.

4 oz. (¾ c. or 125 g.) mixed dried fruit	¼ tsp. dried marjoram
	Pinch of dried thyme
1 oz. (2 tbs. or 25 g.) sugar	¼ tsp. dried basil

The herbs should be fairly finely crushed. Combine fruit, sugar, and herbs with the flour.

1 *egg, beaten*   ¼ *pt. (150 g.) milk*

Use these to mix the dry ingredients to a soft cake consistency. Turn into the prepared tin, smooth the top and bake until firm in the centre. Turn out on a rack to cool and when quite cold, put it in a polythene bag. Keep for 24 hrs. before cutting.

ORANGE LOAF WITH EAU DE COLOGNE MINT

COOKING TIME 1 hr.   TEMPERATURE E. 350° (180°C.) G.4
QUANTITIES FOR a 1 lb. (½ kg.) loaf. Grease the tin.

8 *oz. (1½ c. or 250 g.) self-raising flour*   ½ *tsp. salt*
Put in a mixing bowl.

1 *oz. (25 g.) butter or margarine*
Rub into the flour.

Finely grated rind of 1 small orange (½ tsp.)

1 *oz. (2 tbs. or 25 g.) sugar*   1 *tbs. finely chopped mint*
Mix into the flour.

1 *egg, beaten*   *About* ¼ *pt. (150 ml.) milk*

Use these to mix the dry ingredients to a soft cake consistency, using as much of the milk as needed. Put in the greased tin, spread evenly and bake until cooked through. Turn out on a rack to cool and leave 24 hrs. before cutting.

CHEESE SCONES WITH HERBS

These are delicious to serve at tea-time or instead of bread with a salad meal. Use any of the herbs which go well with cheese: sage, marjoram, thyme, dill, fennel, basil, or savory. Use just one herb or a mixture. Dried herbs are generally more satisfactory than fresh ones.

COOKING TIME 10–15 mins.   TEMPERATURE E. 475° (250°C.) G. 7–8
QUANTITIES FOR 12 scones.

8 *oz. (1½ c. or 250 g.) self-raising flour*   ½ *tsp. salt*
Put in a mixing bowl.

2 *oz. (50 g.) butter or margarine*
Rub into the flour.

2 *oz. (½ c. or 50 g.) finely grated strong cheese*
½–1 *tsp. dried crushed herbs, depending on strength of flavour*

Mix into the flour using your fingers to combine the ingredients.

About ¼ pt. (150 ml.) milk

Use a knife for mixing and add milk to make a very soft, almost sticky dough. Roll out on a floured board to about ½ in. (1 cm.) thick and cut in rounds about 2¼ in. (6 cm.), or cut in squares. Put on a baking tray. Brush the tops with milk and bake until golden brown. Serve hot or warm.

HERB PASTRY

This mixture can also be used for biscuits to serve with cheese or to make a base for canapes and savouries. Bake it at the usual pastry temperature, about E. 425° (220°C.) G.7

It also makes excellent pastry for sausage rolls, allowing 8 oz. (250 g.) of pork sausage meat to this quantity of pastry.

QUANTITIES FOR a 7–8-in. (18–20-cm.) flan or 8 sausage rolls.

4 oz. (¾ c. or 125 g.) plain   ¼ tsp. salt
flour   1 oz. (25 g.) lard
1 oz. (25 g.) butter or
margarine

Mix the flour and salt and rub in the fat.

About 1 tbs. finely chopped fresh herbs

The amount depends on how strongly flavoured the herbs are. Use any herb appropriate to the filling you are using with the pastry or use a mixture of herbs, for example, marjoram, tarragon, thyme, chervil, or dill.

1 egg, beaten

Use enough egg to mix the dry ingredients to a stiff dough. Roll out and use as required.

CARROT AND CHEESE FLAN

COOKING TIME 30 mins.   TEMPERATURE E. 425° (220°C.) G.7
QUANTITIES FOR a 7-in. (18-cm.) flan.

4 oz. (¾ c. or 125 g.) *flour made into short crust or herb pastry or use 6–8 oz. (175–250 g.) ready-made pastry*

Roll the pastry thinly and line a flan ring or pie plate with it. Prick the bottom and put it in the refrigerator while the filling is being prepared.

4 oz. (125 g.) finely grated raw carrot	1–2 tbs. chopped fresh herbs or 1½–2 tsp. dried (marjoram,
2 oz. (⅔ c. or 50 g.) strong cheese, coarsely grated	mint, basil, or savory) Salt and pepper
1 tsp. chopped chives	3 tbs. cream
1 egg, beaten	3 tbs. milk

Mix all the ingredients together and put in the pastry case. Bake until the filling is set and lightly browned. Serve warm or cold.

CORNISH PASTIES WITH HERBS

COOKING TIME 30–40 mins.   TEMPERATURE E. 425° (220°C.) G.7
QUANTITIES FOR 4 small pasties.

  8 oz. (1½ c. or 250 g.) *flour made into short crust pastry or use*
  12 oz. (375 g.) *ready-made pastry*

Form the pastry into a fat sausage and cut it in four equal pieces. Roll each to a circle about ⅛ in. (3 mm.) thick and trim the edges if necessary. Put the filling (see below), on one half of each piece of pastry, moisten the edges with water and fold over, pressing to seal the edges, or roll them together to make an even better seal. Cut a small slit in the top and brush the pastry with milk or beaten egg and water. Bake until the pastry is well browned by which time the filling should be cooked. Serve hot or cold.

FILLINGS

  Allow about 12 oz. (375 g.) filling for 4 pasties; and 1–2 tbs. chopped fresh herbs or ½–1 tbs. dried; season with salt and pepper.

BEEF AND POTATO PASTY

  Chopped or minced raw beef mixed with finely diced raw potato, a little chopped onion, and chopped fresh or dried, herbs, for example, marjoram, thyme, parsley, savory, chervil, or a mixture.

CHICKEN PASTY

  Diced raw chicken, salt and pepper, finely chopped onion, raw grated carrot, chopped mushrooms, and chopped fresh herbs, for example, tarragon, lemon thyme, or fines herbes.

LAMB PASTY

  Chopped or minced raw lean lamb, grated raw carrot or potato, salt and pepper, chopped fresh mint.

CURRANT PATTIES WITH MINT

COOKING TIME 20 mins.   TEMPERATURE E. 425° (220°C.) G.7
QUANTITIES FOR 12 patties.

    6 *oz. (175 g.) flour made into short pastry or use 8 oz. (250 g.)*
    ready-made pastry.

Make the pastry and put it to rest in a cool place while making the
filling.

    2 *oz. (⅓ c. or 50 g.) currants*   3 *tbs. finely chopped mint*
    2 *oz. (¼ c. or 50 g.) brown*
    sugar

Chop or mince the currants and mix them with the sugar and mint.
Roll the pastry about ⅛ in. (3 mm.) thick and trim to a square or
rectangle. Spread the currant mixture over half of it, moisten the
edges with water, and fold over the other half pressing the edges
of the pastry together. Roll over the surface lightly until the fruit
begins to show through. Brush the top with milk or egg and bake
until the pastry is lightly browned. Alternatively, brush the top with
water and sprinkle with granulated sugar before baking. When
cooked, cut into squares or other shapes.

HERB DUMPLINGS

To serve with stews of meat, game, or poultry, or with boiled salt
beef and other boiled meats. Tiny dumplings are also used for
garnishing soups.

COOKING TIME ½–¾ hr. for large dumplings; 15–20 mins. for small
ones.

QUANTITIES FOR 4 large dumplings.

    2 *oz. (6 tbs. or 50 g.) self-*   1 *tbs. fresh chopped herbs or*
    raising flour   ¼–½ *tsp. dried herbs.*
    1 *oz. (4 tbs. or 25 g.) fresh*   ¼ *tsp. salt*
    grated or packet suet

Good herbs to use are thyme, marjoram, savory, tarragon, parsley,
or chervil; or use a mixture. Pulverise dried herbs before using them.

    Mix all the ingredients together thoroughly. Then, using a knife
for mixing, quickly add enough cold water to make a soft dough,
softer than pastry, but not sticky. Flour your hands and roll the
mixture into smooth balls.

    Steaming is the best method of cooking for serving with boiled
meats or stews cooked on the hob. Put the dumplings in a steamer

top over rapidly boiling water. Cover and steam until risen and light. Do not lift the lid for the first 15 mins. of cooking or they may become heavy. Steaming produces a lighter and less sticky dumpling than boiling.

Baking is a good method for a casserole. Put the dumplings in the bubbling casserole about ¾ hr. before the end of cooking. Cover with the lid. If a crisp crust is wanted the dumpling mixture can be shaped in one piece and, when it is risen and set, remove the casserole lid and allow the top to brown, increasing the heat of the oven if necessary.

For soup either boil in the soup or steam separately, as above.

BISCUITS AND CAKES

CARAWAY BISCUITS

COOKING TIME 15 mins. TEMPERATURE E. 350° (180°C.) G.4
QUANTITIES FOR 36 biscuits 2½ in. (5 cm.)

   8 oz. (1½ c. or 250 g.) *plain flour*
   4 oz. (125 g.) *butter or margarine*
Put the flour in a bowl and rub in the fat.

   4 oz. (½ c. or 125 g.) *caster*   1 tbs. caraway seeds
      sugar
   Pinch of grated nutmeg
Mix into the flour evenly

   1 *egg, beaten*   1 *tbs. sherry*
Use the sherry and as much egg as is needed to mix the dry ingredients to a softish dough. Roll out on a floured board to about ⅛ in. (3 mm.) thick and cut in rounds using a plain or fluted cutter. Put fairly close together on lightly greased baking trays and cook until the biscuits are lightly coloured and crisp. Cool on a rack and, when quite cold, store them in an airtight container.

CHEESE BISCUITS

COOKING TIME 15–20 mins. TEMPERATURE E. 400° (200°C.) G.6
QUANTITIES FOR 24 biscuits 2¼-in. (5½-cm.) cutter.

   4 oz. (¾ c. or 125 g.) *flour*   *Pinch of salt*
   Few grains cayenne pepper   *Pinch of dry mustard*
Put in a bowl.

   1½ oz. (40 g.) *butter or margarine*

Rub into the flour until the mixture looks like fine breadcrumbs.

    4 *oz.* (1 *c. or* 125 *g.*) *grated strong cheese*

    1 *tbs. chopped fresh herbs or* 1 *tsp. dried herbs or fennel seeds*

Suitable herbs are sage by itself or sage and chives; mint or marjoram alone or mixed; lemon or common thyme; basil; dill; fennel; crushed coriander seeds; cumin.

    Rub herbs and cheese into the flour mixture to distribute them evenly.

    1 *egg, beaten*

Use the egg to mix to a stiff dough, using only as much as is needed for this purpose. Roll out thinly, not more than ⅛ in. (3 mm.), and cut in shapes. Use any remaining egg mixed with a little cold water, to brush the tops. Bake until crisp and brown.

HERB BISCUITS

To serve with cheese or a savoury spread.

COOKING TIME 15–20 mins.   TEMPERATURE E. 400° (200°C.) G.6

QUANTITIES FOR 24 biscuits 2¼-in. (5½-cm.) cutter or smaller for
    cocktail snacks or canapés.

    8 *oz.* (1½ *c. or* 250 *g.*) *plain flour*   ½ *tsp. salt*

Put in a mixing bowl.

    2 *oz. butter or margarine and* 2 *oz. lard* (125 *g. total*) *or use*
      4 *oz.* (125 *g.*) *soft margarine*

Rub the fat into the flour by hand or machine until the mixture looks like fine breadcrumbs.

    3 *tbs. chopped fresh herbs or* ½–1 *tbs. dried, according to strength*
      of flavour (see below)

Herbs to use are mint, chervil, lemon thyme, basil, sage, dill, fennel, rosemary, powdered anise seed, crushed coriander seed. Rub the herbs into the flour mixture.

    1 *egg, beaten*

Use this to mix the dry ingredients to a stiff dough, using the hands to work it in and only adding water if absolutely necessary to bind the ingredients together. Refrigerate the dough for ½ hr. before rolling it out thinly, about ⅛ in. (3 mm.), and cutting into shapes. Bake until crisp and lightly browned.

ANISETTE GLACÉ ICING

This is a very good way of introducing anise flavour into biscuits, cakes, and pastries. It has the obvious advantage that only some of a batch need to be iced with anise, using another flavour for the anise haters. It is particularly good for coating small petits fours made of Genoese sponge, or for icing larger cakes and any other type of confectionery where a glacé icing is used for decoration. If a caraway flavour is preferred to anise, try flavouring the icing with kümmel instead of anisette.

8 oz. (1½ c. or 250 g.) *icing sugar*   *A little hot water*
1 tbs. *anisette*

Sieve the icing sugar into a basin and use the anisette and water to mix it to a consistency which will coat the back of a spoon without running off. Beat well to make the icing glossy.

ANISE SPONGE

COOKING TIME 20–25 mins.   TEMPERATURE E. 375° (190°C.) G.5
QUANTITIES FOR a tin about 10 in. × 6 in. (25 × 15 cm.)

Oil the tin and line the bottom with non-stick paper; or use a non-stick tin. Two 7½-in. (18-cm.) sandwich tins can be used instead.

3 *eggs*   4 oz. (½ c. or 125 g.) *caster sugar*

Warm the mixing bowl and eggs. Beat until they are light and then beat in the sugar until the mixture is very thick like whipped cream.

3 oz. (⅔ c. or 75 g.) *plain*   1 tbs. *cornflour*
    flour
1 tsp. *ground anise seed*

Sift into the egg mixture and fold in gently.

3 oz. (75 g.) *just melted butter or margarine*

Add to the sponge and fold in thoroughly and gently. Pour into the prepared tin and bake until the sponge just begins to shrink from the sides of the tin. Cool in the tin for a few minutes and then turn out on a cake rack. The cake can be cut in small pieces and iced and decorated for petits fours using an icing flavoured with anisette (p. 242) or a lemon glacé icing. If baked as a sandwich, join together with cream or a lemon filling.

FRUIT CAKE WITH ROSEMARY

Dried crushed rosemary used in place of spice gives an interestingly different flavour to this cake, slightly gingery, but yet not the same as using ginger.

COOKING TIME 1¼ hrs.   TEMPERATURE E. 325° (160°C.) G.3

QUANTITIES FOR a 6-in. (15-cm.) tin lined with paper.

4 oz. (125 g.) butter or margarine   2 eggs
4 oz. (½ c. or 125 g.) caster sugar

Cream the fat and sugar until light and then beat in the eggs one at a time.

4 oz. (¾ c. or 125 g.) plain   ¼ tsp. baking powder
  flour
3 oz. (¾ c. or 75 g.) ground
  almonds

Sift the flour and baking powder into the creamed mixture and add the almonds.

2 oz. (¼ c. or 50 g.) currants   2 oz. (¼ c. or 50 g.) raisins
2 oz. (¼ c. or 50 g.) sultanas   1 oz. (4 tbs. or 25 g.) chopped
1 tsp. dried crushed rosemary   peel

Mix into the cake and put in the prepared tin, spreading the top flat. Bake until a fine skewer inserted in the centre comes out clean. Leave in the tin to become cold.

LEMON VERBENA SANDWICH CAKE

COOKING TIME 15–20 mins.   TEMPERATURE E. 375° (190°C.) G.5
QUANTITIES FOR two 6-in. (15-cm.) sandwich tins, greased and floured, or use non-stick tins.

4 oz. (125 g.) butter or margarine
4 oz. (½ c. or 125 g.) caster sugar

Cream together until very light.

2 eggs

Beat in one at a time beating until the mixture is light.

4 oz. (¾ c. or 125 g.) self-   1 tbs. warm water
  raising flour   1 tsp. dried powdered lemon
Pinch of salt   verbena leaves

Powder the leaves well and then sieve them so that the mixture looks like spice. Mix this with the flour and salt and stir gently into the creamed mixture, adding the water at the end. Divide evenly between the two tins, smooth over and bake until the cake begins to show signs of shrinking from the sides of the tin. Allow to cool for 10 mins. and then turn out on a cake rack. Leave to become cold.

Jam   Sifted icing sugar

Sandwich the sponge with jam and sprinkle icing sugar over the top.

Alternative: Ice the cake with butter or glacé icing flavoured with powdered lemon verbena or lemon juice.

SWEET CICELY BUNS

COOKING TIME 15–20 mins.   TEMPERATURE E. 375° (190°C.) G.5
QUANTITIES FOR 18 cakes.
Grease and flour 18 bun tins or use paper cases.

   4 oz. (125 g.) *butter*   4 oz. (½ c. or 125 g.) *caster sugar*
Cream together until very light and fluffy.

   2 *eggs*
Add one at a time and beat each in very thoroughly.

   6 oz. (1¼ c. or 175 g.) *self-raising flour*
   ½ pt. (250 ml.) *sweet cicely leaves, chopped*
Stir gently into the creamed mixture. Two-thirds fill the cases or
tins and bake until lightly browned and springy in the centre. Turn
out on a wire rack to cool. Serve plain, or ice with Anisette Glacé
Icing (p. 242).

SEED CAKE

This is an old-fashioned recipe which includes spices as well as
caraway seeds and is a big improvement on the usual seed cake.
COOKING TIME ¾–1 hr.   TEMPERATURE E. 325° (160°C.) G.3
QUANTITIES FOR a 6-in. (15-cm.) tin. Line the tin with paper.

   4 oz. (125 g.) *butter*   4 oz. (½ c. or 125 g.) *caster
                                       sugar*

Cream together thoroughly.

   2 *eggs, beaten*
Beat into the creamed mixture gradually.

   3 oz. (⅔ c. or 75 g.) *self-*   1 *tsp. caraway seeds*
   raising flour   ¼ *tsp. ground cinnamon*
   2 oz. (¼ c. or 50 g.) *plain*   ½ *tsp. grated nutmeg*
   flour
Sift flour and spices together and mix in the caraway seeds. Add to
the creamed mixture and stir to blend thoroughly. Put the mixture
in the prepared tin, smoothing the top. Bake until a fine skewer
inserted in the middle comes out clean. Leave in the tin to cool
for about 15 mins. before turning the cake out on a rack to finish
cooling.

DESSERTS

ANISE CREAM

COOKING TIME a few mins. Prepare 8–12 hrs. in advance
QUANTITIES FOR 6, or a 1½ pt. (750 ml.) mould.

1 *egg*	1 *tbs. custard powder*
2 *tbs. sugar*	½ *pt. (250 ml.) milk*
1 *tsp. ground anise seed*	

Put all except the milk in a small basin and whisk until smooth.
Add a little of the milk and heat the remainder to boiling. Pour
into the blended mixture, mix, and return to the pan. Stir until the
mixture boils. Remove from the heat.

2 *tsp. gelatine dissolved in 2 tbs. hot water*

Pour into the custard mixture in a steady stream, stirring vigorously
to combine well. Stand the pan in a basin of cold water to cool it
quickly, giving the custard an occasional stir at the beginning.

½ *pt. (250 ml.) whipping cream*

Soft whip and fold into the cold, but not set custard. Should the
custard have set, whisk to soften it before folding in the cream.
Pour into the mould and refrigerate until set. Unmould and garnish
to taste.

Alternative: Instead of the ground anise seed use 1 tbs. anisette,
adding it to the mixture just before folding in the cream.

APPLE TART WITH FENNEL SEEDS

COOKING TIME 30–45 mins.   TEMPERATURE E. 425° (220°C.) G.6
QUANTITIES FOR an 8-in. (20-cm.) tart.

6 *oz. (175 g.) flour made into short pastry or use 8–12 oz.
(250–375 g.) ready-made*

Divide the pastry into two and roll each piece to a circle. Use one to
line a flan ring or pie plate and the other for a lid. Put in a cool
place while the filling is prepared.

1 *lb. (½ kg.) apples*	4 *oz. (½ c. or 125 g.) sugar*
2 *tsp. fennel seeds*	

Mix the fennel and sugar. More sugar may be needed for a tart
variety of apple, possibly less for a sweet apple. Peel, core, and slice
the apples, not too thinly. Layer them in the lined flan or pie plate
with the sugar. Moisten the edges of the pastry, put on the pastry

lid and mould the edges together carefully, making a small roll, to keep in the juice. Cut small slits over the top of the pastry with the point of a vegetable knife. Brush the top with beaten egg and water, or with milk, and bake until the pastry is lightly browned and the apples tender. Serve hot or cold.

BAKED RICE PUDDING WITH BAY LEAVES

COOKING TIME 2 hrs.   TEMPERATURE E. 300° (150°C.) G.2
QUANTITIES FOR 3–4.

    1 pt. (½ l.) milk   1 *large bay leaf or two small*
    ½ tsp. *crushed coriander seeds*

Put in a pan and bring to the boil. Set aside to infuse and become cool. Strain the milk.

    1½ oz. (3 tbs. or 40 g.) rice   3 oz. (½ c. or 75 g.) *seedless*
    1 tbs. sugar   raisins
    Pinch of salt

Put in a baking dish with the milk and cook slowly, stirring once or twice during the first hour.

    Serve hot or cold with cream, which may be beaten into the cold pudding to make it soft and creamy.

BLANC MANGE

QUANTITIES FOR 4.   Use a 1-pt. mould (½ l.) and prepare the blanc mange 8–12 hrs. in advance and refrigerate it.

    1 *small piece of cinnamon*   ½ tsp. *crushed coriander seeds*
      stick   2 tbs. *sugar*
    ½ pt. (250 ml.) cream   ½ *bay leaf*
    ½ pt. (250 ml.) milk

The cream can be single or double and you can use different proportions of milk and cream to make up the total of 1 pt. (½ l.). Put all the ingredients in a pan and heat to boiling. Remove from the heat and leave to infuse for 5 mins.

    ½ oz. (1½ tbs. or 15 g.) gelatine   3 tbs. (45 ml.) *cold water*

Soak these together while the milk infuses. Add to the milk and stir for a minute or so to dissolve the gelatine. Strain into the mould and leave to become cold. Cover, and refrigerate until set. Unmould and serve plain or with fruit.

CREAMED RICE MOULD WITH LEMON VERBENA

COOKING TIME about 20 mins. QUANTITIES FOR 6.

1 *pt. (250 ml.) milk* 2 *oz. (4 tbs. or 50 g.) sugar*
3 *or 4 top sprigs of lemon*
verbena

Wash the verbena and put in a pan with the sugar and milk. Heat until the sugar dissolves and the milk just comes to the boil. Remove from the heat, cover the pan and infuse for 5 mins. or until the milk is well flavoured. Strain.

1½ *oz. (4½ tbs. or 40 g.) ground rice*   *A little milk*

Blend the rice to a smooth cream with a little cold milk. Stir this into the hot milk and stir until boiling. Simmer gently for 15 mins., stirring frequently. Remove from the heat.

½ *oz. (1½ tbs. or 15 g.) gelatine soaked in 3 tbs. (45 ml.) cold*
water for a few mins.

Add to the hot rice mixture and stir for a few seconds to dissolve the gelatine.

½ *pt. (250 ml.) whipping cream*

Add to the hot rice and stand the pan in a bowl of cold water. Whisk frequently until the mixture is cold and beginning to thicken. The more it is whisked during cooling the lighter the mould will be. Pour into a 1½-pt. (750-ml.) mould and leave to set. Unmould and serve with

Stewed or canned fruit to which a little chopped lemon verbena
has been added

CUSTARD WITH LEMON VERBENA

COOKING TIME ¾–1 hr. or 4 mins. pressure cooking.
TEMPERATURE for baking E. 350° (180°C.) G.4
QUANTITIES FOR 3–4.

¾ *pt. (400 ml.) milk*   3 *sprigs of lemon verbena*

Put in a pan and bring to the boil, remove from the heat and infuse for 15 mins. or until the milk is well flavoured.

2 *eggs*   1 *tbs. sugar*

Beat to mix eggs and sugar. Pour in the strained milk and put the custard in a baking dish. Stand the dish in a baking tin with hot water to come half way up the sides of the custard dish and cook until set. A knife blade inserted near the centre should come out clean. Serve warm or cold.

To pressure cook, put in a suitable-sized basin, on a rack, with

½ pt. (250 ml.) water and cook at 15 lb. pressure for 4 mins. Remove from the heat and leave the pressure to reduce slowly before opening the pressure cooker.

CUSTARD WITH PELARGONIUM

Use the above recipe substituting three pelargonium leaves for the lemon verbena.

EGG CUSTARD SAUCE (to serve warm or cold)

COOKING TIME about 10 mins.   QUANTITIES FOR 4.
  ½ pt. (250 ml.) milk   *½ bay leaf*
  ¼ tsp. crushed coriander seeds

Put in a small pan and bring to the boil. Remove from the heat, cover, and leave to infuse for about 5 mins.
  1 egg or 2 yolks   *½ tbs. sugar*

Beat to mix sugar and egg. Strain in the milk, stir well and return to the pan. Cook over a very gentle heat, stirring all the time until it begins to thicken a little and just coats the back of the wooden stirrer. Remove at once from the heat and pour into a jug. If it is to be served cold, stand the jug in a bowl of cold water to cool the custard quickly, then cover and refrigerate.

This is the consistency of thin cream. If a thicker custard is preferred, add 1–2 tsp. blended custard powder with the egg and just bring to the boil.

EGG JELLY WITH PINEAPPLE AND LEMON VERBENA

COOKING TIME 15–20 mins.   QUANTITIES FOR 4.
  ½ oz. (1½ tbs. or 15 g.) gelatine   1 pt. (½ l.) water
  Yellow rind of 2 lemons   3 oz. (6 tbs. or 75 g.) sugar

Put in a pan and heat without boiling, until the gelatine and sugar are dissolved. Remove from the heat, cover and infuse for 10 mins.
  4 eggs   *Juice of 2 lemons*

Beat together to break up the eggs. Add the hot liquid. Stir, and strain into the pan. Stir over a gentle heat until the mixture thickens slightly.
  2 tbs. sherry, marsala, or 1 tbs. rum

Flavour to taste and pour into four individual moulds. Cool, and then refrigerate until set.

4 *rings fresh or canned pineapple*
1 *tsp. chopped fresh lemon verbena*

Turn the jellies out, each onto a ring of pineapple, and sprinkle with the chopped lemon verbena.

GOOSEBERRY FOOL WITH SWEET CICELY

The anise-like flavour of sweet cicely gives a pleasant variation to the usual gooseberry flavour. A similar effect could be got by using a few drops of anisette liqueur. Prepare the fool several hours in advance and chill it in the refrigerator.

QUANTITIES FOR 4.

1 *lb. (½ kg.) fresh or frozen gooseberries*
4 *oz. (½ c. or 125 g.) sugar or to taste*
¼ *c. (75 ml.) of sweet cicely leaves*

Wash the gooseberries and sweet cicely and put them in a pan with the sugar. Cook over a very gentle heat, or in a casserole in the oven until the gooseberries are reduced to a pulp. Do not add any water or the pulp will be too thin for a successful fool. Sometimes the gooseberries themselves are unusually watery and, if there seems rather much juice, strain some off before making the purée by rubbing the fruit through a nylon or stainless steel sieve. It should give about ½ pt. (250 ml.) of thick purée.

½ *pt. (250 ml.) double cream or use ¼ pt. (150 ml.) thick*
custard plus ¼ pt. (150 ml.) double cream

To make the custard use 2 tbs. custard powder to ¼ pt. (150 ml.) milk. Stir the custard frequently as it cools. This helps to keep it smooth. Whip the cream until thick but not buttery and fold in the purée. If custard is used, beat smooth and whisk in the purée, then fold in the whipped cream. Put the mixture in individual glasses, cover, and refrigerate.

GRAPEFRUIT AND MINT

Prepare halves of grapefruit for serving in the usual way. Either sprinkle with sugar and chopped fresh mint, or with a mixture of dried mint and sugar. Leave for a little while to allow the flavours to mingle before serving.

LEMON JELLY WITH CORIANDER

QUANTITIES FOR 4.

1 *tbs. crushed coriander seeds*   ½ *pt.* (250 *ml.*) *boiling water*

Pour the water over the seeds, stir, cover, and infuse until cold, then strain.

1 *pkt. lemon jelly or* 1 *pt.* (½ *l.*) *home-made*
2 *tbs. sherry*

Use the coriander liquid and sherry with additional water, to make 1 pt. (½ l.) of lemon jelly. Pour into a mould and leave to set. Unmould and serve with

Cream

LEMON SORBET WITH MINT

QUANTITIES FOR 6.

3 *strips of lemon rind*   ¼ *pt.* (150 *ml.*) *water*

Put in a small pan and bring to the boil. Strain.

3 *oz.* (6 *tbs. or* 75 *g.*) *sugar*

Return the strained liquid to the pan, add the sugar, stir until dissolved, and boil for 5 mins. Cool a minute.

4 *tbs. honey*   1 *tsp. gelatine soaked in* 1 *tbs.*
                                    cold water

Add to the hot syrup and stir until dissolved.

½ *pt.* (250 *ml.*) *mint leaves, lightly packed*
¼ *pt.* (150 *ml.*) *water*

Wash the leaves and put in the electric blender with the water. Process to chop the leaves finely. Strain into the other liquid. If no blender is available, boil the water and infuse the leaves in it until cold, then strain.

¼ *pt.* (150 *ml.*) *lemon juice*

Add and leave the mixture to become cold, then chill in the refrigerator and finally freeze until almost firm. Remove to a basin, beat to break up.

1 *egg white, beaten stiff*

Beat into the frozen mixture and finish freezing. Thaw until fairly soft and stir before serving.

ORANGE AND MINT SORBET

QUANTITIES FOR 6.

4 *oz.* (½ *c. or* 125 *g.*) *sugar*   ½ *pt.* (250 *ml.*) *water*

Put in a small pan and heat to dissolve the sugar. Then boil for 5 mins. Remove from the heat.

1 *can, about 6 oz. (175 ml.) of frozen concentrated orange juice*

Add to the syrup, stir to mix well, and melt the orange.

½ *pt. (250 ml.) eau de cologne mint leaves, lightly packed*

Wash and drain the leaves. Put them in the electric blender with the liquid and process to chop the mint finely. Strain and leave to become quite cold. If no blender is available the mint can be infused in the hot syrup until cold and then strained before adding the thawed orange juice.

When the mixture is cold, chill it in the refrigerator.

1 *egg white*

Add to the orange mixture and whisk just enough to mix the egg in. Freeze until it is almost frozen turn out into a basin and whisk by hand until the mixture is thick and smooth. Continue freezing until firm.

PEARS WITH GINGER AND NASTURTIUM FLOWERS

COOKING TIME 5 mins.   QUANTITIES FOR 4.

2 *oz. (6 tbs. or 50 g.) sugar*   ½ *pt. (250 ml.) water*

Boil in a small pan for 5 mins. Allow to become cold and then pour into a serving dish.

4 *large ripe pears*   *Chopped crystallised ginger*

Peel and core the pears and slice them thinly, putting them at once into the syrup to prevent them from discolouring. Sprinkle with chopped ginger, amount according to taste. Chill in the refrigerator.

4–6 *nasturtium flowers*

Wash each flower carefully under running water and drain in a sieve. Add them to the salad just before serving it.

PLUM COMPÔTE WITH SWEET CICELY

COOKING TIME 10–20 mins.   QUANTITIES FOR 4.

4 *oz. (½ c. or 125 g.) sugar*   ½ *pt. (250 ml.) water*

Put in a pan large enough to let the plums lie in a single layer. Bring to the boil, stirring to dissolve the sugar.

1 *lb. (½ kg.) red plums*

¼ *c. (75 ml.) or more of scissor-snipped sweet cicely leaves*

Wash the plums and herb and add to the syrup. Poach gently, turning occasionally, until they are just tender but not collapsed. Lift out carefully into a serving dish. If there seems to be too much syrup boil it rapidly to reduce it before pouring it over the plums. Leave the sweet cicely pieces in the syrup as these help to add flavour, which is slightly of anise and a very pleasant change from plain plums.

RHUBARB WITH ANGELICA

COOKING TIME 15 mins. or more depending on the method of cooking.
QUANTITIES FOR 2–3 or for ½ pt. (250 ml.) purée.

1 *lb.* (½ *kg.*) *rhubarb*
4 *oz.* (½ *c. or* 125 *g.*) *sugar, more or less*
½ *oz.* (15 *g.*) *chopped angelica leaves or* 1 *oz.* (25 *g.*) *young
   stems cut in small pieces*

Wash and trim the rhubarb and cut in pieces. If you like a fair amount of juice begin by making a syrup with the sugar and a little water. Poach the rhubarb and angelica in this until just tender but not broken. If there is too much syrup at the end, lift out the rhubarb and boil the syrup hard to concentrate it before pouring it over the rhubarb.

For cooking in the oven in a casserole or over a gentle heat, put the ingredients in the pan or casserole with just one or two spoons of water, or none at all. Cover and cook gently until tender, to a pulp if you want it for a purée. Sieve or put in the electric blender to make the purée. Use it for making a rhubarb fool or other cold sweet such as a mousse or cream.

RHUBARB AND LEMON BALM CASSEROLE

COOKING TIME 25–35 mins.   TEMPERATURE E. 400° (200°C.) G.6
QUANTITIES FOR 4–6.

2 *lb.* (1 *kg.*) *rhubarb*   6–8 *oz.* (175–250 *g.*) *sugar*
12 *small sprigs of fresh balm or less according to taste*

Cut off the leaves and trim the root ends of the rhubarb. Cut it in pieces about 2 in. (5 cm.) long. Wash the balm and put in a casserole in layers with the rhubarb. Use either young growths of balm or the top halves of taller stems. Sprinkle the sugar on top and cover the casserole. Bake until the rhubarb is tender but not mushy. Remove the sprigs of balm before serving the fruit. Serve warm or cold.

RHUBARB WITH SWEET CICELY

Use two sprays or one handful of sweet cicely leaves and cook the sprigs with the rhubarb as in the recipe above. Leave the sprigs in the rhubarb as it cools and then remove them before serving. Alternatively, the leaves can be scissor-snipped before cooking and left in when the fruit is served.

CHAPTER SIXTEEN

Drinks

HERB TEAS

Herb teas are part of ancient folk medicine but many are also used just because they are pleasant refreshing drinks. Those made from culinary herbs are among the best, with mint tea perhaps being the favourite. Others, such as lemon balm and bergamot, are sometimes mixed with Indian tea to give a perfumed flavour.

The majority of herb teas are better made with dried leaves but some, such as lemon balm, mint, sage, sweet cicely, and bergamot are equally good with fresh leaves.

QUANTITIES

1 tbs. scissor-snipped fresh leaves per cup or 1 tsp. dried crushed leaves (not powdered); or seeds

Finely powdered leaves are almost impossible to strain out of the tea and spoil its appearance. These quantities can be varied according to taste, perhaps using less of the stronger herbs.

METHOD

Heat the tea pot in the usual way, add the herb and pour in boiling water. Stir and leave to brew for 5 mins. Stir again and strain into cups.

Optional additions are lemon or orange juice (1–2 tsp. per cup, or a small slice), and sugar. Some like mint tea very sweet. Other herbs suitable for making a sweetened tea are lemon balm, lemon verbena, bergamot, sweet cicely, sage, and rosemary. The rest are usually too spicy for sugar but this is a matter of taste.

HERBS SPECIALLY RECOMMENDED

Bergamot (fresh or dried leaves)
Lemon balm (fresh or dried leaves)
Lemon verbena (fresh or dried leaves)
Lemon verbena with eau de cologne mint in equal quantities
Mint (fresh or dried leaves)
Sage (specially with lemon or orange juice)
Sweet cicely (very good if you like an anise flavour)

Dill seed
Lovage
Catmint
Rosemary
Savory (strong but good)
Thyme (a strong flavour)

MILK DRINKS FLAVOURED WITH HERBS

These are very refreshing for hot weather drinks and much more interesting than plain cold milk.

The quantity of herb can be varied according to taste and the steeping time will naturally make a difference to the flavour.

QUANTITIES FOR ½ pt. (250 ml.) cold milk.

> 2 *small sprigs of lemon verbena or eau de cologne mint, or*
> 3 *sprigs of burnet*

Put the milk in a jug, add the washed herb, cover and infuse for at least an hour in the refrigerator. Strain before serving.

Using lemon verbena gives the milk a delicious perfumed lemon taste, the eau de cologne mint is very pleasant but, for a stronger mint flavour, you can use one of the ordinary culinary mints. The burnet is perhaps the best of all, a slight flavour of cucumber, plus other flavours.

I have tried the milk with young borage leaves but, to me, they seem to produce a slight fishy taste, plus the usual cucumber flavour of borage.

YOGURT AND MILK DRINK

QUANTITIES FOR 4 glasses.

> ½ *pt. (250 ml.) cold water*
> ½ *pt. (250 ml.) thick yogurt   Pinch of salt*

Put the yogurt in a bowl and whisk it until smooth, then beat in the water, and salt to taste. Alternatively, mix the ingredients for a few seconds in the electric blender.

> 8-10 *leaves of fresh mint or a pinch of dried powdered mint*

Either chop the fresh leaves finely and add, or blend the leaves with the yogurt for a few seconds to chop them finely. Put the drink in a jug, cover, and refrigerate until well chilled.

HERBS FOR FLAVOURING WINE CUPS AND CHILLED FRUIT DRINKS

Those most frequently used are mint, borage, and balm, but some others are good too (see below).

To impart its flavour to the drink, the herb needs to be infused for some time with the other ingredients. When a sugar and water syrup is used as the basis for the drink, the herb can be added to the hot syrup and infused for about 15 mins. or longer. Such an infusion can be made in advance and stored in the refrigerator (see Mint syrup, below).

Alternatively, add the herbs (bruised or scissor-snipped), to a cold drink and infuse while the drink is being chilled in the refrigerator for an hour or so.

When a drink is to be chilled by adding ice cubes or crushed ice, it is best to introduce the herb flavour by using a herb syrup as already described. This can be used hot or cold.

In all cases the herbs are strained out before serving the drink. Small fresh leaves and flowers are often added as a final garnish.

If you make the herb wine flavourings described on p. 88, these can be added to fruit and wine drinks, particularly useful for individual drinks made with chilled fruit juices. The possibilities for making your own personal blends are obvious and wide-ranging.

RECOMMENDED HERBS FOR WINE CUPS AND CHILLED FRUIT DRINKS
Angelica leaves, for a muscatel flavour
Balm, use plenty, ¼ pt. (150 ml.) leaves to ½ pt. (250 ml.) liquid
Basil, the tender young tips
Bergamot, leaves or flowers
Borage, leaves and flowers
Burnet, young leaves for a cucumber flavour
Clary sage, young leaves for a grapefruit flavour
Costmary, tiny pieces for a bitter, minty flavour
Mint leaves, any kind
Rosemary, leaves and flowers
Verbena, lemon, for a perfumed lemon flavour.

MINT SYRUP

This may be diluted with water to make a refreshing cold drink, or used to flavour other drinks. It is also very good for flavouring the syrup for fruit salads and fruit cocktails. It can be made in advance and will keep for a week or more in the refrigerator.

QUANTITIES FOR ½ pt. (250 ml.) syrup.

½ pt. (250 ml.) water   6–8 *oz.* (175–250 *g.) sugar*

Bring to the boil, stirring to dissolve the sugar, then boil gently for 5 mins. Cool a little.

½ pt. (250 ml.) lightly packed mint leaves

Use eau de cologne mint or any other mint you have. The simplest way of extracting the flavour of the mint is to blend warm syrup and leaves in the electric blender, then strain through muslin. This will give a stronger flavour than the alternative method which is to scissor-snip the leaves into the hot syrup, cover, and infuse until cold before straining.

¼ pt. (150 ml.) lemon juice or to taste

Add to the cold syrup, cover and store.

Alternative: Omit the lemon juice if the mint syrup is to be used for flavouring milk drinks or fruit drinks already containing lemon juice.

HOCK CUP

QUANTITIES FOR 2¼ pt. (1¼ l.).

     1 *oz.* (2 *tbs. or* 25 *g.) sugar*

     ½ pt. (250 ml.) lemon balm leaves

     ½ pt. (250 ml.) boiling water

Put the sugar and balm in a heat-resistant jug and pour in the boiling water. Cover, and leave to infuse for 15 mins.

     1 *small glass sherry*   1 *bottle hock or chablis*

Add to the jug and leave to stand for an hour. Strain, and then chill in the refrigerator.

     Chilled soda water (about ½ pt. or 250 ml.)

Add just before serving.

VERMOUTH WITH SODA WATER AND HERBS

About a quarter fill tumblers with French or Italian vermouth. Fill up with iced water or soda water, add a slice of lemon, a lump of ice, and sprigs of either mint, lemon balm, or lemon verbena.

TOMATO JUICE COCKTAIL WITH HERBS

QUANTITIES FOR 6 or more.

1 *pt.* (½ *l.*) *tomato juice*
2 *tbs. lemon juice*
½–1 *tsp. salt*
Worcester sauce
2 *tsp. finely chopped fresh basil or* 1 *tsp. dried*
2 *tsp. chopped chives or a little chopped onion*

1 *tbs. orange juice*
2 *tsp. sugar*
Paprika pepper
2 *tsp. chopped fresh tarragon*
2 *tsp. scissor-snipped fresh savory*

Combine the ingredients, cover, and leave in the refrigerator to steep for an hour or so until the tomato juice is flavoured to taste. Strain before serving.

MINT JULEPS

The only thing that the hundreds of mint julep recipes seem to have in common is the mint. Some are non-alcoholic, the ingredients being fruit juices and sugar, orange, lemon, pineapple, or any other juice. The alcoholic juleps may contain sherry, brandy, cider, ale, whisky, or beer.

All juleps are served chilled, with sprigs of mint as a garnish.

NON-ALCOHOLIC MINT JULEP

QUANTITIES FOR 8.

6 *oz.* (¾ *c. or* 175 *g.*) *sugar*   ½ *pt.* (250 *ml.*) *water*

Heat to dissolve the sugar and bring to the boil. Boil for a minute or two.

3 *tbs. chopped fresh mint*

Add to the hot syrup and leave to cool. Then cover and store in the refrigerator to chill it well.

¼ *pt.* (150 *ml.*) *lemon juice*   1 *qt.* (1¼ *l.*) *dry ginger ale*
¾ *pt.* (400 *ml.*) *orange juice*

Put these in the refrigerator to chill. When ready to serve the julep, strain the mint syrup into a jug and add the chilled juices and ginger ale. Serve well chilled and garnished with

Sprigs of mint, eau de cologne, or other variety

GRAPEFRUIT AND MINT (for the blender)

QUANTITIES FOR a little over 1 pt. (½ l.).

1 *medium-sized grapefruit*

Peel off the yellow rind thinly and put it in the blender goblet. Remove as much of the white pith as possible and discard it. Cut the fruit in pieces and put it in the goblet.

2 *oz.* (4 *tbs. or* 50 *g.*) *caster*   ¼ *c.* (75 *ml.*) *mint leaves*
  sugar, or to taste   1 *pt.* (½ *l.*) *cold water*

Add to the grapefruit and blend until the grapefruit is pulped and the mint finely chopped. The mixture will then be a pale green. Strain into a jug, cover and refrigerate until well chilled. Garnish each glass with

A *small sprig of mint*

LEMON AND MINT

Make as the above recipe but substitute 2 lemons for the grapefruit and increase the amount of sugar.

Index